EDUCATION IN SOUTH ASIA

REFERENCE BOOKS IN
INTERNATIONAL EDUCATION
(General Editor: Edward R. Beauchamp)
VOL. 3

GARLAND REFERENCE LIBRARY
OF SOCIAL SCIENCE
VOL. 390

Reference Books in International Education

Edward R. Beauchamp
General Editor

EDUCATION IN SOUTH ASIA
A Select Annotated Bibliography

Philip G. Altbach
Denzil Saldhana
Jeanne Weiler

GARLAND PUBLISHING, INC. · NEW YORK & LONDON
1987

Library of Congress Cataloging-in-Publication Data

Altbach, Philip G.
    Education in South Asia.

    (Reference books in international education ; vol. 3)
(Garland reference library of social science ; vol. 390)
    Bibliography: p.
    Includes index.
    1. Education—South Asia—Bibliography. I. Saldhana,
Denzil. II. Weiler, Jeanne. III. Title. IV. Series.
V. Series: Garland reference library of social
science ; v. 390.
Z5815.S654A47 1987 [LA1144.5]   016.37′0954   86-29548
ISBN 0-8240-8453-5

Printed on acid-free, 250-year-life paper
Manufactured in the United States of America

CONTENTS

FOREWORD

Good bibliographies are indispensable but often taken for granted. There is also a mistaken, if widely held, view that the compilation of a good bibliography is a relatively low level academic activity requiring no special skills.

The fair-minded reader who takes the trouble of carefully examining the structure and organization, as well as the enormously useful citations found in this volume, will reach a different conclusion. Philip Altbach and his colleagues have given us an extremely valuable resource that will be welcomed by scholars, students, and others interested in education in South Asia. The compilers of this volume have not only carefully constructed a useful conceptual framework for their citations, they have successfully taken on the very difficult task of judiciously choosing only those items which are of greatest importance to the thoughtful researcher. To compile an exhaustive bibliography on a subject is a task requiring perseverance and patience. To sift through the literally thousands of items on education in South Asia, but, selecting only those which their experience tells them are of the greatest significance is, indeed, a work of scholarship.

Finally, I would like to call the reader's attention to Professor Altbach's excellent introductory chapter in which he not only provides a fine, up-to-date analysis of educational research in South Asia, but also raises many provocative questions having relevance for educational researchers in other parts of the globe.

This volume, one of a continuing series on education in different parts of the world, is particularly intended to serve the needs of students and scholars. The general editor and the publishers, therefore, welcome readers' suggestions for making the series more useful, as well proposals for future volumes.

Edward R. Beauchamp
University of Hawaii
August 1986

ACKNOWLEDGMENTS

A book of this magnitude is necessarily the work of many people. The authors would like to acknowledge the assistance of the following: Kowsar Chowdhury, a doctoral student in comparative education at SUNY-Buffalo, was helpful in collecting materials on Bangladesh and in assisting with the early stages of the work. The reference and Interlibrary Loan staffs of Lockwood Library, SUNY-Buffalo, provided valuable assistance. In India, we are grateful to the Tata Institute of Social Sciences for providing a research grant that partly covered the cost of data collection. Sandhya Srinivasan, Rita Sharma and Anita Haladi assisted in collecting materials on India at different stages of the project and Ms. Janaki Velayudhan typed the preliminary draft. We are indebted to the staffs of the University of Bombay libraries at Fort and Kalina and of the Tata Institute of Social Sciences library. The final text was typed by Pat Glinski and Nancy Myers of the Quantitative Analysis Laboratory, Faculty of Educational Studies, State University of New York at Buffalo.

This project is a joint undertaking of the Comparative Education Center, SUNY-Buffalo and the Unit for Research in the Sociology of Education, Tata Institute of Social Sciences, Bombay. We thank Hugh Petrie, Dean of the Faculty of Education Studies, SUNY-Buffalo, and Suma Chitnis, Head of the Unit for Research in the Sociology of Education, TISS, for their support.

Philip G. Altbach, Jeanne Weiler
Buffalo, New York

Denzil Saldanha
Bombay, India

July, 1986

PREFACE

This bibliography comprises 1,419 items arranged in 35 chapters. About 40 percent of the listings include annotations. The bibliography includes material in English mainly for the period from 1960 to 1985. In a few instances, important items published earlier are listed. The volume covers the major South Asian nations of Bangladesh, India, Nepal, Pakistan, and Sri Lanka.

Our effort has been to list books, journal articles, and published reports of major governmental or international agencies. We have not included doctoral dissertations, in part because there is a comprehensive guide to dissertations done in American universities and in part because theses are difficult to obtain internationally.[1] We have not included newspaper articles and in most instances we have chosen articles of more than ten standard journal pages in length. We have deliberately not listed materials, such as reports by local institutions, that we felt would be difficult to obtain. And while our selection of journals is fairly wide, we have tried to include publications that are likely to be available in South Asia and in North America.

This bibliography is selective in several respects. It includes material only in English. This is a significant limitation, since published material on education exists in the various South Asian languages and does not appear in this bibliography. There are several reasons for the exclusion of non-English materials aside from the linguistic limitations of the compilers. Access to material in South Asian languages is very difficult. Bibliographies are rare and there is generally no central depository of books or journals. Relatively few researchers outside the region are fluent in these languages. And it is still the case that the bulk of the original research in education and in the social sciences is published in English. Nevertheless, the exclusion of material in such languages as Bengali, Sinhala, Marathi, Hindi, Urdu, and Malayalam is a significant weakness. By the year 2000, it is very likely that a bibliography that aims at a thorough coverage of the field of education will need to include at least some of the languages of the region. It is hoped that bibliographical controls of material in these languages will keep up with the production of research. This volume is more complete with regard to books than to articles. We attempted to include every book relating to education that we could locate. We were considerably more selective with regard to journal articles, choosing materials we thought had a lasting significance and excluding articles shorter than ten pages in most instances.

It is likely that this volume reflects more complete coverage of India than of the other South Asian countries. The compilers are most familiar with the Indian literature and have better access to

Indian sources. North American libraries tend to have better collections of Indian materials. Bibliographical controls in India are significantly better than for the other South Asian nations. It is furthermore true that India produces a much larger amount of research than the other nations of the region, and this imbalance is naturally reflected in the bibliography. Yet, the literature on education in South Asia, especially India, is very vast. India has been called the "research superpower" of the Third World and the large number of journals and publishers and a significant research community in education and the social sciences has meant that its literature on education in quite large. We have tried to provide as comprehensive a listing as possible, but useful items have been inevitably left out.

The chapters reflect several choices. On the one hand, we feel that the chapters reflect important topics in the field of education and we have chosen them for this reason. On the other hand, the chapters also reflect the nature of the literature. On some topics, such as educational policy and planning, there is a large amount of literature. On others, there has been less written. Thus, our topical selection reflects a combination of the nature of the literature and our own view of the relevance of particular areas. The reader is urged to search among related topics to locate relevant materials.

We have put together what we feel is a selective yet reasonably comprehensive bibliography of books, articles, and reports relating to education in South Asia. This bibliography is a guide to the literature, but it does not include everything written on a topic. For such a complete listing, the researcher will need to consult materials in the languages of the region--and in a few cases, other European languages, especially German and French. The researcher would also have to consult specialized bibliographies on particular aspects of education. This bibliography has a chapter listing such references. Yet, we are inclined to believe that this volume comprises the most complete available overview of the various fields of education.

1. Franklin Parker, ed. American Dissertation on Foreign
    Education: Vol. 2: India (Troy, New York: Whitston, 1972).

RESEARCH ON EDUCATION IN SOUTH ASIA

Philip G. Altbach

This volume is a selective guide to research on education in a region whose population numbers about one billion people--a fifth of mankind. The major countries of the region--Bangladesh, India, Nepal, Pakistan, and Sri Lanka--are culturally and religiously diverse. Each has a long history and a distinctive "high culture." Each, in its way, is multifaceted and complex. Each has a colonial past rooted in the British tradition, and each has an educational system that stems from the British colonial period but which has developed significantly since Independence. It is not possible in this essay to outline either the complex cultural traditions of the region or chronicle the historical development or contemporary problems of the educational systems. Rather, this essay will focus on several of the common elements of the countries of the region and on the emergence and development of research on education. The reader will have to turn to some of the excellent studies listed in the bibliography for specific details about educational systems and practices.

Unity and Diversity

South Asia has the world's only Hindu kingdom--Nepal. It contains two of the world's most populous Islamic countries-- Bangladesh and Pakistan. Sri Lanka, with its Buddhist majority, represents another religious tradition. And India, the behemoth of the region, is the world's largest democracy and has a majority Hindu population in the context of a multicultural secular state. India and Sri Lanka are parliamentary democracies. Bangladesh and Pakistan have military regimes, while Nepal is a monarchy with parliamentary trappings. Each of the countries in the region is faced with serious political, ethnic, or religious tensions.

All of the countries of the region face daunting problems of development and modernization. Per capita incomes are low--in the case of Bangladesh among the very lowest in the world. Levels of literacy are also low--ranging from about half to under 20 percent. Each of the countries of the region has placed great stress on education as a means of modernization and has spent large sums on educational development. Education is a topic of considerable importance in politics and society and is seen by many as a key to social mobility and to success. Modernization is an ongoing process in each of the countries of the region. India has had considerable success in developing an industrial and technological base, allowing India to produce virtually every industrial product--from computers and steel to nuclear weapons. But this technological infrastructure sits on top of a society which remains 80 percent rural and, is, in

1

many ways, just emerging into the twentieth century. Yet, there are significant variations in India's rural sector, with a few parts of the country having developed a prosperous and productive agricultural sector while others are still at a level of subsistence farming. India has the most diverse and the most successful economy in the region. Bangladesh remains almost totally agrarian. A large and rapidly growing population in a country with few natural resources has caused severe immediate and long term economic problems. Pakistan has lagged behind India in industrial development, but it has made considerable progress. Sri Lanka has a fairly diverse economy and the highest per capita income in the region--but the current civil war between the Sinhalese Buddhist majority and the Tamil Hindu minority has severely disrupted the nation. Nepal remains an economic backwater, dependent on India in most respects.

Historical Commonalities

The five nations of the region are quite diverse--culturally, politically, economically, but their history has one important common element--British colonialism. Many would argue, in fact, that the existence of the three separate nations of India, Pakistan, and Bangladesh is a legacy of British colonial policy and that, had different colonial decisions been made, the subcontinent might not have been divided among three powerful nations. The legal system in all South Asian countries is deeply influenced by British law and, while modifications have been made in the post-independence period, the basic structure of the British legal tradition remains. The bureaucratic traditions of the British colonial civil service remain, and with few exceptions, the basic structure of the colonial bureaucracy is in place almost a half century after the departure of the British. The military traditions of the British also influence the countries of the region although the concept of the apolitical military has been broken in both Bangladesh and Pakistan--while it has been, thus far, maintained in the other three countries of the region.

The heritage of the English language is one of the key aspects of the colonial tradition. From the perspective of this bibliography this is a key factor, since the bulk of research and scholarship is written in English in all of the countries of the region. While much of the education system has slowly shifted over to South Asian languages, a significant amount of higher education remains in English, and a majority of teaching and research at the post-baccalaureate level is in English. The large majority of scholarly publishing is in English. It is possible that the most lasting feature of British rule will be the English language. The continued use of English as the language of scholarship means that the results of research can be easily communicated outside the region--but there are problems of ensuring that such research has a wide impact within the country. In India, for example, about 2 percent of the total population is literate in English, yet about half of the books published in India are in English and most academic, political, and scientific journals appear in English. This means that most literate Indians do not have access to the bulk of what is published. A growing number of teachers and other education professionals are not able to read much of the research on educational issues that is published in English. The situation, however, is slowly changing in all of the countries of the region as journals and other publications are appearing in the regional languages.

Indian materials tend to be fairly widely circulated (although not much in Pakistan), but publications from the other countries in the region are not frequently found in India. Publications from South Asia can find a market outside the region, since English is the major language of scholarship worldwide. Books and journals from India have some influence in other Third World nations although materials published in the other countries of the region are not much in evidence outside their countries of origin. South Asian libraries purchase large numbers of books and journals from overseas, particularly from Britain and the United States, and the impact of research done in the West is considerable in South Asia. Many South Asian researchers and academics work overseas, both in the West and in other Third World countries. More than most Third World regions, South Asia is involved in the international knowledge network.

Educational Traditions

Modern education in South Asia stems from several important forces. The rich traditions of traditional education have virtually been eliminated from the mainstream of contemporary education. Remnants remain, however, in the shape of Islamic educational institutions, which mainly serve religious education needs, and in the Ayurvedic medical schools in India, which train practitioners in traditional Indian medicine. The educational system has few such traditional elements and is based on the Western models imposed by the British. The colonial educational model has been significantly adapted to contemporary realities and dramatically expanded, but other aspects of education have also been altered.

The rich cultural, religious, and educational traditions of the region continue to play a role despite the presence of the Western models. The stress on learning in Hindu tradition combined with the control of education and religious scholarship by the Brahman castes has made modern schooling readily accepted by Indians. Both access to education and access to the teaching profession have been traditionally linked to caste. In Pakistan and Bangladesh, the

Islamic educational tradition has been important and, in today's atmosphere of Muslim revivalism, Islamic elements have become more important in education. The fact that the "high cultures" of South Asia--Hindu, Islamic and Buddhist--all stress education and access to written knowledge has made it easier for Western education to take root in the region--and eventually to dominate. As with so much else in South Asia, there is an important interplay between traditional and modern elements. What seems to be entirely "modern" has strong elements of traditional values and norms.

The impact and history of traditional educational ideas and practices in South Asia have been largely ignored in the literature. There has been some research on the Islamic madrassas, on traditional Hindu educational ideas, and on Buddhist educational practices, but the vast bulk of the literature relates to "modern" schooling in its many forms. The lack of attention to the traditional roots of education has meant that an important part of the historical heritage of the South Asian nations has been neglected. Recently, with a revival of interest in religious ideologies, there has been some resurgence of interest in the historical and religious underpinnings of education. Further, some traditional religious educational institutions may have grown, and this may also trigger more research.

The educational systems of the South Asian nations are basically patterned on Western models. The organization and curriculum of schooling, from kindergartens to universities, is Western in nature. There are many reasons for this fact. The impact of British colonialism on education in South Asia can hardly be exaggerated. The British model was inherited and none of the countries found it either desirable or possible to make a sharp break following Independence. They were concerned with the expansion of education, with improving rates of literacy and the like and did not place shifting the models of education as a high priority. Only Mahatma Gandhi argued forcefully for a basic change in the ideology and practice of education, and he was not influential in post-Independence debates. Most of the nationalist leadership was educated in British-model schools and many were more at home speaking English than their mother tongues. Muhammad Ali Jinnah, the founder of Pakistan, could hardly speak Urdu and Jawaharalal Nehru was more eloquent in English than in Hindi.

The colonial experience had much to do with the dominance of Western patterns of schooling in South Asia. Western models of education are dominant everywhere in the world, and, thus, it is not surprising that the South Asian nations would retain the colonial pattern. Indeed, the fairly widely diffused British-style school system in the region may have given the nations some advantage in the post-Independence development of education. No Third World nation has jettisoned Western educational models and either returned to indigenous roots or started entirely anew. A few have attempted to incorporate elements of educational schooling, and one or two have experimented with new approaches, but these efforts have not been very successful. China, for example, tried several times, most recently during the Cultural Revolution, to build an indigenous revolutionary educational orientation but these efforts failed and China has reincorporated Western practices and orientations into its school system.

The specific heritage of the British, however, is distinctive in South Asia. English provides a "link language" for the elites of the countries of the region and as a regional means of communication as well. As the major international language of scholarship, technology, commerce, and diplomacy, English also gives an advantage to the region in the international sphere. However, the widespread use of English means that the large majority of the populations in South Asia is virtually cut off from positions of power. The British, while permitting the establishing of a wide range of private schools, did not spend large sums on the establishment of education in their colonies. Thus, an elitist approach by the British was combined with a laissez-faire attitude toward the growth of schools that were not funded by government. Schooling in the British colonies was largely limited to the urban areas and upper socioeconomic groups. Some have argued that for India the rate of illiteracy was actually higher under the British than earlier. The British had specific educational goals for South Asia: The training of an effective and loyal civil service ranked as quite important among them. The bias of the educational system was toward the liberal arts. Science and technology were not integral to education.

While educational policy was dominated by the colonial authorities, there was considerable influence from indigenous groups. The nationalist movements had some influence on the educational system. Indigenous groups sponsored schools and colleges. In South Asia, many groups, including religious, political, caste, and others, had ideas about education and a willingness to sponsor schools. These groups have an impact on the education during the colonial period and after as well.

There has been a substantial amount of research on the history of education in South Asia so that it is possible to discern in considerable detail the nature of historical patterns to education and the interplay of traditions, colonial policy and education in the region. Indeed, it is likely that the richness of the research permits more generalizations concerning South Asia than about most other Third World areas. There has been a stress on the historical development of education in the British colonial period and especially on policy issues. Researchers have neglected curricular concerns and other school-related topics. Nevertheless, it is

possible to obtain a fairly thorough understanding of the
educational traditions of South Asia based on the available
literature.

The Configuration of Research

This bibliography deals with all of the South Asian countries,
but approximately 80 percent of the material concerns one country--
India. India is the largest nation in the region, with a population
that is more than double the combined total of the other South Asian
nations. It has the longest academic tradition--with universities
dating back more than a century. India also has a very large
academic system, with more than 120 universities and 4,000,000
students at the post-secondary level. The Indian academic community
is at least five times larger than the rest of the region combined.
India also has a well-developed infrastructure of journals and
publishers. The other nations of the region are less well endowed
with outlets for research and scholarship. Finally, the Indian
academic system, especially in the universities, stresses research
and scholarship for promotion, and academic staff are under some
pressure to do research and writing.

The sociology and economics of scholarship have a good deal to
do with the nature of the research materials that are available.
India has an active publishing industry and a number of journals,
including several specifically devoted to research on education, and
scholars can be assured of a place to publish their work. In turn,
the publishers and journals can survive because of the large
academic system which purchases their products.

India has been called the "research superpower" of the Third
World. In many fields, Indian scholars are among the most important
producers of research in the Third World. According to the
Institute of Scientific Information, India accounts for more than
one-quarter of research output cited in major scientific journals
from the Third World. Thus, the Indian academic community has
achieved an important place in Third World science. While there are
no statistical studies relating to the field of education in this
respect, it is our impression that India holds an equally important
place in this field.

The other South Asian nations have shorter academic traditions
and much smaller academic communities. They produce a much smaller
amount of research. Yet, each of the countries of the region has a
well-developed university system, a strong interest in education,
and a small research community in the field of education development
and related social sciences. Sri Lanka, with a small academic
system (seven universities with some 18,000 students), has an active
research community and several journals. Senior academics tend to
write in English and are involved in research. Pakistan, with eight

universities and about 150,000 students and Bangladesh, with six
universities and more than 150,000 students, also have significant
academic communities. Nepal has one university. In addition to the
universities, there are a number of Institutes of Education
(responsible mainly for teacher training) in each of the countries.
The region's post-secondary institutions are modeled on the Indian
universities (it should be remembered that Pakistan and Bangladesh
were part of India until partition in 1947).

    All Third World nations are at a disadvantage with regard to
the dissemination of research, since the major libraries, data
bases, and journals are located in the industrialized nations and
tend to neglect Third World scholarship and publications. Yet, in
this context, India has a considerable advantage. It has a
relatively well-developed network of libraries, a number of
bibliographical resources, and its scholars are frequently tied into
the international networks. As a result, Indian scholarship is more
widely recognized and used than is the case for the other South
Asian nations or, for that matter, most of the Third World. It is
possible that this bibliography reflects an overrepresentation of
Indian materials simply because access to relevant books and
journals is easier. It is also quite likely that a scholar seeking
to use this bibliography will find it easier to obtain materials
from India than from the other countries of the region.
Unfortunately, education journals from South Asia generally will be
relatively difficult to obtain in the West, but journals from
Bangladesh, Pakistan, and Sri Lanka are virtually impossible to
locate. Several key Indian journals have a significant
international circulation. The Economic and Political Weekly,
Education Quarterly, and several others can be found outside of
India. It is also significant that the region's scholarly journals
are not easily located in the other countries of the region. While
some Indian journals and books are obtainable in the other South
Asian nations, it is rare, for example, to find a Bangladeshi
journal in India or a Pakistani publication in Sri Lanka.

Research Trends

    It is very difficult to characterize educational research and
publication in a region as diverse as South Asia and with a
literature as large as that reflected in this bibliography. A large
proportion of the research was undertaken by individual scholars or
research teams with little, if any, external funding available.
There have been few "directives" concerning research on education.
Thus, research reflects the interests and concerns of the scholars
undertaking the work. These scholars are, of course, guided by many
factors, including their own research interests, international
trends in research, national issues, and the concerns of
governmental or other agencies. Funding for educational research
has been fairly limited, with some of the funding coming from

foreign agencies such as the Ford Foundation or UNESCO and some from
national organizations. Thus, there is a complex nexus of
interests, concerns, and orientations. This very complexity makes an
accurate mapping of the research over time and in a contemporary
context all the more difficult.

Despite the eclecticism and variety of educational research in
South Asia, much of the research reflects the major issues of debate
in the region over the post-Independence period. Researchers and
analysts have been concerned with questions that have had policy
impact, that have caused problems in educational systems and with
apparent contradictions and difficulties in education. There have
also been issues, such as the history of education and curricular
research, that have had a continuing but relatively modest
attraction for researchers over the years. Points of crisis have
accounted for a significant proportion of research and writing on
education. The following discussion reflects India somewhat more
than the other South Asian nations, but since problems have been
similar throughout the region, research trends are similar, with the
bulk of publication much greater for India than for the other South
Asian countries.

Writing on South Asian education varies in quality and
orientation. There is, of course, much research-based analysis and
discussion of education issues. However, government officials,
journalists, and educators frequently write on education topics
without a research base. This non-research writing is influential
in public debates. Indeed, it seems to this observer that the press
in South Asia, and in other Third World areas, features education
more frequently than is the case in the industrialized nations, a
fact that probably reflects the importance of education in the lives
of those who read newspapers and magazines. The bibliography that
follows reflects both research and non-research-based writing, but
it does not include newspaper and other journalistic accounts.

It is not surprising that some of the major themes reflected in
the literature relate to flashpoints of educational controversy in
South Asia. A good example of such a topic is student political
activism. Student activism has been a disruptive influence on both
educational institutions and politics in virtually all of the
nations of South Asia. Activism, or "indiscipline" as it is called
in India, has been endemic in India and a considerable force
elsewhere. Student unrest has triggered major political crises in
India--including riots in defense of the use of English in South
India, demonstrations against political corruption, and, quite
recently, violent protests against the reservation of places in the
colleges and the civil service for students from poor sections of
the population. In the Punjab, Sikh students have been among the
most militant in the current unrest. Historically, students were in

the forefront of nationalist movements and were active in Indian,
Pakistani, and Bangladeshi nationalism.

The literature on students is a good example of the development
of research and analysis. The growth of the literature paralleled
the growth of unrest and protest and the attention paid to this
protest in the press and among decision makers. Much discussion
appeared in the press and in magazines during the "early stage" of
concern with student unrest. A second phase of concern was
characterized by research studies relating to student activism.
Funding agencies provided resources for a number of research studies
which permitted researchers to develop adequate methodologies and
conduct scientific studies. This "research phase" featured many
studies related directly to understanding activism and coping with
its implications. A number of studies dealing with students but not
directly with political unrest were also undertaken. Concern with
the psychological and social problems of college students, with
student living conditions and with the class and religious
backgrounds of students all resulted in research studies. The data
and analysis of these research efforts became part of the debate
concerning student activism. A third phase in the literature on
student unrest saw the use of the research studies in an effort to
formulate policy relating to students.

A number of generalizations can be made about this literature.
First, without the incidents of unrest and campus disruption,
student political activism would have received very limited
attention in the literature. Second, very little literature or
analysis was produced by those directly involved in the issue--the
students--although academic administrators, also involved, did write
quite a bit. Third, journalists and politicians began to write
about the topic without the benefit of expert data or analysis, but
when the data began to be produced by research scholars, it was
used, at least to an extent, by others. When governmental and
academic bodies attempted to formulate policies, they frequently
(but not always) made use of the research and other, more
journalistic, accounts. It is not possible to quantify the impact
of the research and analysis on student unrest on policy making, but
it seems fairly clear that the scholarly literature and analysis had
some impact on decision makers and on academic leaders, and perhaps
also on student leaders.

The development of educational policy has been a persistent
theme in the literature in South Asia. From the time of Independence
it has been clear that the nations of the region needed to develop
educational policies to cope with new demands on educational
systems, to create a national system of education out of the
colonial heritage, and to plan for future developments. The
countries of the region inherited colonial-based elitist educational
systems and immediately had to expand educational opportunities

dramatically and quickly train a cadre of administrators, teachers, and officials. All of the nations of the region, especially Bangladesh and Pakistan, entered the period of Independence with a very small research base in education. Policy was made on the basis of few facts and limited knowledge of most aspects of educational development. Even such basic information as rates of literacy, rates of enrollment, the number of teachers in rural areas, and the like were lacking. Policy makers had to move quickly to build a research and information base.

Educational policy has been a continuing concern precisely because there is a need to make decisions that affect educational development and policy makers have called on the education research community to provide a base for policy making. Frequently, researchers have been asked for recommendations concerning specific policy decisions. On occasion, and especially in India, educational policy is made in the context of the five-year planning process, and this has given the research community sufficient lead time to provide detailed research aspects of policy development.

Related to the development of educational policy is a large literature on the administration of education. The problems of managing schools, of providing supervision to rural schools, and of administering a rapidly expanding school system have all been addressed in a variety of studies. Most of this literature is aimed at dealing with the practical problems of South Asian education and not with providing theoretical insights into the field. It is also the case that much of the literature uses models and practices from the West and no distinctively South Asian patterns of educational administration have emerged. Yet, the bulk of material is large and the research has permitted expanding educational systems to more effectively cope with growth.

The bibliography shows that the literature relating to post-secondary education is larger than that relating to primary or to secondary education. This seems a misallocation of research, since higher education is by far the smallest segment of the educational system. Higher education received considerable emphasis in the first years after Independence for a number of reasons. The articulate middle classes, concentrated in the cities, demanded access to higher education for their children and governments found it difficult to resist the demands of this articulate group. Further, it was necessary to quickly train personnel for a rapidly expanding public sector of teachers and government officials, all of whom re-quired some kind of post-secondary education. Finally, the interna-tional foreign assistance agencies stressed the importance of higher education in rapid socioeconomic development.

As a result of these and other factors, higher education grew very rapidly in South Asia following independence. India saw the

quickest growth, both in proportional and absolute terms, and the
Indian academic system is now the third largest in the world, after
the United States and the Soviet Union. Indeed, the very size of
the Indian university system accounts for the key role of Indian
scholarship not only in South Asia but in the Third World generally.
The university system generated research on itself and also provided
a research cadre. The rapidly expanding post-secondary system also
required a good deal of research in order to solve its own problems.
The literature on student unrest, mentioned above, is an example of
how crisis in higher education stimulated research and writing.
Additional work on the administration of higher education, on the
academic profession, on the curriculum of higher education, on the
highly controversial examination system, on language issues and on
many other topics has been done.

Topics which have perplexed South Asian societies have
naturally received a good deal of attention in the literature, and
the research can be useful to other Third World countries. Language
issues have been important in all of the South Asian countries and
have received much attention in the literature. The heritage of
English and efforts to provide alternatives have been researched.
The problem of providing curriculum and textbooks in indigenous
languages has been considered. The politics of language and its
relationship to schooling have also attracted considerable attention
from researchers. The problem of educating backward classes,
castes, and minority groups generally has been a key issue in South
Asia, and particularly in India. Indian efforts to provide special
reserved places in schools and colleges for these groups have
attracted quite a bit of research. Studies of how to most
effectively meet the needs of these groups as well as the impact of
the programs that have been implemented are part of an extensive
literature. The other South Asian countries, although there are
similar problems, have seen much less research, perhaps because less
attention is paid to the problems of the education of minorities.
The current conflict in Sri Lanka between the majority Sinhalese and
the minority Tamils may reflect this lack of long-term concern. A
related issue that has received only limited attention in the
literature is rural education. All of the South Asian countries are
at least 80 percent rural, and while schools have been impressively
extended to the rural areas, it is the urban 20 percent that
benefits most from education. Few opportunities for secondary or
higher education exist in the villages, and the problems of rural
education are serious and multifaceted. There has been some
research on this topic but, given its magnitude and importance,
surprisingly little.

Women's education has received a remarkably large amount of
attention in the past decade. Stimulated to a considerable extent
by international concern for women's education, as well as a
recognition of the issue within the South Asian region, research has

grown impressively. In India and Bangladesh, particularly, an active research community of women scholars and journalists has contributed most of the writing. Agencies such as the Indian Council for Social Science Research and foreign organizations such as the Ford Foundation and UNESCO have provided funding for research on women's education. Journals provide outlets for this research. The research has covered many facets of women's education--from women in textbooks to curricular matters to the role of women and girls in the educational systems of South Asia.

Fields of research which are well established and perhaps even dominant in Western educational research, of course, exist in South Asia, but they seem to be much less important. Educational psychology and measurement, for example, is by no means the largest area of research in education, as it appears to be in the United States. Further, the methodological approaches of the measurement experts and psychologists do not dominate the scene, as is frequently the case in the West. Given the importance of testing in all of the South Asian educational systems, it is surprising that the research is not more dominant. There is also a modest amount of research on aspects of the curriculum, on curriculum development and on the role of curriculum in education. Again, it is surprising that this research is not more extensive.

With the close relationship among education, the allocation of scarce resources, and the importance paid to planning in South Asia, it is surprising that there is relatively little research on the economic costs and benefits of educational expenditures. There has been a recent growth of research on the economics of education, on the economic aspects of educational planning, and to a small extent on cost-benefit analysis of specific educational programs, and there has been a recent emphasis on this research approach. This area can be expected to grow, and it is surprising that so little research has been done to date.

The Research Network

It is important to focus on who produces research and how it is disseminated in South Asia and abroad. As has been mentioned earlier, the English language dominates research on education throughout the region. This has had many consequences. For one thing, it permits research to be easily disseminated regionally and internationally. It is fair to say that India dominates the region's research and the other South Asian countries look to India, as well as to the industrialized nations, for research. It is also the case that South Asian educational research has relatively easy access to the international knowledge network because it appears in English, although South Asian scholars pay closer attention to research trends abroad than the industrialized nations pay to literature from South Asia.

The large bulk of research-based analysis is done by South
Asian scholars working in universities and research institutions
although politicians, journalists, and educators also write quite a
bit, but their work is not usually based on research. The research
community in India is quite large. Agencies like the National
Council of Educational Research and Training (NCERT) in New Delhi
are major producers of research. They sponsor important journals
and publish books and monographs. Many of the universities in South
Asia have departments of education which are active in research. A
few scholars in teacher training institutions are also active. In
addition, educational issues have attracted the interest of many
social scientists and psychologists, sociologists, historians,
political scientists and others. By Third World standards, there has
been a good deal of money available for research on education, both
from governmental and academic agencies within the region and from
foreign funding sources. The indigenous research community
concerned with education in South Asia is large and experienced.
There is an infrastructure of expertise, institutions, and concerns
in all of the region with the possible exception of Nepal.
Researchers are being trained in local institutions, and an internal
community of scholars is at work. India dominates the region, but
political differences and economic problems have meant that there is
less personal contact among scholars in the region that might
otherwise be the case. Direct contact between Indian and Pakastani
researchers is rare as is collaboration between Bangladesh and
Pakistan. Nepal is very dependent on India. All of the countries
of the region have direct contacts with Western social scientists
and are influenced by research and methodological trends in the
West, particularly in the United States and Britain.

Much Third World educational research has been done over the
years by Western scholars although this trend is changing in many
countries. The domination by Western researchers has been less
evident in South Asia than other areas with a less-well-developed
academic infrastructure. Even at the time of Independence, all of
the countries of the region (with the partial exception of Nepal)
had an active university system and at least a small cadre of
researchers. Education has long been a concern in the region.
Thus, indigenous scholars were active in research from the
beginning. For example, the classic history of education in India
is by two Indian scholars, Syed Nurullah and J. P. Naik, A Students'
History of Education in India, and it was published in the early
1950s. Yet, Western scholars and Western methodological
orientations have been important in educational research in South
Asia. The most indirect but perhaps most important long-term impact
from the West is the influence of both methodological and topical
elements. The basic methodologies of research in virtually all
scientific fields, including education, are shaped in the
industrialized nations and legitimated by researchers in the West
and by Western journals and books. The trends in educational

research in the major industrialized nations, particularly the
United States and Britain, where many South Asian scholars have been
trained, are very important in South Asia. Even where these
approaches might not be directly relevant to local needs, they are
influential. Foreign researchers have done considerable work in
South Asia over the years, and this research has entered the
mainstream of local scholarship. In India, particularly, Western
scholars are able to publish their work locally, so it is relatively
easy to obtain access to it. During the 1950s and 1960s, when South
Asian educational research was in a fairly early stage and when
funds from the U.S. PL480 and other foreign-sponsored programs were
easily available, the number of Western scholars working in South
Asia was significant. Later, funding cutbacks in the West and
restrictions on access to research placed by the governments of the
region dramatically lowered the number of Western researchers.

Despite these major influences, however, the fact remains that
the large bulk of writing on South Asian education has been done by
local scholars and published in local books and journals. This, in
itself, places South Asia well ahead of many other parts of the
Third World in terms of research orientation and output. Today,
most of the scholars who have the most influence on education in
South Asia are indigenous scholars and while Western methodologies
are important, they are filtered through local researchers, who are
now able to ensure that the methods used are relevant to local
needs.

The impact of foreign sources, however, continues to be
important. Not only are intellectual influences from abroad
powerful, but books and journals published abroad--particularly in
the United States and Britain- ·are widely circulated in the region.
Many scholars feel that material published abroad is somehow more
valuable than locally published work, and research published in the
major international publications gets a wider circulation than work
published within the country of origin. This is particularly true
for Bangladesh, Pakistan, and Sri Lanka but also for India to some
extent. Local scholars often want to take advantage of the higher
prestige and often the greater financial remuneration of publishing
abroad. Foreign scholars who have worked on South Asian education
also tend to publish in their own countries, thus increasing the
amount of work published outside of the region. Thus, a large body
of research on South Asian education is published in the West. The
balance, especially for India, is on the side of indigenous
publication and the trend is increasingly in that direction, but it
is impossible to ignore research and scholarship published outside
the region.

Several key South Asian institutions have been active in
sponsoring research on education. These agencies sometimes also
sponsor journals. In India, the National Council of Educational

Research and Training (NCERT) is the agency responsible for school-related educational research. It has concerned itself with curriculum development, educational administration, the expansion of schools, the education of minority groups, and a wide range of other issues. NCERT is a Government of India agency and its financing comes from the Ministry of Education. The Indian Council for Social Science Research (ICSSR) has also taken an interest in education and has funded many research projects, mostly by social scientists, relating to education. In Bangladesh, the Foundation for Research on Educational Planning and Development (FREPD) has been active in sponsoring and publishing research. In Sri Lanka, the Marga Institute has included education among its subjects of research. In Nepal, the Institute of Education at Tribhuvan University has been responsible for a good deal of educational research. In all of the South Asian countries, the ministries of education have been instrumental, both directly and indirectly, in research on education. Much of the research on education has resulted from the initiative of individual scholars or small groups of researchers, sometimes with external financial assistance. For example, much of the research on women's education in India is the work of feminist scholars in Bombay and in New Delhi, with the support of the Ford Foundation and the ICSSR.

Publications are somewhat difficult to obtain. Many agencies publish their own documents, frequently in mimeographed (cyclostyled) format, and these publications are very difficult to obtain as they are neither cataloged nor distributed properly. This is true of many government reports. It is particularly unfortunate that educational documents are not widely distributed in the region, and it is frequently easier to locate a document published in Sri Lanka or Bangladesh in New York or London than in New Delhi or Karachi. There are few sources of bibliographical materials on education in the region or even within the individual countries. Doctoral dissertations, a source of much original data, are hard to locate. In short, access to information on education is one of the most serious problems in South Asia.

Despite these problems, a small number of journal and book publishers take a major interest in educational research. These are prominently featured in the bibliography that follows this essay. In India, several key journals are particularly valuable in keeping abreast of educational research. Economic and Political Weekly frequently publishes articles relating to education. Education Quarterly is the publication of the Ministry of Education, and the Journal of Indian Education is issued by the NCERT. The Journal of Higher Education is published under the auspices of the University Grants Commission and features material relating to post-secondary education, as does New Frontiers in Education. A number of smaller publications also exist. Among the publishers in India that publish on education are Vikas, S. Chand, Sterling, and Oxford University Press.

In the past decade, a large number of Indian publishers, mostly in New Delhi, have published social science monographs, and education is a prominent subfield of publication. The other South Asian nations do not have as prominent a center for publishing activity in education, and thus relevant materials are more difficult to locate. It is also more difficult in these countries for an author to gain access to publications since choices are more limited. As in India, most, but not all, of the material is published in English.

Conclusion

Research on education in South Asia is diverse, complex and diffuse. Among Third World regions, South Asia is one of the most active in terms of research and publication and is dominated by India, with its large university system and plethora of journals and publishers. India is indeed a "research superpower." The fact that the region uses English as the main medium of communication in research and scholarly writing gives it a special advantage in terms of communicating with the outside world as well as in intraregional communication. Yet, it is surprising that there is so little regional collaboration or even regional use of books and journals. Indian materials are used to some extent throughout the region, but India itself does not pay much attention to what is going on elsewhere in the region. For all of the South Asian nations, there is considerable reliance on research trends and publications from the industrialized world, but little regional consciousness. Part of the problem, of course, results from political disagreements among the countries of the region, but the lack of regional cooperation is common in the Third World.

This essay has pointed out some of the major trends in educational research in South Asia and has discussed the configuration of research and publication in the region. The bibliography that follows provides a concrete overview of research on education. It is hoped that this volume will permit the reader to understand not only the research on education but also the context in which that research was produced.

The Bibliography

CHAPTER 1

HISTORY OF EDUCATION

INDIA

Books

1. Apte, D. G. Universities in Ancient India. Baroda: M.S.
    University, Faculty of Education and Psychology, undated.

    An account of four famous universities in ancient India--
    Takshasila, Nalanda, Valabhi, and Vikramasila--existing
    between 1000 B.C. and the twelfth century A.D. Gives a brief
    description of function, finances, courses taught, famous
    students and teachers, and reasons for the demise of the
    universities.

2. Basu, Aparna. Essays in the History of Indian Education.
    New Delhi: Concept, 1982.

    A series of essays on aspects of the history of education
    in India, this volume includes discussions of such topics as
    the origins and operations of the Indian education system,
    1757-1947, the indigenous system of education in the early
    nineteenth century and its decline, technical education in
    India between 1854 and 1921, comparative colonial educational
    policies, the education of civil servants during the Company
    period, and an overview of the history of Indian education.
    The author draws on original sources as well as the work of
    other historians in India and abroad.

19

3.   Basu, Aparna. The Growth of Education and Political
      Development in India, 1898-1920. Delhi: Oxford
      University, 1974.

      The rapid expansion of English education at all levels in
      the first two decades of this century set the pattern for
      future development. This appraisal of the interplay of
      politics and educational policy examines the motivations of
      the administration's educational policy during this period
      and the socioeconomic factors such as caste, religion, and
      region which determined the pattern of literacy that emerged
      and in turn generated political overtones.

4.   Bhatnagar, S. K. History of M.A.O. College, Aligarh. Delhi:
      Asia, 1969.

5.   Bhatt, B. D. and J. C. Aggarwal. Educational Documents in
      India, 1813-1968: Survey of Indian Education. New Delhi:
      Arya Book Depot, 1969.

      A collection of extracts from leading official educational
      documents arranged chronologically so as to present a
      perspective in the development of public education. Covers
      the period from the Charter Act of 1813 to the National
      Policy on Education. The concluding chapter presents a
      historical calendar on education.

6.   Biswas, A., and Surendra Agrawal, eds. Indian Educational
      Documents Since Independence: Committees, Commissions,
      Conferences. New Delhi: Academic, 1971.

7.   Bose, Anima. Higher Education in India in the 19th Century:
      The American Involvement, 1883-1893. Calcutta: Punthi
      Pustak, 1978.

8.   Brockway, K. N. and Marjorie Sykes. Unfinished Pilgrimage:
      The Story of Some South Indian Schools, 1823-1923, 1923-
      1973. Madras: Christian Literature Society, 1973.

      This is a history of St. Christopher's Training Colleges
      and related institutions in the broader context of South
      Indian educational movements. It uses material from A Larger
      Way for Women and A New Day for Indian Women, supplemented
      and updated.

9. Chatterji, Reena. Impact of Raja Ram Mohan Roy on Education
    in India. New Delhi: S. Chand, 1983.

    An evaluation of the contribution of Raja Ram Mohan Roy
    which presents his educational ideas, his role in
    establishing educational institutions and his contributions
    in the field of literature and journalism, in the context of
    the history of Indian education and the impact of the West.
    Ram Mohan Roy is seen as an advocate of Western scientific
    education as a way of modernizing and rejuvenating the Indian
    system.

10. Chaube, S. P. A History of Education in India. Allahabad:
    Ram Narain Lal Beni Madho, 1965.

11. Das, Sisir Kumar. Sahibs and Munshis: An Account of the
    College of Fort William. New Delhi: Orion, 1978.

    A history of a significant educational institution,
    covering the period from its foundation in 1800 to its demise
    in 1850. Discusses other important aspects of an
    institution, founded primarily for the general education of
    British civil servants, such as the development of Indian
    language prose, printing, publishing, and language teaching
    methods. Uncovers the tensions between the utilitarian
    function of training in administration and scholarly
    interests, and sheds light on the relationships between
    Indians and Europeans, both teachers and students.

12. Das Gupta, Debendra Chandra. Educational Psychology of the
    Ancient Hindus. Calcutta: University of Calcutta, 1949.

    A treatise on the contributions of the ancient Hindus--
    including Buddhists and Jains--to educational psychology.
    Traces developments from the time of Rig Veda to the twelfth
    century A.D., however, in a topical rather than chronological
    manner. Sources used are Brahmanic, Buddhistic, and Jaina,
    in originals and translations.

13.   Dharampal. The Beautiful Tree: Indigenous Indian Education
       in the Eighteenth Century. New Delhi: Biblio Impex, 1983.

       This is a comprehensive study of archival materials,
       relating particularly to what was known during colonial rule.
       The author has shown that the indigenous system of education
       at the end of the eighteenth century compared more than
       favorably with the system obtaining in England at about the
       same time, in respect to the number of schools and colleges
       proportionate to the population, the number of students
       attending these institutions, the number of years spent by
       students in school and college, the diligence as well as the
       intelligence of students, the quality of teachers, the
       financial support provided from public and private sources,
       the high percentage of lower class (Sudras and others)
       students receiving education as compared to upper class
       (Brahmin, Kshatriya, and Vaishya) students, and the range of
       subjects taught.

14.   DiBona, Joseph, ed. One Teacher One School. New Delhi:
       Biblio Impex, 1983.

       The Adam Reports on indigenous culture in early nineteenth
       century Bengal have long been recognized as a unique record
       of Indian institutions before the British influence extended
       to all the interior villages. What Adam did was to carefully
       document the existence of this system of schools in a way
       that would rival the best empirical efforts today. What may
       be most difficult to comprehend from a modern perspective is
       how the small schools (each school had but one teacher) with
       limited resources were able to train quality professionals
       and specialists for the wide range of social needs in Bengali
       society. These village schools turned out the accountants,
       the lawyers, the doctors, the priests, the logicians, and the
       bureaucrats that were required in nineteenth century Bengal.
       The decision by T. B. Macaulay supported by the Governor
       General that Western education in the English language was to
       be imposed on the diverse cultures of India brought many
       unexpected results. The majority of poor villagers were cut
       off from access to the most prestigious jobs in government
       and industry. The alienation of educated Indians from the
       land is another theme that runs through discussions of Indian
       education; the other consequence that is really an aspect of
       the same condition is the erosion of traditional culture.
       The evidence of the demise of indigenous culture is closely
       associated with the elimination of indigenous schools. As
       traditional schools disappeared so too did the folklore and
       history that gave the rural community its stability and
       appeal. The suggestion that the English language itself has
       been a barrier to economic and social progress is likely to

be dismissed as malicious by those benefitting most from
English education. The fact that Japan has been able to
modernize without benefit of a Western language or Israel
resurrecting Hebrew for contemporary purposes notwithstanding, there remains resistance to the suggestion that the
adoption of English continues to serve as a barrier to social
and economic progress in South Asia.

15.   D'Souza, A. A. Anglo-Indian Education: A Study of its
      Origin and Growth in Bengal up to 1960. Delhi: Oxford
      University, 1976.

16.   Education in Ancient India. Varanasi: Nand Kishore, 1965.

17.   Ghosh, Suresh Chandra, ed. Development of University
      Education, 1916-1920. (Selections from Educational
      Records, New Series, Vol. 2). New Delhi: Sterling, 1977.

18.   Jaffer, S. M. Education in Muslim India. Lahore: Ripon,
      1964.

19.   Jaffer, S. M. Education in Muslim India, Being an Inquiry to
      the State of Education During the Muslim Period of Indian
      History 1000-1800. Delhi: Indrah-c-Adabiyat-i, 1973.

20.   Jha, Hetukar. Colonial Context of Higher Education in India:
      Patna University from 1917 to 1951, A Sociological
      Appraisal. New Delhi: Usha, 1985.

21.   Keay, Frank E. A History of Education in India and Pakistan.
      London: Oxford University, 1959.

      First published in 1918 as: Indian Education in Ancient
      and Later Times. A history of India's indigenous educational
      systems from ancient times up to the introduction of Western
      education.

22.   Mookerji, Radha Kumud. Ancient Indian Education. London:
      Macmillan, 2nd ed., 1951.

      A scholarly account of Brahmanical and Buddhist educational
      theories and practices from Vedic times to about A.D. 1000.

23.   Mukherji, S. N. History of Education in India (Modern
      Period). Baroda: Acharya Book Depot, 1974.

24. Mukhopadhyay, Gopal. Mass Education in Bengal: (1882-1914).
     Calcutta: National, 1984.

     Explores how the problem of elementary education of the
     masses in Bengal was handled by the British government, the
     Christian missionaries and the leaders of Bengali society,
     from the Hunter Commission of 1882 to 1913 when the new
     education policy was announced. Discusses the impact of
     modernization on different classes in Bengali society, with
     special reference to mass education. Based on original
     sources.

25. Naik, J. P. and S. C. Ghosh. Development of Educational
     Service, 1859-1879. New Delhi: Sterling, 1977.

26. Naik, K. C. and S. Sankaram. A History of Agricultural
     Universities. New Delhi: Oxford and IBH, 1972.

27. Nurullah, Syed and J. P. Naik. A Students' History of
     Education in India. Bombay: Macmillan, 1962.

     The history of the evolution of the modern system of
     education in India has been discussed from different angles.
     The background of the study is provided not only by the
     social political and constitutional history of India but also
     by the sociopolitical and educational developments in
     contemporary England. How the planning of institutions in
     India was influenced by institutions in England and how
     changes in the educational policy of England were reflected
     in Indian education are discussed. Further, how the function
     of English education was viewed both by British and the
     Indian elites and why the system was popular is analyzed. An
     attempt has been made in this book to show the conflict
     between traditional and Western education policies and to
     trace its history. The major influence and interrelationship
     between three major groups, the missionaries, the European
     officials of the education department, and the Indian people
     are highlighted.

28. Pandit, K. G. The Deccan Education Society: 1885-1960.
     Poona: Deccan Education Society, 1960.

     An abridgement of the larger history of the society
     compiled by P. M. Limaye and published in 1935. Covers the
     aims and objects of the society which has founded several
     educational institutions, its progress over seventy-five
     years, and a retrospective evaluation.

29.   Parasnis, N. R. The History and Survey of Education in Thane
        District. Bombay: University of Bombay, 1967.

        A history of educational changes since 1818, concentrating
        on primary and secondary education, problems in the education
        of tribals, and the existing facilities. Based primarily on
        government documents.

30.   Rai, B. C. History of Indian Education. Ahmadabad:
        Prakashan Kendra, 1965.

31.   Rao, V. Y. Education and Learning in Andhra under the East
        India Company. Secunderabad: undated.

32.   Ray, Krishnalal. Education in Medieval India. Delhi: B.
        R., 1984.

        Surveys the education system in medieval India during the
        period of Muslim rule. Both the Hindu and the Islamic system
        are examined.

33.   Richey, J. A., ed. Selections from Educational Records, Part
        II (1840-1859). Delhi: Manager of Publications,
        Government of India, 1965.

34.   Sangma, M. S. History of Education in Garo Hills. Guwahati:
        Spectrum, 1985.

35.   Seth, R. R. and J. L. Mehta. A History of the Punjab
        University: 1947-1967. Chandigarh: Punjab University,
        1968.

36.   Sharib, Zahurul Hassan. The History and Prospects of Rural
        Education in India. Bombay: All India Institute of Local
        Self-Government, 1982.

37.   Sharma, N. K. Linguistic and Educational Aspirations under a
        Colonial System: A Study of Sanskrit Education During the
        British Rule in India. New Delhi: Concept, 1976.

        Presents a systematic illustration of the development of
        Sanskrit education during the colonial period. Evaluates the
        claims of the Anglicists that they could revive Sanskrit
        education in India on better lines by introducing scientific
        methods in its teaching and study. Also examines the
        criticism of the Indian Orientalists and reformers that the
        British destroyed the finest points of Sanskrit education,
        replacing individual and direct method of instruction by mass

method, the sacred ties of the teacher and the students by materialistic relationship, and Sanskrit as medium of instruction by English, for their own convenience.

38.   Singa, S. P. English in India: A Historical Study with Particular Reference to English Education in India. Patna: Janaki Prakashan, 1978.

39.   Singh, R. P. Education in an Imperial Colony. New Delhi: National, 1979.

It is argued that educational policy in Britain had an impact on British colonial policy in India and other colonial areas such as Ireland. The book examines the evolution of British educational policy and the nature of British society in the nineteenth century and then relates these developments to India. The nature of British colonial policy and practice is discussed in detail.

40.   Singh, R. P. A Model for Studying Colonial Systems of Education with Particular Reference to India. New Delhi: National Council of Educational Research and Training.

41.   Tikekar, Aroon. The Cloister's Pale: A Biography of the University of Bombay. Bombay: Somaiya, 1984.

An account of developments in the University of Bombay in the context of the changing city, from 1857 to 1982. Based primarily on university records, biographical, and autobiographical sources.

42.   Toppo, Sita. Dynamics of Educational Development in Tribal India. New Delhi: Classical, 1979.

An anthropological approach to the study of the growth of education and its impact on culture among the Oraon tribe in Bihar, from the most primitive and informal to the modern and formal types of education. Includes a discussion on the traditional system of Dhumkuria, the reasons for its disintegration, as well as a description of a system that attempts to synthesize the Dhumkuria with modern education. Evaluates the contribution of Christian Missionaries and of the Adim Jati Seva Mandal and carries out an in-depth empirical study of five contemporary schools. Asserts the significance of education in social change.

Articles

43.   Acharya, P. "Indigenous Vernacular Education in Pre-British
      Era: Traditions and Problems." Economic and Political
      Weekly 13 (December 2, 1978): 1981-88.

44.   Chakrabarty, D., and R. Dasgupta. "Functions of the
      Nineteenth Century Baman: A Document." Economic and
      Political Weekly (August 31, 1974): M-73-75.

45.   Datta, Bhabhatosh. "Presidency College Calcutta." Journal
      of Higher Education 4 (Autumn 1978): 145-56.

46.   DiBona, Joseph. "Indigenous Virtue and Foreign Vice:
      Alternative Perspectives on Colonial Education."
      Comparative Education Review 25 (June 1981): 202-15.

47.   Hay, S. "Growing Up in British India--Indian Autobiographers
      on Childhood and Education Under the Raj." Journal of
      Asian Studies 44, no. 3 (1985): 658-59.

48.   Higginson, J. H. "Dependence or Independence in Higher
      Education: Comments on the 1917 Calcutta University
      Commission." Pp. 95-107 in Dependence and Interdependence
      in Education: International Perspectives, ed. Keith
      Watson. London: Croom Helm, 1984.

      Compares certain efforts of the ruling power at the time
      when Mohandas Karamchand Gandhi was just beginning to emerge
      as a politically significant figure in India. The author
      identifies four problems as living realities facing Gandhi as
      he pursued his political negotiations and as he evolved an
      educational theory to be expressed in the Wardha Scheme of
      Basic Education. These four issues are: the consequences of
      creating an intellectual, jobless proletariat; the need for a
      change of attitude about vocational development; prejudices
      arising from multicultural problems; and the education of
      women.

49.   Kooiman, Dick. "The Gospel of Coffee: Mission, Education
      and Employment in 19th Century Travancore." Economic and
      Political Weekly 19 (September 1, 1984): 1535-43.

50.   McDonald, Ellen. "English Education and Social Reform in
      Late Nineteenth-Century Bombay: A Case Study in the
      Transmission of a Cultural Ideal." Journal of Asian
      Studies 25 (May 1966): 453-70.

The content of higher education, in most societies, has formed a culture the monopoly of which has served to set the highly educated apart from the common man. Thus the system of higher education forms a well-recognized institutional avenue approach, not only to a society's high literary culture, but to prestige and power as well. These prospects of higher educational systems suggests that the content of higher education may have a social utility for the educated elite quite apart from its informational value. This article examines the relationship between the college curriculum and the social reform activities of the educated elites of one Indian province, Bombay, in the late nineteenth century.

51.   Minault, G., and D. Lelyveld. "Campaign for a Muslim University, 1898-1920 (Muslim University, Aligarh)." Modern Asian Studies 8 (April 1974): 145-89.

This article concentrates on the movement of establishing a Muslim University at Aligarh, India between 1898 to 1920. For the authors, the Muslim University campaign was both political and educational in nature. The campaign was a good example of the confluence of education and politics in modern India.

52.   Sardesai, Gargi. "Some Aspects of the Education of Women in Maharashtra in the 19th Century." Journal of S.N.D.T. Women's University 6 (1977): 184-99.

53.   Shah, Gunvant B. "Genesis of Women's Education in India." National Institute of Education Journal 9, no. 3 (1973): 1-9.

Article reviews history of female education in India from eighteenth through early twentieth centuries. It discusses efforts of missionaries, social reformers, and the government in female education.

54.   Singh, Amrik. "Indian Education Since 1947: An Assessment." Prospects 5, no. 3 (1975): 312-22.

Assesses Indian education since independence. The various aspects and impact of all the five national plans for education and the Education Commission Report (1964-66) have been evaluated in the sociopolitical and economic context of India.

55.   Thaarakan, P. K. Michael. "Socio-Economic Factors in Educational Development: Case of Nineteenth Century Travancore." Economic and Political Weekly (November 10 and 17, 1984): 1913-28 and 1959-67.

PAKISTAN

Books

56.   Khan, Mohammad Hameeduddin. History of Muslim Education,
      1751 to 1854. Karachi: All Pakistan Education Conference,
      Academy of Educational Research, 1973.

57.   Pakistan. Development of Education in Pakistan, 1973-75.
      Islamabad: Ministry of Education, 1975.

58.   Zaman, Umme Salma. Banners Unfurled: A Critical Analysis of
      Developments in Education in Pakistan. Karachi: Royal,
      1981.

      Covers the historical background of education in Pakistan
      and the economic, geographical, and religious factors having
      a bearing on education. An analysis has been made of prob-
      lems related to the impact of new technology, multilingualism
      and political instability, educational planning, and
      bureaucracy.

SRI LANKA

Books

59.   Chelliah, J. V. A Century of English Education.
      Vaddukoddai: Jaffna College, 1984.

60.   Education in Ceylon: From the Sixth Century B.C. to the
      Present Day: A Centenary Volume. 3 vols. Colombo:
      Ministry of Education and Cultural Affairs, 1969.

      This Centenary volume on education looks at the educational
      tradition in Ceylon from the sixth century B.C. to present
      day. The volume contains over 100 chapters contributed by
      eminent scholars, educationists, historians, sociologists,
      and political scientists and is published in three separate
      parts. Arranged in chronological order, Part One contains a
      study of education and its achievements in ancient Ceylon; a
      look at educational growth and development up to the
      fifteenth century; and an inquiry into education under
      Portuguese and Dutch rule. Part Two contains a comprehensive
      discussion of issues in education during British Colonialism,
      and a study of the current phase of education. Part Three

looks at educational traditions among Buddhists, Hindus and Muslims, and an examination of auxiliary services in education such as museums, libraries, radio, press, and cinema. Includes bibliography on education in Ceylon.

61.   Jayasuriya, J. Early History of Education in Ceylon: From Earliest Times up to Mahasend. Colombo: Dept. of Cultural Affairs, 1969.

62.   Jayasuriya, J. Education in Ceylon Before and After Independence, 1939-69. Colombo: Associated, 1970.

63.   Jayasuriya, J. Educational Policies and Progress during British Rule in Ceylon (Sri Lanka), 1796-1948. Colombo: Associated, 1976.

This book, comprising sixty-five chapters in seven sections and presented in numbered paragraphs, is a comprehensive history of education in Ceylon (Sri Lanka). Its history has been divided into five periods and for each the relevant political and social background, information regarding the agencies and documents having significant impact during the period, descriptions and statistics for the various types of schools in existence during the period, a statement of the various issues leading to controversy (some carrying into subsequent periods) are provided. In most sections the curricula, examinations, language problems, school finance, and administration are dealt with in detail.

Discusses how the indifferent British attitude toward education contributed to numerous dualities that existed throughout the period: the existence of schools under government management and schools under denominational and private management; a linguistic division in the medium of instruction between English and the vernacular; the advantages of urban education in contrast to rural education; the English-medium schools leading to lucrative employment and higher education in contrast to the vernacular-medium schools leading only to menial employment; the relatively high fees charged in the English schools as compared with the absence of tuition in the vernacular schools (thus creating an economic duality). The result of these dualities was that educational provision was unplanned, unevenly distributed, wasteful of human and financial resources, and that, above all, access to a quality education was by and large denied to the mass of the rural population and the urban poor.

64.   Ruberu, Ranjit T. Education in Colonial Ceylon: Being a Research Study on the History of Education in Ceylon for the Period 1796 to 1834. Kandy: Kandy, 1962.

Traces the history of the development of education in Ceylon (Sri Lanka) during the first thirty-eight years of British occupation. All educational development in the country throughout this period culminating with the implementation of the educational reforms of the Colebrooke Commission in 1834 has been traced and presented elaborately. The significant role played by the Christian Missionary Societies in the field of education in Ceylon during this period has been discussed in detail. Attempts have been made to bring to light the educational policies of the authorities responsible for education, namely the British Government, the Ceylon Government, and the Christian Missionary Societies.

65.   Sumathipala, K. H. M. History of Education in Ceylon, 1796-1965: With Special Reference to the Contribution Made by C. W. W. Kannangard to the Educational Development of Ceylon. Colombo: Tisara Prakasakayo, 1968.

66.   Van Goor, J. Jan Kompenie as Schoolmaster: Dutch Education in Ceylon 1690-1795. Groningen: Wolters-Noordhoff, 1978.

Articles

67.   Ames, M. M. "The Impact of Western Education on Religion and Society in Ceylon." Pacific Affairs 40 (1967): 19-42.

68.   Corea, J. C. A. "One Hundred Years of Education in Ceylon." Modern Asian Studies 3, no. 2 (1969): 151-76.

69.   Jayaweera, S. "British Educational Policy in Ceylon in the Nineteenth Century." Pedagogica Historica 9 (1969): 68-90.

70.   Ruberu, Ranjit. "Educational Traditions Indigenous to Ceylon." Pedagogica Historica 14, no. 1 (1974): 106-17.

71.   Ryan, B. F. "Status, Achievement, and Education in Ceylon: An Historical Perspective." Journal of Asian Studies 20 (1961): 463-76.

72.   Watson, K. "Educational Policies and Progress During British Rule in Ceylon." Compare 9, no. 1 (1979): 86-92.

73.   Wills, J. F. "Kompenie, Jan as Schoolmaster--Dutch Education in Ceylon, 1690-1795." American Historical Review 85, no. 1 (1980): 196.

74.   Wood, H. R. "Educational Policies and Progress During
      British Rule in Ceylon." Comparative Education 22, no. 3
      (1978): 517-18.

CHAPTER 2

EDUCATION AND SOCIETY

BANGLADESH

Books

75.   Foundation for Research on Educational Planning and
       Development (FREPD). The Study on the Situation of
       Children in Bangladesh. Dhaka: FREPD, 1981.

       This study is based mainly on primary data generated on the
       needs of children and the major problems they face in the
       areas of education, health, nutrition, and social welfare,
       through field surveys conducted in eight selected rural loca-
       tions, two from each of the four administrative divisions of
       Bangladesh. It was found that only about 40 percent of the
       five-fourteen age group population have been enrolled in
       schools in the survey areas. Widespread poverty, low
       educational status of the adult members, malnutrition among
       the child population, high infant mortality, serious
       incidence of disease and sickness coupled with general
       ignorance of the population have created extremely
       uncongenial and adverse economic, environmental, and physical
       conditions for the education of children. Hence, the low
       enrollment ratio.

76.   Islam, Taherul. Social Justice and the Educational System in
       Bangladesh. Dhaka: Bureau of Economic Research,
       University of Dhaka, 1975.

       This study throws light on the problem of the slow progress
       of literacy in Bangladesh. Official statistics being
       deficient in quality as well as in coverage, Islam's study,
       based on a survey of two rural areas, provides an interesting
       analysis of the causes of low enrollment of school-age
       children in primary school. Discussed at some length is the
       problem of financing education and in particular the role of
       public expenditure in promoting equality. Generally public

expenditure on education is justified by the concept that
education is an equalizing institution in society. It is
believed that public financing of education ensures equality
of opportunity to all social classes by permitting all able
individuals of whatever social background to rise in the
social structure. At subsidized prices, even poorer students
are able to receive education and thus equality of
educational opportunity is believed to be ensured by
budgetary financing of education, economic disadvantages of
the poorer families notwithstanding. The author argues,
however, that the financing of education which seems to be
progressive does not, in fact, allow education to act as an
essential social factor preventing the transformation of
socioeconomic differences into social stratification. It
rather favors the development of the richer social strata at
the expense of the poorer in a developing country like
Bangladesh. This is so because even though public
expenditure reduces tuition fee, other costs of education
which are still to be privately borne by students may prove
too heavy for the poorer families. Though the study is
mainly limited to the primary level of education, it is
reasonable to expect that the picture in the second and third
level of education is also the same, if not more
disappointing for poor people. The process of social
selection of students from economic groups, which starts from
the primary level of education, continues, perhaps, in a more
rigorous form, right up to the third level of education.

Articles

77.   Chowdhury, A. K. M. "Education and Infant Survival in Rural
         Bangladesh." Health Policy and Education 2, nos. 3-4
         (1982): 369-74.

78.   Dove, Linda. "The Political Context of Education in
         Bangladesh 1971-80." Pp. 165-82 in Politics and
         Educational Change: An International Survey, P. Broadfoot
         et al. London: Croom Helm, 1981.

         Discusses the political context of educational development.
         It is widely believed both by national leaders and the
         international community that education is a critical need if
         Bangladesh is to develop economically and socially. This
         article assesses why policy implementation was defective,
         partly in terms of variables within the educational system
         itself. Also examines the national and international factors
         affecting the course of Bangladeshi development.

INDIA

Books

79.   Bhatnagar, G. S. Education and Social Change: A Study in
       Some Rural Communities in Punjab. Calcutta: Minerva
       Associates, 1972.

       Seeks to identify the role of education in social
       structural, attitudinal and behavioral change, with reference
       to three villages in Ambala District, Punjab state. The
       villages differ in educational facilities, population size,
       and proximity to urban centers. Finds that education is one
       of the most important factors in social change. The study is
       based mostly on interviews which seek to establish the
       relation between educational background and attitude towards
       and knowledge of socioeconomic issues.

80.   Chitnis, S. Drugs on the College Campus. Bombay: Tata
       Institute of Social Sciences, 1974.

81.   Dave, J. P. Our Changing Schools: A Research Profile.
       Ahmedabad: New Order, 1969.

82.   DeRebello, Daphne. Formal Schooling and Personal Efficacy.
       New Delhi: Sterling, 1977.

83.   D'Souza, A. Indian Public Schools: A Sociological Study.
       New Delhi: Sterling, 1974.

84.   Gandhi, M. K. Problem of Education. Ahmedabad: Navjivan,
       1962.

85.   Gore, M. S. and others. Field Studies in the Sociology of
       Education: All India Report. New Delhi: National Council
       of Educational Research and Training, 1970.

       The general report of an extensive all-India survey is
       presented on the social background and social values of the
       major participants in education, with the question of
       equality in educational opportunity being an accompanying
       focus of interest. Based on data compiled from
       questionnaires administered during 1964-67 to a sample of
       students, parents, teachers, and heads of institutions

connected with primary schools, secondary schools, and colleges in eight states: Andhra Pradesh, West Bengal, Gujarat, Maharashtra, Mysore, Orissa, Punjab and Rajasthan. Reports for the different states are published separately, as are papers presented at seminars preparatory to the survey.

86.   Gore, M. S., I. P. Desai, and Suma Chitnis. Papers in the Sociology of Education in India. New Delhi: National Council of Educational Research and Training, 1975.

The papers in this book seek to answer a series of questions related to modernization, democracy, and education. The goals of democracy and modernization have created new rights and responsibilities. What are the implications of this to the education system in India? What was the focus of formal ·education in the Vedic, the Buddhist, the Moslem, and the British periods? Do modernization and a democratic way of life call for a major change in the traditional outlook on education? What is modernization? What is the role of education in society, and particularly in a changing society? How can the sociologist help define this role? How does the sociologist explain student indiscipline? What are the implications, to education, of the acceptance of the ideal of an equality of opportunity? Does education foster equality and social mobility? Are opportunities for tribals, backward castes, and women unrestricted and equal in India?

87.   Haq, S. Education and Political Culture in India: The Limits of the Schooling System and Political Socialization. New Delhi: Sterling, 1981.

Discusses some aspects of democratic political culture and socialization and their relation to the political function of education. On the basis of a sample of 600 respondents-- students, teachers, and parents--drawn from three representative schools in Delhi, the author makes a comparative analysis of the sources--textbooks, teachers, parents, and the mass media--and consequences of political socialization in terms of political orientation, i.e. political awareness, commitment, and participation. Data are collected from questionnaires, interviews, observations, and content analysis of textbooks. The family in a structured society, rather than the school, is found to be the most important source of political socialization determining the choice of school and exposure to mass media. The school reinforces the influences of nonformal and primary institutions. The two major patterns of political orientation, the "articulate-moderate" and the "inarticulate-

militant," represent the hierarchical traditions of society
and schools. A common school system is suggested as one way
of promoting an integral democratic culture in India.

88. Jindal, B. L. Schooling and Modernity. New York: Apt,
     1984.

     An investigation of modern aspects of education in a sample
     of urban and rural adolescents from Hissar, India. The role
     of the teacher and the impact of student participation in
     extra-curricular activities are also considered.

89. Kamat, A. R. Education and Social Change in India. Bombay:
     Somaiya, 1985.

90. Mathur, S. S. A Sociological Approach to Indian Education.
     Agra: Vinod Pustak Mandir, 1973.

     Analyzes the weaknesses of the Indian educational system in
     the context of its establishment with inadequate
     consideration of the special characteristics of society and
     its distance from real needs. Discusses the social bases of
     education in various institutions such as the family,
     religion, state, and social stratification. Draws out the
     relation between educational programs and socioeconomic
     progress and the role of education in achieving the ideal of
     a socialistic pattern of society.

91. Mazumdar, Vina. Education and Social Change. Simla: Indian
     Institute of Advanced Study, 1972.

92. Mehta, S. The School and the Community in India. New Delhi:
     S. Chand, 1974.

93. Mohanty, Jagannath. Indian Education in the Emerging
     Society. New Delhi: Sterling, 1982.

     A discussion of the changing character of Indian education
     from the post-Independence period, in terms of new values,
     problems, and methods, and the contributions of Gandhi,
     Tagore and Aurobindo. Outlines the changing role of
     education in the context of issues such as national
     integration, international understanding, population control,
     vocationalization, and youth unrest. Concludes with a
     presentation of new philosophical and sociological
     perspectives on education.

94.   National Council of Educational Research and Training. Case
      Study on the Drop-out Problem in India Sponsored by the
      UNESCO Regional Office for Education in Asia and the
      Pacific. New Delhi: NCERT, 1982.

95.   Nayana Tara, S. Education in a Rural Environment. New
      Delhi: Ashish, 1985.

96.   Paliwal, M. R. Social Change and Education: Present and
      Future. New Delhi: Uppal, 1984.

97.   Panchmukhi, P. R. Inequality in Education. Dharwar: Center
      for Multi-disciplinary Research, 1981.

      Based on data relating to socioeconomic characteristics
      and performance of a sample of primary and secondary school
      students and facilities in the schools in Dharwar. Concludes
      that even in a relatively educationally advanced city, access
      to and participation in education are unequally distributed,
      mainly due to socioeconomic factors outside the scope of
      educational policy. Suggests ways in which short-term steps
      toward greater equality may be taken, within the given
      constraints.

98.   Prasad, S. N., ed. Education and World Hunger. Delhi:
      Mittal, 1985.

99.   Raza, Moonis; Aijazuddin Ahmad and Sheel Chand Nuna. School
      Accessibility in India: The Regional Dimension. New
      Delhi: National Institute for Educational Planning and
      Administration (NIEPA), 1984.

      The present paper attempts to portray the inter-regional
      variations in the population coverage by schools of different
      levels within the range of distances perceived as walkable.
      The paper also computes the weighted mean distances to
      schools of different levels for each district of the states
      of the Indian Union and analyzes their spatial pattern.
      While highlighting the role of physical factors in
      determining the pattern of accessibility, the study reveals
      that the areas with inhospitable physical conditions are
      characterized by poor accessibility to schools.

100. Rudolph, Susanne H. and Lloyd I. Rudolph, eds. Education and
      Politics in India: Studies in Organization, Society and
      Policy. Cambridge: Harvard University Press, 1972.

Identifies and analyzes the institutions and processes that
shape educational policy and performance in India. Critical
problems in the relationship between politics and education
are identified and concepts and methods for their
investigation are explored.

101. Ruhela, S. P., ed. Contributions to Sociology of Education
      in India: Vol. 1 University Education In India. New
      Delhi: Jain Brothers, 1969.

102. Ruhela, S. P., ed. Social Determinants of Educability in
      India: Papers in the Sociological Context of Indian
      Education. New Delhi: Jain Brothers, 1969.

      A collection of twenty-four contributions by social
      scientists on the problems of education in India and their
      roots in the socioeconomic and cultural situation. The
      underlying principle is that there are elements both in
      society and in the educational system that determine the
      educability of different groups. Discusses a number of
      related topics, such as the environmental limitations on
      educability, special education of the gifted, of delinquents,
      of tribals, of scheduled castes and of rural and urban
      communities. While presenting the results of studies based
      on primary and secondary sources, the collection contains a
      conceptual framework and a review of research in this field,
      from an interdisciplinary social science perspective.

103. Saberwal, Satish, ed. Towards a Cultural Policy. New Delhi:
      Vikas, 1975.

      Comments on basic differences between the struggles and
      movements in India before 1947 and those after that year,
      viz. the former were concerned with cultural issues whereas
      the latter are not. Contributions are concerned with matters
      connected with the formulation and implementation of a
      cultural policy for India.

104. Saini, Shiv Kumar. Development of Education in India:
      Socio-Economic and Political Perspectives. New Delhi:
      Cosmo, 1980.

      An interdisciplinary study of the development of education
      in India from 1921 to 1947, in its social, economic and
      political context. Traces the role of the intellectual and
      elite during the period of the Independence movement, while
      analyzing developments at different stages of education and
      aspects such as women's education, educational research,
      policy making, administration and finance.

105. Salamatullah and S. P. Ruhela, eds. Sociological Dimensions of Indian Education. New Delhi: Raaj Prakashan, 1971.

106. Sargent, Sir John. Society, Schools and Progress in India. Oxford: Pergamon, 1968.

Society, Schools and Progress in India describes many educational turning points. They include crises of quantity, quality, resources, and orientation. The institutions of a vast and complex civilization are challenged by the need to catch up with the material achievements of the outside world, as well as the tasks of independence and of a newer concept of human dignity. Two alternatives to parliamentary democracy and to the "Western way of life" are found on India's borders. In the past, India has been the battle-ground of conflicting cultures yet has produced her own amalgam; the present study reveals how that process may be repeating itself now.

107. Seetharamu, A. S. Education in Slums. New Delhi: Ashish, 1983.

A study of the participation of slum dwellers in education, based on data regarding the social, economic, demographic and other characteristics of 500 families of dropouts and 500 families of regular attenders in twenty slums in Bangalore city. Compares the backgrounds in terms of occupation, income, religion, caste, health, family size and educational level; examines the contributions of dropouts to family incomes and the utilization of special educational facilities such as the midday means scheme, scholarships and free textbooks, by regular attenders. Policy implications are drawn out.

108. Seetharamu, A. S., and M. D. Ushadevi. Education in Rural Areas. New Delhi: Ashish, 1985.

A study of school participation in rural areas covering several school and nonschool factors. Data have been collected from a sample of drop out households and primary schools from sixty-two villages in ten talukas, selected from five different ecological regions. Draws out conclusions that are considered relevant to educational policy.

109. Shah, A. B., ed. The Social Context of Education: Essays in Honor of J. P. Naik. New Delhi: Allied, 1978.

A collection of articles presented by the J. P. Naik Festschrift Committee on the occasion of the seventy-first birthday of the notable educator. The twenty contributors are eminent educators from India and abroad who write on the interaction between education and society from the standpoint of social justice. Also includes a quasi-humorous article by J. P. Naik on what he would do if he were the educational dictator of India.

110. Shah, Beena. Sociology of Educational Development. Nainital: Gyanodaya Prakashan, 1984.

A study of the sociological and academic characteristics of graduate students of the Kumaun region grouped on the basis of caste, so as to reveal underlying psychological factors. Educational development is found to be influenced more by sociological variables than by a stable category like caste belongingness in itself. Education appears to play a limited part in bringing about a change in the ethos of Kumaun society.

111. Sharma, Sita Ram. American Influence on Indian Education. New Delhi: Raaj Prakashan, 1979.

A historical analysis of the development of education in post-Independence India, as it is related to the economic and cultural influences of U.S. foreign policy. Influences of an ideological, practical and institution-building character are seen with respect to secondary, higher, and teacher education. Aspects discussed are the educational context for government to government aid, the determinants of American aid, American educational trends as influencing the contribution to Indian education, and the actual impact on specific areas of Indian education.

112. Shils, E. The Intellectual Between Tradition and Modernity: The Indian Situation. Hague: Mouton, 1961.

113. Sivakumar, Chitra. Education, Social Inequality and Social Change in Karnataka. Delhi: Hindustan, 1982.

Explores class- and caste-based social inequalities and access to educational opportunity through an in-depth study of some colleges in Mysore city. Aspects of social change have been viewed in the perspective of a history of education in the state. In discussing the educational system, its organizational structure and process of socialization, problems such as student unrest are also covered. The last theme analyzed is the relation between students' social origins and their attitudes on caste, vocation, and marriage. Attitudinal change is seen as a reflection of wider societal changes.

114.   Taneja, V. R. Tryst with Education in the Technetronic Society: National Lectures Sponsored by the University Grants Commission. New Delhi: Sterling, 1983.

Three lectures on the problems of education analyzed in their changing societal context. Presents a brief history of educational developments, with a focus on policy changes after Independence. Appraises the state of primary, secondary, and higher education. Holds that present problems of education are related to India's becoming a technetronic society in which the political, economic, social, and cultural environment is influenced greatly by science and technology, and suggests an "ecological approach" which assumes an intimate relation between education and the social system.

115.   Veeraraghavan, J., ed. Education and the New International Order. New Delhi: Concept, 1983.

Articles

116.   Acharya, Poromesh. "Politics of Primary Education in West Bengal: The Case of Sahaj Path." Economic and Political Weekly (16 June 1981): 1069-75.

This paper attempts to study the agitation in West Bengal against the left front government's education policy, particularly the agitation over Sahaj Path, in the context of problems of appropriate primers to ensure universal literacy.

It traces the origins and growth of modern education in Bengal since the colonial intervention and notes that the historically exclusivist character of modern Bengali language and the existing system of education has meant that the benefits of modern education, including those accruing from learning Bengali as it has evolved in the nineteenth century, have been appropriated by the 'middle order'.

Viewed thus, both the introduction of Sahaj Path in 1969 by the united front government and the preparation of the new primer in 1980 by the left front government only appear as measures meant to help the masses; and the opposition parties have only taken advantage of the inconsistencies and contradictions in government's policy and have made an issue of Sahaj Path because it is likely to sell best.

117. Ahmad, Karuna. "Towards a Study of Education and Social
      Change." Economic and Political Weekly (14 January 1979):
      157-64.

      The sociology of knowledge may throw light on some of the
      perplexing aspects of the relationship between education and
      social change. For instance, the role of the educated
      Indians in the national movement of independence has been
      outlined time and again, but this remains an impressionistic
      observation. The role of the content of curriculum, the
      organization and the transmission of knowledge may give us
      more reliable and interesting data. More research ought
      therefore to be undertaken by sociologists in this hitherto-
      unexplored area.

      This will also enable us to distinguish between social
      changes at the structural level and those at the level of
      ideas, values, attitudes or what the author calls
      "ideational" change. Structural changes are more likely to
      be generated by politicoeconomic factors and ideational
      change can bring about stability in such a situation.

118. Ahmed, R. "New Education Pattern: Hair Splitting by the
      Privileged." Economic and Political Weekly 12 (December 3,
      1977): 2022-25.

119. Aikara, Jacob. "Education and Politics in India." Indian
      Journal of Adult Education 37 (January 1976): 19-23.

120. Atal, Y. "Professionalization of Sociologists." Economic
      and Political Weekly 6 (February 6, 1971): 431-33.

121. Chitnis, S. "Education and Equality." Pp. 73-106 in
      Education in a Changing Society, ed. A. Klioskowska and G.
      Martionotti. London: Sage, 1977.

122. Chitnis, S. "Parents and Students: Study in Value
      Orientation." Intergenerational Conflict in India, ed. M.
      P. Sinha and K. K. Gangrade. Bombay: 1977.

123. Desai, I. P. "Western Educational Elites and Social Change
      in India." Economic and Political Weekly 19, no. 15 (April
      14, 1984): 639-47.

124. Dhanagare, D. N. "Interdisciplinary Approach to Social
      Reality." Journal of Higher Education 7 (Monsoon 1981):
      97-109.

125. Forrester, D. B. "Western Academic Sophistry and Third
      World." Economic and Political Weekly 9, no. 40 (October
      5, 1974): 1695-1700.

126. Gould, Harold. "Educational Structures and Political
      Processes in Faizabad District, Uttar Pradesh." Pp.
      99-120 in Education and Politics in India, ed. S. H. Rudolph and
      L. I. Rudolph. Delhi: Oxford University Press, 1972.

127. Gusfield, Joseph. "Education and Social Segmentation in
      Modern India," The Social Sciences and the Comparative
      Study of Educational Systems. Edited by J. Fischer, pp.
      240-76. Scranton, Pa.: International Textbook Company,
      1970.

128. Kamat, A. R. "Education and Social Change: A Conceptual
      Framework." Economic and Political Weekly (17 July 1982):
      1237-44.

This article examines the different trends of thought on
the relationship between education and social change. It
rules out the idealistic approach to this connection. Yet it
underscores how, even as the educational structure is not the
prime mover of social change, education can in certain
situations contribute to the awakening of a new social
consciousness among individuals and groups who may be the
harbingers of change.

129. Kumar, Krishna. "Reproduction or Change?: Education and
      Elites in India." Economic and Political Weekly 20 (July
      27, 1985): 1280-84.

130. Lewis, James Mark. "Educational Involvement in Indian
      Poverty." Indian Educational Review 13 (April 1978): 1-
      20.

Poverty in India is well known. It is so common that it
has been, in the past and present, commonly unattended to.
The poor now are angry. Their resentment of the inequalities
of the past has been stirred to a point of action--social,
civic, economic and political.
Assuming that increased education with marketable skills
will eventually alleviate poverty in India, the present paper
attempts to build an action-oriented, long-range
instructional model. While doing so, it takes into account
research findings from India and abroad on the effects of
poverty on the instructional system. An attempt is also made
to combine all the ramifications of poverty--economic,
political and social--within a workable educational
structure. Such a model, it is felt, is required for any

systematic planning. At least a beginning has to be made now, if the poor of India are to reach the promised land.

131.   Lindsey, J. K. "School, State, Caste, and Class in Bombay." Canadian and International Education 7 (December 1978): 64-80.

In this article a theory of the capitalist state, especially in regard to the individualization of members of the society, is briefly outlined. The place of the educational system is located within the state and its differing roles in advanced capitalist and developing countries specified. The social class and caste structure of Bombay are briefly described and related to certain aspects of the school system in general. Then, four school variables are studied in more detail: dropouts, choice of language of instruction, choice of type of school, and the child's age in a given standard grade. These results are integrated into the more general theory of the state in attempt to specify more precisely the role of education in the transition from the caste-based traditional society to a social-class-based capitalist society.

132.   Lindsey, J. K. "Social Class and Primary School Age in Bombay: The Role of Education in the Transition to Capitalism." Canadian and International Education 6 (December 1977): 75-97.

In western capitalist countries, universal education plays an important role in reproducing existing social class relationships. But, in developing countries, the question is rather if and how such relationships are being produced for the first time, within a more "traditional" context. Does or will mass education serve this function in such countries? This study indicates how children fall behind in primary schools in Bombay. Children from the social classes not central to capitalism--the lumpenproletariat, artisans and shopkeepers--have been found to have random distributions of ages within a given standard (grade), while the others do not. Because of the economic precariousness of their situations, and the lack of integration into the capitalist ideology, these families appear not to start their children in school or to keep them there consistently. However, children of artisans and shopkeepers do have lower average ages in a given standard than working-class children. This indicates that at least those children from these two social classes who do stay in school may be integrated fairly rapidly into the capitalist system, and will have more chance of social mobility than members of the working class.

133.   Mohan, Dinesh.   "Indian Education: The Anti-Cultural
        Involution."   Journal of Higher Education 9 (Monsoon 1983):
        21-34.

134.   Saberwal, Satish.   "Education and Inequality: An Essay in
        Political Sociology."   Economic and Political Weekly (7
        February 1972):   409-12.

        Of every five-primary-school-age children in India, about
        two are out of school.   This fact must be considered in light
        of the exaggerated regard for a university education; in a
        highly inegalitarian social and economic system, the rewards
        for 'higher' education are excessive.
        This essay argues that the critical path both for
        quantitative expansion at the primary level and in
        qualitative reform in the universities lies through an
        egalitarian social transformation.

135.   Saberwal,   Satish.   "Education,   Inequality   and
        Industrialisation."   Journal of Higher Education 1 (Autumn
        1975):   189-198.

        Consists of three parts: The first is a review of a book
        by Professor Raymond Boudon, the second examines the critical
        influences available for raising standards in higher
        education, and the third argues that India's historic
        position has closed the capitalist path to industrialization.

136.   Saberwal, S.   "Sociologists and Inequality in India: The
        Historical Context."   Economic and Political Weekly (14
        February 1979):   243-54.

137.   Seshadri, C.   "Equality of Educational Opportunity - Some
        Issues in Indian Education."   Comparative Education 12
        (October 1976):   219-30.

        Discusses the general problems arising in connection with
        the relationship between education and society, the meaning
        of equality of educational opportunity, expansion of
        secondary and higher educational opportunities, the claims of
        quality and quantity in education, and the implementation of
        a common school system.

NEPAL

Books

138.   Sharma, Prayag Raj, ed. Social Science in Nepal: A Report
        on the Seminar on Social Science. Kirtipur: Tribhuvan
        University, 1974.

139.   Wood, Hugh Bernard. The Development of Education in Nepal.
        Washington: U.S. Department of Health, Education and
        Welfare, Office of Education, 1965.

        Discusses history of education in Nepal from early
        development to the modern period. Provides general
        organization and planning for education, types of financial
        support, sources of revenue and administration of educational
        finance. Provides the elaborate description of various
        levels and types of educational system.

Articles

140.   Ashby, J. A. "Equity and Discrimination Among Children --
        Schooling Decisions in Rural Nepal." Comparative Education
        Review 29, no. 1 (1985): 68-79.

141.   Murray, Margaret Y. "Nepal's Great Educational Leap Forward
        -- to What?" Compare 10, no. 1 (1980): 31-46.

        This article discusses educational development since the
        restoration of power to the Royal Family in 1951. Education
        is still a novelty, lacking sophisticated communication
        systems, traditions of learning and exploration, and
        suffering widespread adult illiteracy. In rural areas,
        schools are faced with the task of launching the child from
        an impoverished environment into a bewildering world of
        modern outlooks, ideas, and technology. For the child, the
        differences between his background and the environment
        introduced to him by the school are extremely confusing. For
        the educator, it is extremely difficult to maintain a balance
        between the preservation of an ancient cultural heritage and
        foretaste of the world at large and national manpower
        requirements. Nepal is therefore emphasizing producing
        educable, adaptable people who will be able to cope with the

myriad of changing conditions, rather than people who are
simply "educated."

142.   Vir, D. "Education and Social Stratification in Nepal."
        Indian Journal of Social Work 43, no. 3 (1982): 321-26.

PAKISTAN

Books

143.   Hakim, Mohammad Said. Understanding the Co-operation in
        Educational Scientific and Cultural Field. Karachi:
        Hamdard National Foundation, 1977.

144.   Kalim, M. Siddiq. Pakistan, an Educational Spectrum.
        Lahore: Arslan, 1978.

        This book contains a collection of articles written by the
        author for the educational column of the Pakistan Times. The
        articles cover the full range of education in Pakistan and
        address such problems as universalization of basic education,
        making secondary education semiprofessional, and evolving a
        new pattern of higher education. The author's approach is
        analytical and pragmatic and bears an educational viewpoint
        that is based on socioeconomic and political-cultural
        contexts. The book is divided into five sections:
        educational activity, curriculum development, modes of
        education, cultural activity, ideals of education.

145.   Mahmud, Husain. Education and Culture. Karachi: National
        Book Foundation, 1976.

146.   Rooman, Anwar. Education in Baluchistan. Quetta: Gosha-e-
        Adab, 1979.

147.   Zaki, W. M. Education of the People. Islamabad: Peoples
        Open University, 1975.

SRI LANKA

Books

148. Kariyawasam, T. A Report on a Study of Early School Drop-
      Outs in the Secondary Schools of Underprivileged Areas in
      the City of Colombo. Colombo: Task-Force on Non-Formal
      Education, National Councils of YMCAs of Sri Lanka, 1977.

      According to this survey the majority of dropouts are
      repeaters. The high proportion of dropouts indicates that
      the educational system is not developing in harmony with the
      family, community, economy, and value systems. The findings
      of this study imply that the tone of the school and its
      vigor, purpose, traditions, and temper of work can motivate
      children to want to be and to stay in school.

Articles

149. Gajanayake, Stanley. "Sri Lanka." Integrated Education 20
      (November-December 1983): 38-39.

      Reviews educational concerns in Sri Lanka, including the
      dropout rate, children who have never enrolled in schools,
      inequalities between urban and rural schools, the elitist
      nature of university education, and higher education's
      affirmative action area quota system for the ethnic majority.

150. Jayaweera, S. "Religious Organizations and the State of
      Ceylonese Education." Comparative Education Review 12
      (1968): 159-70.

151. Laiq, Jawid. "Prelude to Partition in Sri Lanka?:
      Segregated Education and Politics, 1945-67." Economic and
      Political Weekly (20 April 1985): 765-68.

      This is a sketch of how populist politicians in Sri Lanka
      used the emotive issues of language and white-collar
      government employment to create a segregated system of
      education. In prompt return, this system produced communal
      demands which were further encouraged by political leaders
      seeking to mobilize communal followings. Expanded higher

educational opportunities seem to have fueled communal
virulence rather than promoted communal harmony.
The mix of sectional education and communal politics in the
early decades of Sri Lanka's independence seems to mark the
origins of the violent confrontation being witnessed today
between the Sinhalese majority and the Ceylon Tamil minority.

152. Oberst, Richard. "Democracy and the Persistence of
      Westernized Elite Dominance in Sri Lanka." Asian Survey 25
      (July 1985): 760-62.

CHAPTER 3

EDUCATION AND DEVELOPMENT

Bangladesh

Books

153. Education for Development. London: Commonwealth Foundation, 1977.

154. Integrated Rural Development and the Role of Education. 2 Volumes. Dhaka: National Foundation for Research on Human Resource Development, 1979.

155. Solaiman, Mohammad. The Comilla Rural Education Experiment. Comilla: Bangladesh Academy for Rural Development, 1975.

INDIA

Books

156. Acharya, P. Education and Agrarian Relations: A Study of Four Villages in West Bengal--Part I--Draft Report. New Delhi: Indian Council of Social Science Research, 1980.

157. Chaudhri, D. P. Education, Innovations and Agricultural Development: A Study of North India (1961-72). New Delhi: Vikas, 1979.

Studies the relationship between education, agricultural productivity, diffusion of innovations and the expansion of farmers' institutional facilities during the Green Revolution in the wheat-growing areas of Punjab and Haryana. Using a simultaneous equations model, the study concludes that general education up to the secondary level, not mere literacy and lower primary education, influences the diffusion of technology and agricultural productivity. Increasing production also raises the demand for education.

51

158.   Di Bona, Joseph, ed. The Context of Education in Indian
        Development. Durham, North Carolina: Commonwealth Studies
        Center, Duke University, 1974.

159.   Goel, S. C. Education and Economic Growth. Delhi:
        Macmillan, 1975.

        This analytical study deals with education and economic
        growth in India during the period 1950-51 to 1970-71. The
        main focus of the study is on such questions as the
        consumption and investment aspects of education, the
        contribution of education to national income, the
        relationship between per capital income and education,
        variance in educational growth in the states of the Indian
        Union, equality of opportunity, manpower planning, and cost-
        benefit analysis of education in India. The aim of the study
        is to examine the role of education as an agent of economic
        and social change. The significant findings and conclusions,
        that have implications for educational planning and policy,
        make a substantial contribution to the education and economic
        growth in India.

160.   Kapoor, D. R. Education and National Development.
        Chandigarh: Kohli, 1984.

        A view of the relation between education and development,
        tracing the impact of different aspects of development on
        education. Presents a critical assessment of the
        possibilities of various innovations in education influencing
        development programs.

161.   Nair, P. R. G. Primary Education, Population Growth and
        Socio-Economic Change. New Delhi: Allied, 1981.

        Analyzes the interrelationships among school education,
        demographic variables, employment and occupational structure
        and mobility, and emigration in Kerala, accompanied by inter-
        state comparisons. Discusses both the socioeconomic forces
        underlying educational progress and the impact of changes in
        the educational system on society. Presents a comparative
        perspective of the costs of education in terms of pupil
        years. The author attributes the economic and political
        changes and the decline in death and birth rates in Kerala,
        primarily to the educational development in the state.
        Concludes that even though education promotes development and
        equality to a limited extent, educational expansion, with
        direct and indirect benefits, is possible even in backward
        societies.

162.   National Seminar on Education and Rural Development, 19-21
        February 1982. Seminar Papers. Pune: Indian Institute of
        Education, 1982.

        The papers presented concentrated on the following themes:
        education for rural development; rural institutions and the
        role of education in adapting them for social and economic
        change; inequalities in education in the context of rural
        development; socioeconomic context of education in rural
        development.

163.   Radhey, Mohan, ed. Education and National Development. New
        Delhi: Indiana, 1975.

164.   Rahman, A. and K. D. Sharma, eds. Science Policy Studies.
        Bombay: Somaiya, 1974.

        The eight sections cover such themes as science policy,
        science and planning, science manpower, science organization,
        science and industry, science and economic development.
        Emphasizes the contribution which science and technology can
        make to national development, eradication of poverty, and
        solving some of the problems of India and other developing
        countries.

165.   Ruhela, Satya Pal, ed. Educational Challenges in Socialist
        India. Delhi: Kalyani, 1975.

        A collection of fourteen papers on issues and problems in
        education, in relation to the goal of a socialist, democratic
        state. Covers stages of education, pre-school education,
        teacher education, equalization of educational opportunities,
        the crisis of higher education, the role of social
        scientists, and student activism.

166.   Seetharamu, A. S. Education and Rural Development. New
        Delhi: Ashish, 1980.

        Discusses the rural response from people of different
        educational levels to twenty-one mainly production oriented,
        development programs in Karnataka. Data were collected from
        a sample of respondents from eighty-nine villages in two
        talukas representing different educational characteristics.
        Education is found to be one of the significant factors in
        development responsiveness, defined in terms of awareness of
        programs, the interest shown, and the degree and quality of
        involvement. Awareness of the programs is what characterizes
        the educated, with the latter two aspects depending on
        factors other than education, since the illiterate are also

found to participate in certain programs. Suggests a rural educational program that is development oriented and that generates a culture of development.

167.   Sharma, S. L. Modernizing Effects of University Education. New Delhi: Allied, 1979.

Evaluates the modernizing effects of university education on value orientations, through an empirical study of a sample of students drawn from the rolls of day classes of teaching departments of Punjab University during 1973-74. Attempts to specify the differential effects of various aspects of the educational system and to identify the circumstances under which the select source variables of modernity will have the most impact. On the methodological front, the study devises a standard scale for measuring psychosocial modernity in India, as part of an attempt at conceptualizing the socializing role of education in a developing country. The higher informational inputs provided by education are found to have a limited effect on attitudinal modernity, since only specific aspects of the latter are amenable to influence by the former. The quality and content of education and the type of early schooling, rather than education per se, are found to play a part in modernizing attitudes.

168.   Singh, Brig Pal. Educational Progress and Economic Development in Punjab. Patiala: Punjabi University Press, 1979.

Attempts to relate the progress of education with economic development. Comments that the proper content of education in conjunction with a conducive socioeconomic climate leads to capital formation and emphasizes the need for enrichment of content and curtailment of the mushroom growth of education. Concludes that the educational system is largely unproductive and carries a considerable amount of miseducation and misdirection of resources and that it has created excess capacity capable of being utilized at a marginal cost.

Articles

169.   Adiseshiah, Malcolm S. "Education and Productive Work in India." Prospects 4 (Summer 1974): 143-51.

Discusses what is meant by productive work and how a doctrine of productive work can be applied to the educational

system of India. In order to redeem the pledges in the Fifth
Plan of India, the author begins with a number of
constructive suggestions of action.   The programs suggested
are: the functionalization of school, development of out-of-
school and out-of-college education, functional literacy for
illiterate adults, vocationalization of education, de-
schooling and de-training the unemployable young men and
women and re-educating and re-training them in various forms
of productive work.   Finally, he suggests that 1)
democratization of society and power of the elites, 2)
empowerment of the rural masses to make their own decision,
3) closure of the high schools, universities and colleges for
two years to induct students into National Service schemes,
youth corps with other rural development programs where they
would have the privilege and opportunity of working
productively on the farm or factory.

170.   Adiseshiah, Malcolm S.   "Role of Universities in
       International Co-operation for Development." New Frontiers
       in Education 14 (April-June 1984):   55-65.

171.   Aikara, Jacob. "Education and Rural Development." Indian
       Journal of Social Work 39 (January 1979):   399-408.

172.   Aikara, Jacob, and John Kurrien.   "Mass Education for
       Development in India: Evolution and New Strategies."
       Indian Journal of Social Work, 40 (January 1983):   439-54.

173.   Ananthkrishnan, M. V. "Science-Technology Interaction: A
       Systems Model for Education." Journal of Higher Education
       9 (Autumn 1983):   229-33.

       Comments on the effectiveness of the educational system and
       training programs and their dependence on economic and
       cultural developments.   Makes a reference to India which
       started with an agricultural base to slowly become an
       industrialized nation.   A study of the societal milieu and
       the science technology interaction is made with a special
       reference to the interdependence of science and engineering
       education.

174.   Deshpande, S. H.   "Innumeracy and Economic Behaviour."
       Economic and Political Weekly (March 1981, Annual Number):
       501-13.

       Stresses the need for studying the relationship between
       mathematical ability of a community and its economic life.
       The economic consequences of innumeracy are discussed in the
       context of the Warlis, a backward tribe in Maharashtra.

175.   Dias, Patrick V. "Educational Science, Educational Aid and
        Development in the Third World." New Frontiers in
        Education 14 (October-December 1984): 54-64.

        Discusses the role of the education system in the social
        development countries, the sociohistorical factors affecting
        education, and the promotion of education as part of the
        development process. Comments on education and human capital
        formation and whether education can be an obstacle to
        development. Criticizes the weakness in the organization of
        learning and the content of syllabii.

176.   Diwan, Romesh. "Development, Education and the Poor:
        Context of South Asia." Economic and Political Weekly (12
        February 1977): 401-08.

        The development efforts of the countries of the Third
        World, in spite of their enormity and even when successful,
        have followed a path that has led to the intensification of
        the problems of poverty, unemployment, and inequality.
        The solution of the problems of poverty, inequality, and
        unemployment requires a different strategy. Elements in this
        strategy involve the provision of opportunities for "self-
        defined" work, encouragement of production of "use-values,"
        and strengthening of small organizational structures that are
        not based on the principle of pure exchange.
        A reordering of the development effort on these lines
        requires that development be understood not only in terms of
        GNP, material goods and use-values, but also as a "state of
        mind." To understand the existing "state of mind"--which
        values goods, activities, policies and programs, that lead to
        increases in poverty--one has to examine the system of
        education in the developing countries.

177.   Gill, Sarjit Singh, and T. S. Randhawa. "Role of Colleges in
        Rural Development." Journal of Higher Education 10
        (Monsoon-Autumn 1984): 73-6.

        Suggests the possibility of a significant contribution to
        rural development by educated youth. Highlights certain
        priority areas: transmission of technology, timely provision
        of adequate inputs, credit and marketing facilities, and the
        formation of regulatory measures and policies. Provides a
        model of developmental projects for college-based youth
        clubs.

178.   Johl, S. S. "Relevance of Agricultural Research in India."
        New Frontiers in Education 14 (October-December 1984): 18-
        27.

Quantifies the increase in food production and the simultaneous increase in imports during the period 1961-62 to 1983-84. Suggests that scientists and policy makers should pay greater attention to increasing food production using improved technology. Suggests a change in research policy from a traditional approach to a new one and criticizes the existing research methods.

179.   King, A. D. "Higher Education and Socio-Economic Development." Comparative Education 5, no. 3 (1969): 263-81.

180.   Naik, J. P. "Equality and Quantity: The Elusive Triangle in Indian Education." International Review of Education 25, no. 2-3 (1979): 167-86.

The simultaneous pursuit of equality of opportunity and improvement of standards in the face of scarce resources confronts Indian education with a dilemma common to many countries. Equality and quality are relatively new values for education in India stimulated by the British system and the influence of the ideals of nationalist leaders like Gandhi, but they only gain ground slowly. The modernization process has introduced some changes into class and caste structures in the social and economic context of education, but the situation of the rural masses remains essentially unchanged. In the drive for equality of opportunity, there has been a visible advance in the enrollment of girls, though this may not reflect a real change in status. The same may be said of the education of the lower intermediate and scheduled castes. Regional disparities within the country also continue.
The high rate of adult illiteracy has only recently been seen as a major problem, requiring massive government action. In primary education there has been rapid growth, despite continued wastage, but the effects of the power structure on the allocation of resources to education are seen in the reckless expansion of secondary and higher education. Examination of the quality aspect reveals the dual nature of the system, with high standards in a small group of institutions and a less favorable situation in the majority. The major obstacle here is the lack of resources.

181.   Naik, J. P. "The New Indian Programme: Science and Technology for Development." Minerva 11 (1973): 537-70.

182.   Nair, P. R. G. "Decline in Birth Rate in Kerala: A Hypothesis About the Inter-Relationship Between Demographic Variables, Health Services and Education." Economic and Political Weekly (February 1974): 325-36.

183.   Padmanabhan, C. B. "Integration of Education with Economic
       Needs." New Frontiers in Education 12 (January-March
       1982): 37-49.

       Reviews the extent of development expenditure on education
       in successive Five Year Plans. Comments on the requirements
       of economic development and analyzes the time trend of public
       expenditure on education within this context. Discusses the
       problems of balancing different levels of education.

184.   Pillay, Subramania G. "Linkage of Higher Education with
       Environment." Journal of Higher Education 4 (Spring 1980):
       373-80.

185.   Raina, B. L. and S. C. Panigrahi. "Education and
       Development." Education Quarterly 37 (Summer 1985): 1-7.

186.   Rama, G. W. "Education and Democracy." Journal of Higher
       Education 9 (Monsoon 1983): 1-20.

187.   Tilak, Jandhyala B. G. "Planning Education for Economic
       Development." Perspectives in Education 1 (January 1985):
       35-47.

188.   Tilak, Jandhyala B. G. "Utilisation of Resources for
       Educational Development in India." Man and Development 6
       (December 1984): 144-62.

189.   Yadav, M. S. and others. "Integrating Education with
       Development in the Community: Role of University
       Teachers." New Frontiers in Education 14 (April-June
       1984): 43-51.

190.   Yadav, R. K. "Problems of National Identity in Indian
       Education." Comparative Education 10 (October 1974): 201-
       09.

       Discusses and evaluates the role of education in solving
       the problems of psychological and spritual unity of India,
       where conflict between religious, caste, and various
       linguistic groups was a major impediment for development.
       The author concludes that too much has been expected from
       education and instead of national integration, there are
       areas of conflict where clashes of interest exacerbated
       antagonism. He argues education for national integration is
       not merely "extra-curricular" or "cocurricular" activity. It
       should prepare people for searching of hearts and re-
       evaluation of the "ancient" and "cherished" values and the
       "glorious heritage."

NEPAL

Books

191.   Aryal, Krishna Raj. Education for the Development of
        Nepal. Kathmandu: Shanti Prakashan, 1970.

        The study is an attempt to look into the problems of
        development and planning, exploring the socioeconomic and
        political events that have affected the development of
        education in the past. Some present conditions which
        challenge the educators are an imported educational system,
        crisis in societal values, general lack of consciousness
        among the people about education, and financial constraints.
        Some suggestions to better planning of education are:
        clearly defined national objectives which correspond to
        Nepal's socioeconomic situation, a total and comprehensive
        plan, not section-wise, more vocationally oriented where
        appropriate, production of locally written, and published
        textbooks.

192.   Kasaju, Prem, and G. S. Pradhan, eds. Education and
        Development, 1980. Kathmandu: Research Center for
        Educational Innovation and Development, Tribhuvan
        University, 1980.

193.   Mohsin, Mohammad, and Prem Kasaju, eds. Education and
        Development. Kathmandu: National Education Committee,
        1975.

        The main body of the volume is divided into three sub-
        headings: Education and National Development, Education,
        Manpower and Economic Development, and Views and Reviews. A
        section on educational data and country data is included in
        the Appendix. The main focus of the book is on highlighting
        the rationale of the National Education Plan and offering
        critical analyses of its implications and current reform
        areas of Nepal's attempts at developing relevant educational
        programs.

194.   Reed, Horace B., and Mary J. Reed. Nepal in Transition:
        Educational Innovation. Pittsburgh: University of
        Pittsburgh Press, 1968.

        Describes the problems and milieu within which Nepal's
        educational system related to overall national development.
        Provides an overview of the Nepalese society both traditional
        and in transition. Problems of educational innovation are
        discussed and suggestions are made. Much of the discussion
        on culture-education relationships confined to observations
        and suggestions.

195.   Sellar, Peter O., and others. U.S. Aid to Education in
        Nepal: A 20-Year Beginning. Washington, D.C.:
        U.S.A.I.D., 1981.

        This evaluation measured the impacts of United States aid
        to education in Nepal. It differs from other Agency for
        International Development (AID) Impact Evaluations in that,
        rather than a single project, a series of projects (1954-
        1975) were evaluated, dealing with primary education, teacher
        training, vocational and secondary education, curriculum
        materials and development, and the institutional development
        of the entire education system. Following the introduction,
        the background/setting, and accomplishments/
        problems/analyses of results are discussed, the latter
        focusing on the areas previously indicated. In addition,
        impacts on education, agriculture, family planning, health,
        people's attitudes/behaviors, women, equity, and the Nepalese
        society and body politic are discussed. Major conclusions
        indicate that: (1) AID's assistance to Nepal has had positive
        impact; (2) there is an urgent need to find more efficient
        and effective approaches to educational problems through
        experimentation with innovative approaches; (3) vocational
        programs are more successful if training is started early;
        and (4) AID should continue its influence on basic education
        programs in this country. Eight appendices and three tables
        include evaluation methodology, analyses of questionnaires,
        bibliography, photographs and other supporting
        data/information.

196.   Sharma, Surseh Raj, et al., eds. Education and Development,
        1982. Kathmandu: Tribhuvan University, 1982.

Articles

197.   Jamison, D. T. and P. R. Moock. "Farmer Education and Farm
        Efficiency in Nepal--The Role of Schooling, Extension
        Services, and Cognitive Skills." World Development 12, no.
        1 (1984): 67-86.

198.   Pudasaini, S. P. "The Effects of Education in Agriculture --
        Evidence from Nepal." American Journal of Agricultural
        Economics 65, no. 3 (1983):   509-15.

199.   Reed, Horace B. "Nepalese Education Related to National
        Unity, Economic Development and Social Justice."
        Comparative Education 15 (March 1979): 43-61.

        This essay applies a model in order to guide an analysis of
        the goodness-of-fit between national plans and educational
        plans. The model is described through application to a Third
        World country (Nepal). In the process, fairly detailed in-
        formation is collated on Nepal's twenty-five years of
        educational efforts and the reciprocal relationship to
        national development.

PAKISTAN

        Books

200.   Curle, Adam. Educational Problems of Developing Societies:
        With Case Studies of Ghana, Pakistan, and Nigeria. New
        York: Praeger, 1973.

        This book is concerned with development; the progress made
        by nations in building institutions--a whole social order--
        qualified to tackle effectively their problems of poverty,
        disorder, hunger, ignorance, disunity and oppression. It
        deals, in general, with some of the social and particularly
        the educational issues which arise in the process of change.
        It examines some ways in which change might contribute to
        development and the conditions under which, conversely,
        change might either fail to contribute or do actual damage to
        the development potential.

201.   National Conference on Women's Participation in Scientific
        and Technological Development Papers. Islamabad: Women's
        Division, Government of Pakistan, 1984.

202.   A Profile of 20 Villages in the Islamabad Federal Area.
        Islamabad: Experimental Pilot Project Integrating
        Education in Rural Development, Ministry of Education,
        1978.

203.   Quddus, Syed Abdul.   Education and National Reconstruction
        of Pakistan.   Lahore: S. D Gilani, 1979.

        A study of the role of education in nation-building with a
        look at such agencies as films, teachers, students, women and
        family which have bearing on individuals. The book begins
        with a chapter on Islam and education and proceeds with
        chapters on the school system and its separate levels and
        various socioeconomic problems. How education, and rational
        social action can lead to a stronger nation by strengthening
        the intellectual and moral characters of its people is also
        discussed.

204.   Rauf, Abdur.   West Pakistan: Rural Education and
        Development.   Honolulu: East West Center Press, 1970.

        Article

205.   Freeman, D. M. and H. Azadi.   "Education, Power Distribution,
        and Adoption of Improved Farm Practices in Pakistan."
        Community Development Journal 18, no. 1 (1983):   60-67.

SRI LANKA

        Book

206.   Education and Socio-economic Development of Sri Lanka.
        Colombo: Sri Lanka Foundation Institute, 1977.

        Article

207.   Hewage, Lankaputra and David Radcliffe.   "Sri Lanka: The
        Relevance of Culture in Adult Education and Development."
        Convergence 10, no. 2 (1977):   63-74.

        The middle path approach to development--a recognized trait
        in the Buddhist culture of Sri Lanka and one that has
        traditionally emphasized adult education--attempts to
        maintain a balance between the socioeconomic and religio-

cultural aspects. It is in this context, that the authors describe how Sarvodaya Shramadana, a non-governmental voluntary movement, integrates and translates deeply enshrined Buddhist values into a contemporary direction program for self-reliance and cooperative rural development.

CHAPTER 4

ECONOMICS OF EDUCATION

BANGLADESH

208.   Puttick, Edwin B., and Others. The Finance of Non-Government
       Schools in Bangladesh. Berkeley: University of
       California, Program in International Education Finance,
       1975.

       The educational system in Bangladesh is unique in its
       finance and management structure. Elementary and higher
       education are mostly publicly financed, while secondary and
       intermediate education are mainly private organized. This
       study concentrates on private schools at the secondary,
       intermediate, and college levels; and the difference in
       access between males and females and between urban,
       semiurban, and rural areas. The data were obtained from
       questionnaires sent by the National Commission on Manpower
       and Education (NCME) in 1968-69 to each known private school
       in what was then East Pakistan. A detailed analysis is made
       of the private schools in the areas of finance, costs, and
       enrollments. The size of government grants to private
       schools is explored, and information is given on the fee
       requirements of pupils of public schools. Per-pupil-
       expenditures are surveyed in order to examine the
       quality/cost relationship. Enrollment practices and size
       distribution of schools are analyzed. A copy of the
       questionnaire and frequency distribution tables are contained
       in the appendixes. (Author/MLF)

INDIA

Books

209.   Azad, Jagdish Lal. <u>Financing</u> <u>of</u> <u>Higher</u> <u>Education</u> <u>in</u> <u>India</u>.
       New Delhi: Sterling, 1975.

       Identifies the strong and weak points in policies and
       procedures of governmental subsidies to institutions
       imparting higher education and the administrative machinery
       managing them.   Recommends certain policy measures to
       improvise the system and to curtail costs without impairing
       its growth.

210.   Azad, J. L. <u>Government</u> <u>Support</u> <u>for</u> <u>Higher</u> <u>Education</u> <u>and</u>
       <u>Research:</u> <u>A</u> <u>Critical</u> <u>Study</u> <u>of</u> <u>Patterns,</u> <u>Procedures</u> <u>and</u>
       <u>Policies</u>. New Delhi: Concept, 1984.

       An analysis of state and central government pattern, poli-
       cies and procedures for financing higher education
       institutions and research activities. Based on a micro-level
       investigation of institutions in Andhra Pradesh, Gujarat,
       Haryana, and Orissa, representing four regions in the
       country.   Maintains that despite increased financial support,
       institutional needs are not adequately met due to lack of
       clear policies and inter-institutional/interdisciplinary
       disparities in financing.   Challenges the notion that higher
       education financing is increasing at the cost of primary and
       secondary education.
       Deficit budgets are found in 38 percent of the
       universities, during the period under review.

211.   Azad, J. L. <u>Government</u> <u>Support</u> <u>for</u> <u>Higher</u> <u>Education</u> <u>and</u>
       <u>Research</u>. New Delhi: National Institute of Educational
       Planning and Administration, 1984.

       This study highlights the patterns, procedures, and poli-
       cies of financing higher education and research evolved by
       the federal and the state governments and their specialized
       agencies.   Certain basic policy issues pertaining to
       government support for higher education based on micro-level
       investigations of four states: Andhra Pradesh, Gujarat,
       Haryana and Orissa are discussed along with an analysis of
       the problems of higher education finance with particular
       reference to government support for research.   Some
       suggestions are given for revamping the financial policies
       and procedure of the central and the state governments.

212.   Basu, Partha, Kajal Lahiri, and Amlan Datt. Report on the
        Economics of Education in Some West Bengal Colleges With
        Special Reference to Size, Techniques and Location.
        Calcutta: World Press, 1974.

213.   Garg, V. P.   Cost Analysis in Higher Education: A
        Theoretical Frame, Empirical Results.   New Delhi:
        Metropolitan, 1985.

214.   Heyneman, Stephen P.   Investment in Indian Education:
        Uneconomic? Washington: World Bank, 1978.

215.   Kamat, A. R.   Two Studies in Education.   Poona: Gokhale
        Institute of Politics and Economics, 1968.

        Two studies, one on internal and external assessment of
        students and the other on unit institutional costs in higher
        education, are combined in this book.
        The first study, based on the Pre-Degree Examination, 1962,
        of the University of Poona, makes a detailed analysis and
        comparison of the two assessments and examines the effects of
        the introduction of the scheme of internal assessment on the
        results of Pre-Degree Examination.
        The second study discusses the methodology for finding
        current institutional costs per student in institutions of
        higher education and works out costs in the undergraduate and
        postgraduate courses of the University of Poona in its con-
        stituent colleges and its postgraduate departments.

216.   Kamat, A. R. and A. G. Deshmukh.   Wastage in College
        Education. Bombay: Asia, 1963.

        The book consists of two studies in education based on the
        performance in examinations of the students of the Poona
        University. The first study estimates wastage and stagnation
        in college education in arts and science by considering a
        three-year entry of students to the Fergusson College, Poona.
        Wastage and stagnation are also analyzed by important factors
        such as S.S.C. marks, age, sex, etc.   The second study
        examines the large number of failures in the Pre-Degree
        Examination of the University with a view to indicate the
        problem areas where remedial measures are needed.

217.   Majumdar, Tapas.   Investment in Education and Social Choice.
        Hyderabad: Orient Longman, 1984.

218.   Mathew, E. T.   University Finances in India: A Case Study of
        Kerala University. New Delhi: Sterling, 1980.

Traces the growth of the Kerala University from the establishment of the Travancore University in 1937 to the present, as a backdrop to an analysis of the sources of finances and the composition, pattern, and objectives of expenditure. The relation between finances and academic objectives is brought out, as also the role of the University Grants Committee (UGC) since the early 1960's and of the State and Central Governments in financing and regulating the university. Concludes with a detailed examination of the receipts and expenditure for the year 1974-75. Part of an all-India research project--"Study of University Finances," sponsored by the UGC and the Indian Council of Social Science Research in 1971.

219.   Misra, Atmanand. _Financing of Indian Education_. Bombay: Asia, 1967.

220.   Modi, Buddhish M. _Income Patterns and Education_. Ahmedabad: Sonal, 1984.

Determines the relation between the level of education and socioeconomic status, based on a sample of persons from different occupations in eighteen districts--urban and rural--in Gujarat state. Data were collected on the basis of interviews and questionnaires using the normative survey method. Includes a comparative study of the socioeconomic status of blood brothers in relation to their educational qualifications and brings out the positive impact of education on agricultural practices, productivity, and income.

221.   Mukerji, K. _Study of the Finances of the Calcutta University_. Calcutta: Firma KLM, 1976.

A study of the finances of the university, covering the period 1947-48 to 1970-71. Provides an analytical framework for the income and expenditure of the university, by categories and over time, so that the financial analysis is related to activities. Also studies the trust funds which once contributed to the postgraduate departments and presents a detailed cross-sectional analysis of the income and expenditures for the year 1970-71.

222.   Nanjundappa, D. M. _Working of University Finances_. New Delhi: Sterling, 1976.

Focuses on how the various components of revenue and expenditure have shaped themselves over the years in Indian universities and their resultant implications for the growth of higher education. Refers to the functioning of the UGC in this context. Suggests an alternative financing system for universities, viz., allocating a larger share of public funds directly to students and, in turn, making them pay the full cost of their education.

223.   Padmanabhan, C. B. Economics of Educational Planning in India. New Delhi: Arya Book Depot, 1971.

224.   Padmanabhan, C. B. Financial Management in Education. New Delhi: Select Books, 1984.

225.   Panchamukhi, P. R. Economics of University Finances: Basic Principles and Practice. Dharwar: Centre for Multidisciplinary Research, 1977.

Critically evaluates the use of resources in higher education and evolves general principles of resource mobilization concerning donations, fees, and public grants and their use in 'non-profit' institutions of higher education. Examines the working of finances of Bombay University, one of the oldest universities in the country, and of other universities in Maharashtra. An attempt is made to relate the general discussion with the particular assessment of finances.

226.   Pandit, H. N., ed. Measurement of Cost, Productivity, and Efficiency of Education. New Delhi: National Council of Educational Research and Training, 1969.

227.   Rao, V. K. R. V. Education and Human Resource Development. Bombay: Allied, 1966.

The book discusses the role that education can play in human resource development. After discussing the connection between economic growth, human resource development, and education, it deals with such specific problems as manpower planning, education as investment, the place of higher education, and the technology of education. Throughout, the accent is on development rather than education in the abstract. Though the book is written in the Indian context and contains a section on some purely Indian problems and an appendix on the author's thinking on educational planning in India's Fourth Plan, the policies it deals with, the logic it contains, and even the facts which are used for illustration, all have their relevance to the developing economies in general, and especially to the developing countries in Asia and Africa which are trying to accelerate their economic growth through planned effort.

228.   Research in Economics of Education--India.   New Delhi:
        Association of Indian Universities, 1979.

229.   Shah, A. B., ed.   Educational Finance.   Bombay: P. C.
        Manaktala, 1966.

230.   Shah, K. R. and S. Srikantiah.   Education, Earnings and
        Income Distribution: An Inquiry into Equity Issues
        Involved in the Government Financing of Higher Education in
        India--A Study of the M.S. University of Baroda.   New
        Delhi: Criterion, 1984.

        A study of the impact of government financing of higher
        education and of related questions of equity, within the
        framework of human capital theory.   The empirical work is
        based on questionnaires answered by a sample of graduates of
        four benchmark years of the M.S. University of Baroda, as to
        education and earnings of the respondents and their families.
        The limited effect of education on earnings because of wider
        economic constraints and the value of specific educational
        subsidy directed at particular sections, are some of the
        conclusions.   The analysis of costs, rates of return, and
        efficiency of investment are found to broadly confirm the
        predictions of human capital theory in that rates of growth
        of earnings are found to be associated with growth rates of
        education; earnings are subject to diminishing marginal re-
        turns and the efficiency of investment in education is found
        to be increasing.

231.   Sharma, G. D.   Institutional Costs of University Education:
        A Study of Costs and Efficiency of Indian University Sys-
        tem.   New Delhi: Association of Indian Universities, 1980.

        Examines the structure and unit costs of university
        education in terms of teaching inputs, student welfare,
        examinations, administrative and supporting services, in
        addition to capital costs.   Also presents a comparative view
        of structure and unit costs per student for different types
        of universities, so as to test the economies of scale
        hypothesis.   Administrative and supporting services are found
        to claim a larger proportion of the operating budget, while
        there is a decline in the costs of student services.

232.   Sharma, G. D.   Resource Allocation on Education: An Inter,
        Intra-Country and Inter-Temporal Pattern Analysis.   New
        Delhi: Association of Indian Universities, 1978.

Attempts to examine the manner and pattern of resource allocation in education, changes over the 1971-72 and 1975-76 period, and their relation with economic indicators. Comparisons between states within the country and between countries are provided. Among the conclusions are that India allocates a smaller proportion of its GNP on education than some developed and underdeveloped countries, despite having a larger number of pupils in educational institutions. The rate of return to investment in education also appears higher in India. However, high wastage and stagnation suggests that investment is below the minimum requirement to educate large numbers. Planning of resource allocation at state and national level is found to be deficient. Policy implications are suggested.

233.   Sharma, G. D. and Mridula. Economics of College Education. New Delhi: Association of Indian Universities, 1982.

234.   Singh, Amrik and G. D. Sharma, ed. University and College Finances: Seminar Papers. New Delhi: Association of Indian Universities, 1981.

A collection of papers, partly revised, originally presented at a seminar on the subject. Covers areas such as the basic issues of educational financing discussed from socio-political and economic perspectives; different funding agencies and their methods; case studies of university finances in Karnataka, Bombay, Rajasthan, Baroda, Delhi, and Punjab; and discussions of alternative methods of financing higher education.

235.   Singh, Balgit. Economics of Indian Education. Meerut: Meenakshi Prakashan, 1983.

236.   Singh, Parmanand. Financing of University Education. Delhi: B. R., 1982.

Discusses the role of education in economic development and the objectives of higher education in India as spelled out by the Education Commission--internal transformation, qualitative improvement, and expansion of facilities on the basis of manpower needs. The constraints experienced by university administrations in achieving these objectives, with special reference to the universities in Bihar State, are analyzed with respect to the variables of enrollment, expenditure, and sources of income. Assesses the achievements in the field of higher education in India with suggestions for greater investment and elimination of wastage.

237.   Sodhi, T. S. Education and Economic Development: A Treatise
        on the Problems of Economics of Education.   Ludhiana:
        Mukand, 1978.

        Articles

238.   Adiseshiah, Malcolm. "Education's Pay Off." New Frontiers
        in Education 13 (October-December 1983):   92-7.

        Defines payoff in the context of education and attempts to
        do so in terms of the following: (a) character building, (b)
        learning, (c) traditional payoff measures, and (d) equity
        payoff.

239.   Bhagwati, Jagdish. "Education, Class Structure, and Income
        Equality." World Development 1 (May 1973):   21-36.

        Two questions are posed to examine in this article in the
        context of a Third World country--India. First, given the
        initial income distribution, the working of labor markets,
        and other related characteristics of the economic system in a
        society, can the expansion of educational facilities and the
        educated labor force improve income distribution in the sense
        of reducing income inequality? Second, given the political
        system, particularly in the sense of the class structure and
        its influence on the pattern and level of educational
        expenditures and subsidization by the State, can educational
        expansion be expected to improve income distribution? The
        author argues that the benefits of the State (in capitalist
        LDCs) subsidies accrue disproportionately less to the poorer
        groups at each level of education. The higher the
        educational level being considered, the higher is the average
        income level of the groups to which the students belong; and
        the rate of governmental subsidization to higher education is
        greater than that to primary education.

240.   Bhandari, R. K. "Financing of Education." Education
        Quarterly 34 (January 1982):   1-7.

241.   Bhandari, R. K. "Investment in Education." New Frontiers in
        Education 14 (April-June 1984):   97-111.

242.   Bhatia, C. M. and Vijay K. Seth. "Hierarchy in the System of
        Schools: Political Economy of Education." Sociological
        Bulletin 24 (March 1975):   13-28.

243. Chalam, K. S. "Expenditure on University Education: A Unit Cost Analysis." Journal of Higher Education 4 (Autumn 1978): 201-24.

244. Chitnis, S. "Investment in Higher Education: A Reconsideration." New Frontiers in Education 5 (November 1975): 23-46.

245. Datt, Ruddar. "Cost and Efficiency of the Different Techniques of Education in Delhi University." Journal of Higher Education 6 (1980-81): 71-82.

246. Debi, Sailabala. "Cost Structure of Higher Education: A Case Study of Orissa." Journal of Higher Education 10 (Monsoon-Autumn 1984): 57-72.

247. Garg, V. P. "Cost-Analysis for Educational Planning: Some Basic Issues." New Frontiers in Education 13 (October-December 1983): 40-9.

248. Goel, S. C. "Education and Economic Growth in India." Comparative Education 10 (June 1974): 147-58.

This paper focuses on the relationship between the levels of educational expansion and economic development in India during the period 1950-51 to 1970-71. It examines whether there exists a significant relationship between the growth of education at the primary, secondary, and tertiary levels, on the one hand, and economic development, as measured by the per capita income at current prices on the other. If so, whether this should be interpreted as education-income relationship or as income-education effect. The author concludes that the relationship between education and economic growth is not a causal relationship. Rather the coefficient of correlation establishes a direct or inverse relationship between two variables. And education seems to be more in the nature of an effect of income and less as a cause of economic growth.

249. Heyneman, Stephen P. "Investment in Indian Education, Uneconomic?" World Development 8 (February 1980): 145-63.

In India, where the literacy rate is only three in ten, some believe that there is an economic surplus of education. This article reviews the arguments. In sum, India represents a case in which the presence of unemployment has led observers to the unjustified assumption that the external productivity of education is low. The paper uses new techniques of educational planning: the distribution of per pupil expenditure, examination pass-rates, rate of literacy, trade training, the availability of books, the amount of knowledge acquired in schools, and the degree of impact of school resources on academic achievement. The paper then concludes that there is reason to question the widely held belief that additional investment in Indian education would be uneconomic.

250.   Lakdawala, D. T.   "Financing of Universities in Gujarat." Economic and Political Weekly 20 (May 17, 1975):   795-801.

251.   Nair, P. R. Gopinathan.   "Effective Cost of Primary Education in India."   Economic and Political Weekly (11 September 1976):   1536-40.

The measurement of educational costs is an intricate problem. Since costs are met not only by public agencies, but by private institutions and even households, calculations of costs made solely on the basis of government expenditure will not yield reliable results. There are also dropout and stagnation factors that affect the 'effective cost' per unit of output.
In this paper, an attempt is made to estimate the rates of dropout and stagnation in various Indian states at the elementary stage of education. On the basis of these calculations, a physical index of 'effective cost' is constructed which, it is hoped, is capable of capturing the total cost of schooling per unit of output to society.
An analysis of the physical index of 'effective cost' reveals that the effective costs of primary education are lowest in Kerala, and the states in the northwestern parts of the country. Uttar Pradesh, Bihar, Nagaland, Manipur, Karnataka, Orissa, and Andhra Pradesh are among the states with the highest costs of education per functionally literate person.

252.   Nalla Gounden, A. M.   "Investment in Education in India." Journal of Human Resources 2 (Summer 1967):   347-58.

253.   Padmanabhan, C. B.   "Financing of Education in the Sixth Five-Year Plan."   New Frontiers in Education 13 (April-June 1983):   17-29.

Studies the public policy relating to education and the allocation of resources to education in India under the Five-Year Plans. Reviews the Sixth Five-Year Plan and its policies towards education and its development, the role of the Central Sector Plan in financing elementary and adult education, and the amount of expenditure on education at different levels.

254. Padmanabhan, C. B. "Financing of Education in the Seventh Five-Year Plan." New Frontiers in Education 15 (April-June 1985): 89-97.

255. Pandit, H. N. "Cost Analysis of Education in India: Private and Social Participation." Indian Educational Review 7 (July 1972): 117-57.

The author has attempted to estimate the cost of the resources used up in the educational process during the three Five-Year Plans in India. In this study, the social costs and private costs of education have been estimated separately. The study highlights the importance of neglected inputs, particularly the time spent by the student in education. The growth in costs has been juxtaposed with the growth in the total supply of resources in the Indian economy.

256. Pandit, H. N. "Financing of Education in India: Institutional Framework, Participation and Growth." Indian Educational Review 6 (July 1971): 106-37.

The author describes the institutional framework and the mechanism of educational finance in India. He identifies in the financing of education during three Five-Year Plans (1950-66), the major trends in the participation of the Central government, State governments, local bodies, endowments, households, and international agencies, and analyzes the educational expenditure in relation to the gross domestic product, and total State and Central expenditure on all sectors. He then evaluates the expenditure for 1965-66 as estimated by the Education Commission (1964-66) in relation to the actual educational expenditure.

257. Pandit, H. N. "Financing of School Education." Economic and Political Weekly (7 August 1972): 1653-60.

An attempt is made in this article to review the progress of expenditure on school education and the trends in contributions from private and public sources of finance.
The discussion focuses on the variations in cost per pupil in different types and stages of school education, the place of educational expenditure in budgetary allocations of Central and state governments, the growth in teacher salaries, the estimated burden of private non-tuition costs, and the role of private enterprises in school education.

The review makes it evident that, in the future, education
will have to compete more for resource allocations with other
developmental sectors such as health, irrigation, power,
etc., both at the Central and the state levels. Moreover,
within the educational sector, school education will have to
compete more with higher education. The share of school
expenditure in total educational finance is already showing a
declining trend. The scope for private finance for schools,
as seen here, is also very limited.

Therefore, future growth in school education will depend on
successful experimentation with ways and means to reduce
costs by introducing better management techniques, on explo-
ration of possibilities for public support, and on education
being made more development and growth oriented.

258.   Sachchidananda. "Economic Development, Education and Social
        Change in Arunachal." Man in India 65, no. 1 (1985): 33-
        57.

259.   Shah, K. R. "Expenditure on Elementary Education, 1950-51 to
        1960-61." Economic and Political Weekly 4 (November 22,
        1969): 1809-19.

260.   Tilak, Jandhyala B. G. "Education and Economic Growth in
        India (1950-51 and 1969-70): An Empirical Investigation."
        Indian Educational Review 10 (January 1975): 74-89.

        The author explains how education can boost economic growth
        of a country over a period of time and how it played an
        important role in the development of some European as well as
        Asian countries like Soviet Russia and Japan. In stating how
        much it could contribute to economic growth in countries like
        America he presents several important studies. Then the
        author estimates the extent of correlation between education
        and economic growth in India, considering enrollment and
        expenditures as indicators of the former and Gross National
        Product as an indicator of the latter. By using regression
        analysis he also estimates the magnitude of the impact of
        educational expenditures and of enrollments on national
        income. On the basis of his findings, he makes certain
        recommendations in favor of an apex level of education.

261.   Tilak, Jandhyala B. G. "Political Economy of Investment in
        Education in South Asia." International Journal of
        Educational Development 4, no. 2 (1984): 155-66.

262.   Tilak, Jandhyala B. G. "Unit Cost Analysis of Higher
        Education in India." Journal of Higher Education 5 (Autumn
        1979): 183-94.

NEPAL

Books

263.   Financing of Education in Nepal.   Kathmandu: National
       Education Committee, Centre for Educational Research,
       Innovation, and Development, 1978.

264.   Padhye, Nilakantha R.   Financing First-level and Second-level
       Education in Nepal.   Paris: UNESCO-IIEP, 1976.

PAKISTAN

Books

265.   Ghafoor, Abdul.   The Effects of New Trends in Educational
       Financing on the Plan Objectives: Equity, Quality and
       Efficiency; A Case Study on Pakistan.   Bangkok: UNESCO,
       1982.

       This study discusses some of the current issues in
       educational policymaking, planning, administration, and
       school facilities development in the region.   Also discussed
       are the financing of education under the Fifth Five-Year Plan
       and the mobilization of resources, other than those provided
       by the public sector, for a minimum learning package for all.

Articles

266.   Guisinger, Stephen E. and Others.   "Earnings, Rates of Return
       to Education, and the Earnings Distribution in Pakistan."
       Economics of Education Review 3 (1984):   257-67.

       Examination of earnings and education data for a sample of
       approximately 1,600 workers in Pakistan reveals that the rate
       of return in earnings to schooling is low.   The low rate of
       return appears to be a result of a conscious government
       policy that drastically compressed the skill-wage structure.

267.   Khan, M. A. and I. Sirageldin.   "Education, Income, and
       Fertility in Pakistan."   Economic Development and Cultural
       Change 27, no. 3 (1979):   519-47.

268.   Klitgaard, R. E., K. Y. Siddiqui, M. Arshad, N. Niaz, and M.
       A. Khan.   "The Economics of Teacher Education in Pakistan."
       Comparative Education Review 29 (February 1985):   97-110.

SRI LANKA

     Books

269.   Alles, J. and Others.   Financing and Cost of Education in
       Ceylon: A Preliminary Analysis of Educational Cost and
       Finance in Ceylon 1952-1964.   Paris: UNESCO, 1967.

270.   Hallak, Jacques.   Financing and Educational Policy in Sri
       Lanka (Ceylon).   Paris: UNESCO, International Institute
       for Educational Planning, 1972.

271.   International Bank for Reconstruction and Development.
       Ceylon Preliminary Survey of Education.   Colombo: Ministry
       of Planning and Economic Affairs, 1967(?).

CHAPTER 5

THEORY AND RESEARCH:

PHILOSOPHICAL AND IDEOLOGICAL FACTORS

INDIA

Books

272.   Abduhu, G. Rasool. The Educational Ideas of Maulana Abdul
        Kalam Azad. New Delhi: Sterling, 1973.

        Attempts an evaluation of the educational ideas and outlook
        of Maulana Azad. Sees Azad's attempts to reform Islamic
        education as a compromise between traditional religious
        methods and modern trends based on science and technology.
        Presents his heritage and environment, the evolution of his
        educational outlook, his leadership function in education and
        an examination of his ideas.

273.   Aggarwal, J. C. Theory and Principles of Education:
        Philosophical and Sociological Bases of Education. New
        Delhi: Vikas.

274.   Bhatia, B. D. Theory and Principles of Education. Delhi:
        Doaba House, 1970.

275.   Chaube, S. P. Recent Educational Philosophies in India.
        Agra: Ram Prasad and Sons, 1967.

        A presentation of the educational philosophies of
        Dayananda, Vivekananda, Annie Besant, Aurobindo, Gandhi and
        Tagore; the educational systems associated with them, their
        contributions to education in India and their relevance to
        present problems. Sources used are original writings,
        official reports, bulletins and documents.

276.   Mathur, V. S. Indian Education: Challenge and Hope.
        Ambala: Associated, 1981.

277.   Mukherjee, H. B. Education for Fullness: A study of the
       educational thought and experiment of Rabindranath Tagore.
       Bombay: Asia, 1962.

       This book is a comprehensive, full-length account of
       Tagore's educational thought and activity--a study of which
       is essential to arrive at a precise understanding of the
       creator of Santiniketan and Visva-Bharati. Apart from a
       detailed chronological survey of Tagore' educational writings
       and institutional activities in the perspective of his life
       and thought in general, it also contains a critical
       discussion on almost all the major aspects of his educational
       work; and, in attempting, at the end, an overall evaluation
       of Tagore's unique contribution to education and his message
       to the world, it seeks to correct some common misconceptions
       that have existed from time to time about Santiniketan and
       Visva-Bharati.
       The work is supplemented with a bibliography of the more
       important literature on the subject, and two indexes--
       Tagore's educational writings and a general index.

278.   Navaratnam, Ratna. New Frontiers in East-West Philosophies
       of Education. Calcutta: Orient Longmans, 1958.

       Presents the educational philosophies of the East and West,
       with their modern trends. Holds that present education lacks
       a clear moral focus, which is found necessary for relating
       the individual to his civilization and philosophical outlook.
       Presents an argument for an integral education combining
       features of East and West and towards moral development.

279.   Nazareth, M. Pia. Education: Goals, Aims and Objectives.
       New Delhi: Vikas, 1984.

       Presents a program for educators on the functions and
       process of education. Maintains that educational
       institutions should direct activities towards specified,
       distant goals and evaluate them accordingly.

280.   Oak, L. K., et al. Perspectives of Indian Education: An
       Interdisciplinary Approach. Agra: Sri Ram Mehra, 1975.

281.   Pandey, Ram Shakal. Pragmatic Theories of Education.
       Agra: Lakshmi Narain Agarwal Educational Publishers, 1966.

       Interprets the educative process from the pragmatist's
       viewpoint. Examines the philosophy of pragmatism and
       pragmatic theories such as humanism, instrumentalism,

experimentalism, progressivism and reconstructionism.
Concludes with a critical evaluation.

282.   Parikh, P. C.   Educational Thinking in Modern India.
        Ahmedabad: Shree Mudramalza, 1976.

283.   Patel, M. S.   The Educational Philosophy of Mahatma Gandhi.
        Ahmedabad: Navajeevan, 1953.

        Discusses Gandhi's philosophy of education, his views on
        the aims of education, his precursors, the evolution of his
        theory, his practical contribution such as the idea of basic
        education and the Wardha scheme, as well his views on
        specific issues such as the education of women and the
        language problem.

284.   Reddy, V. Narayan Karan.   Man, Education and Values.   Delhi:
        B. R., 1979.

        A study of the nature of man, the purpose of education and
        the problem of values, as issues in the philosophy of
        education.   Discussed with reference to ancient Indian
        thought and modern Indian thinkers such as Gandhi, Aurobindo
        and Tagore, in particular.

285.   Shrimali, K. L.   A Search for Values in Indian Education.
        Delhi: Vikas, 1971.

        The book highlights the present crisis that faces Indian
        society today.   The crisis has many facets--social, political
        and economic--but the only one which deeply concerns
        education is the moral aspect--which is on the decline.   The
        theme of the book is therefore, to mould the educational
        system to suit the needs of the changing society and at the
        same time to preserve the values of Indian culture.   The
        author diagnoses the causes of the present student unrest and
        suggests remedies.

286.   Taneja, V. R.   Educational Thought and Practice.   New York:
        Apt Books, 1984.

        V. R. Taneja surveys the concept of education in its
        broadest sense.   He decries the dogmatic approach to
        curriculum which has caused intellectual stifling and
        stagnation of many individuals.   The author's approach to ed-
        ucation can, at best, be summarized in his own words: "The
        chief task of philosophy is to determine what constitutes a

life worth living ... the chief task of education is to make
life worth living."

287.   Varma, M. The Philosophy of Indian Education. Meerut:
       Meenakshi Prakashan, 1969.

288.   Vyas, R. N. Education for Political Leadership. New
       Delhi: Ambika, 1978.

       Dwells on the desirability of political education,
       especially given the power wielded by leadership on the
       average man. Tries to establish a linkage between education
       and political leadership and the philosophy underlying such a
       relation, using supportive material from Indian and Western
       sources.

       Article

289.   Shukla, Sureshachandra. "Indian Educational Thought and
       Experiments: A Review." Comparative Education 19 (No. 1,
       1983): 59-72.

       Discusses the concepts or ideas of Indian education, which
       influenced the current trends. The author argues that these
       ideas still have to be taken into account in designing a
       future even if they needed to be modified or negated. The
       influence of the British education system remained intact,
       with an exception of Gandhi's principles of basic education.
       One consequence of this has been the lack of creativity
       within education itself.

PAKISTAN

       Books

290.   Khalid, Tanvir. Education: An Introduction to Educational
       Philosophy and History. Karachi: National Book
       Foundation, 1974.

291.   Lobo, Anthony. Educational Ideas and Their Impact.
       Karachi: Rotti Press, 1975.

292. Rizvi, Syed Jamil Ahmad, comp. Theses on Iqbal: A
     Bibliographical Survey of the Theses on Iqbal, Submitted to
     the University of The Punjab, Lahore, 1950-1976. Lahore:
     Aziz Publishers, 1977.

293. Shami, Parwaiz. Education in Search of Fundamentals.
     Karachi: National Book Foundation, 1976.

294. Siddiqui, Akhtar H. Learned Bodies and Research
     Organizations in Pakistan. Karachi: National Book Council
     of Pakistan, 1978.

Articles

295. Haq, S. "Moral Education in Pakistan." Journal of Moral
     Education 9, no. 3 (1980): 156-65.

296. Roliman, Fzahir. "The Qur'anic Solution of Pakistan's
     Educational Problems." Islamic Studies 6 (December 1967):
     315-26.

SRI LANKA

     Article

297. Ali, Ameer. "Islamic Revivalism in Harmony and Conflict:
     The Experience in Sri Lanka and Malaysia." Asian Survey 24
     (1984): 296-313.

CHAPTER 6

THEORY AND RESEARCH:

METHODOLOGY

BANGLADESH

298. Biswas, Ahsan, ed. <u>Current Scientific and Technological
      Research Projects in the Universities and Research
      Institutions of Bangladesh</u>. Dhaka: Bangladesh National
      Scientific and Technical Documentation Centre, 1978.

      A directory which lists research projects of six
      universities and thirty-eight other research institutions of
      Bangladesh. The compilation gives a short description of the
      institutions and their addresses, the names of the heads of
      the departments, institutes or laboratories for contact
      purposes, and the size of their library collections.

INDIA

    Books

299. Adaval, S. B., ed. <u>Third Indian Year Book of Education:
      Educational Research</u>. New Delhi: National Council of
      Educational Research and Training, 1968.

300. Buch, M. B., ed. <u>A Survey of Research in Education</u>. Baroda:
      Centre of Advanced Study in Education, M.S. University of
      Baroda, 1974.

301. Corey, Stephen M. <u>Some Thoughts about Educational Research</u>.
      Baroda: Faculty of Education and Psychology, Maharaja
      Sayajirao University of Baroda, 1964.

      A monograph that discusses aspects of educational research
      with reference to what is considered as its major purpose:
      problem solving towards improved education. Questions such
      as the use of data sources and statistics are treated within
      this perspective.

302.   Gopal, M. H. <u>Science, Universities and Research in India:</u>
        <u>An Introductory Essay</u>. Mysore: Geeta Book House.

        Comments on the failure of science departments of Indian
        universities in generating relevant research and discusses
        the causes for the failure, viz., bureaucratization of
        universities, manning the faculty with wrong persons and
        political interference. Also discusses the low level of
        achievement of the students and holds the university
        responsible for it.

303.   Institute of Economic Growth. <u>Relevance in Social Science</u>
        <u>Research</u>. New Delhi: Vikas, 1982.

        Discusses the relevance of western approaches, methods and
        techniques for understanding the socioeconomic problems
        facing India. Reviews whether science is divorced from
        policy and the polarity between 'fundamental' and 'problem-
        oriented' research. Attempts to find out whether the
        interests, needs and aspirations of the people have been
        placed as the center of enquiry.

304.   Kaul, Lokesh. <u>Methodology of Educational Research</u>. New
        Delhi: Vikas, 1984.

        Explains methods suited to education and relevant to
        particular educational problems in priority areas. Also
        covers methodological approaches, steps in educational
        research and statistical techniques, with suitable
        illustrations. Each chapter contains a statement of learning
        objectives at the outset and a post-test to evaluate
        knowledge acquired.

305.   Pal, S. K. and P. C. Saxena. <u>Quality Control in Educational</u>
        <u>Research</u>. New Delhi: Metropolitan, 1985.

        Presents and cross-section of current thinking on
        theoretical and methodological issues in educational
        research. Covers a critical survey of present research,
        reasons for deterioration in quality, methodological issues,
        different social science perspectives on educational research
        and suggestions for relevant areas of research.

306.   Sidhu, K. S. <u>Methodology of Research in Education</u>. New
        Delhi: Sterling, 1984.

307.   Thakkar, A., ed. <u>Readings in Educational Research: Report</u>
        <u>on Research Paper Readings</u>. Bombay: University Department
        of Education, 1985.

Articles

308. Datta, Bhabatosh. "Social Science Research: Universities
      and Autonomous Institutions." Journal of Higher Education
      6 (1980-81): 15-24.

309. Ganpathy, R. S. "R and D: Emerging Identity Crisis."
      Economic and Political Weekly 6 (January 2, 1971): 51-4.

310. Joshi, P. C. "Social Science Research and the Institute."
      Journal of Higher Education 8 (Autumn 1982): 155-65.

311. Rao, T. V. "Research on Institutional Environment--A
      Review." Indian Educational Review 6 (January 1971): 126-
      61.

PAKISTAN

312. Siddiqui, Akhtar H. Pakistan in the World of Research and
      Learning: A Guide to Research and Development
      Organizations. Karachi: Pakistan Reference Publications,
      1968.

      The organizations have been grouped according to subject.
      Information provided includes name and address, date of
      establishment, status, functions, library and publications.

CHAPTER 7

PRE-SCHOOL EDUCATION

INDIA

Book

313.   Thakkar, Aruna. Perspectives in Pre-school Education.
        Bombay: Popular Prakashan, 1980.

        Explains the significance of pre-school learning as
        foundation education. Presents a historical perspective on
        pre-school programs, a review of some cognitive programs and
        trends in compensatory education and research abroad, drawing
        out their relevance to the Indian situation through a review
        of the Indian pre-school.

Article

314.   Rajalakshmi, Muralidharan. "Early Childhood Education for
        the Disadvantaged Children in India." Education in Asia
        and the Pacific: Reviews, Reports and Notes, 20 (September
        1983):   21-33.

        A paper presented to the Study Group Meeting on Development
        of New Forms of Pre-School Education in New Delhi which
        discusses the problems of disadvantaged children and
        emphasizes that research shows how well-planned early
        childhood education strategies can foster child development.
        Provides an overview of several pre-existing programs for the
        disadvantaged.

CHAPTER 8

PRIMARY EDUCATION

BANGLADESH

Books

315.   Ahmed, Salehuddin, S. A. Qadir, and Kazi S. Ahmed. Primary
        Education Network in Bangladesh.   Dhaka: National
        Foundation for Research on Human Resource Development,
        1983.

        Assessment of physical and human facilities that exist in
        the country and their utilization.

316.   Bangladesh. Ministry of Education, Bangladesh Bureau of
        Educational Information and Statistics.   Statistics on
        Primary Education. Dhaka: 1980.

        Collection and compilation of data on primary education up
        to 1978.

317.   Chowdhury, Kowsar P. Efforts in Universalization of Primary
        Education: The Case of Bangladesh. Buffalo, New York:
        Comparative Education Center, State University of New York
        at Buffalo, 1984.

        An analysis of the ways in which the Bangladesh Government
        attempted to implement universal primary education in the
        1960s and 1970s. The author points to the problems encoun-
        tered and analyzes the reasons for the difficulties.

318.   Chowdhury, M. K. and A. K. M. Obaidullah. Outdoor Primary
        Education in Bangladesh. Paris: UNESCO, 1980.

        This is a case study of a pilot scheme relating to outdoor
        primary education in Bangladesh. The project, conducted with
        a view of improving the contents and methods of teaching,
        aims at making primary education more practical and
        realistic. The study discusses various aspects of the
        projects and indicates that it was generally well received by
        students, teachers, guardians and others. As a result of a
        Government decision, outdoor primary education was to be
        continued in 500 selected schools in 1977.

319.   Gupta, Debabrata and M. Delwar Hossain. Universal Primary
        Education: Comilla. Comilla: Bangladesh Academy for
        Rural Development, 1980.

320.   Institute of Education and Research. Survey of Primary
        Schools and Evaluation of Primary School Agriculture
        Programme in Bangladesh: A Research Report, Part One.
        Dhaka: The Institute of Education and Research, 1977.

        An analysis of the acute problem of ensuring a minimum
        standard of education in the primary schools spread over some
        66,000 villages of Bangladesh. The primary education sector
        did not receive proper treatment and its share of resources
        in the past and as a result its institutions became
        dilapidated. Consequently, the primary education sector
        could not play its appropriate leadership role within the
        existing infrastructure. Substantial reforms in its
        organizational structure and curricular offerings warranted
        immediate attention. To do so, an evaluation was needed.
        This study has two parts: Part one provides a general
        statistical profile on physical facilities, educational aids,
        teachers, and students of primary schools throughout
        Bangladesh. Part two of the study provides data on agricul-
        tural activities of the schools and also the use of inputs
        supplied by the UNICEF toward the agriculture program.

321.   National Foundation for Resources on Human Resource
        Development. Primary Education Network in Bangladesh:
        Capacity and Utilization. Dhaka: 1979.

322.   Sattar, Ellen. Universal Primary Education in Bangladesh.
        Dhaka: University, 1982.

Bangladesh remains largely illiterate with seventy percent male and eighty-seven percent female illiteracy. The situation is likely to remain so as priority continues to be given to problems of food scarcity, population control, and unemployment. The book is about the state of primary education in Bangladesh at the beginning of the 1980s. It discusses the state of the present system, its functions, problems, curriculum, teachers, administration policy, and planning. Valuable statistics on the situation of primary education are provided. Several innovative models have been described and their implications for the wider system. Some suggestions have been made to improve the situation and aid the drive for universalization. The issue of universalization is fully discussed and with careful distinction made between universal enrollment and universal retention.

The book advocates educational reforms based on the belief that it can create a more equal and just society. The author argues, by the provision and lack of provision of educational facilities, the lives of millions of children will be profoundly influenced. The book identifies the problems in the present system and raises questions of inequality of educational opportunity.

323.   University of Dhaka. Survey of Primary Schools and Evaluation of Primary School Agriculture Programmes in Bangladesh: A Research Report. Dhaka: Institute of Education and Research, University of Dhaka, 1977.

Articles

324.   Abeje, Haile Yesus. "How to Provide Universal Schooling." Prospects 13, no. 2 (1983): 45-9.

Today more children and their parents in developing countries are without any educational opportunities because of the expense and elitist character of traditional education programs. Examples from Bangladesh show how educational opportunities can be broadened by using facilities more intensively and in innovative ways.

325.   Qadir, S. A. "Introducing Universal Primary Education in Bangladesh." Teachers World 12 (Spring 1980): 1-9.

Provides background study on the primary education system in relation to the introduction of Universal Primary education in Bangladesh.

INDIA

Books

326.   Gupta, L. D. Educational Administration at the Elementary
       Level. Chandigarh: Punjab State University Text Book
       Board, 1974.

327.   Kurrien, John. Elementary Education in India: Myth,
       Reality, Alternative. New Delhi: Vikas, 1983.

       Despite the constitutional proclamation of providing eight
       years of free primary education for all children, India is
       far from achieving the goal. The reality is that the educa-
       tional system, as constituted at present or envisaged in the
       future, cannot even provide five years of universal primary
       schooling by the end of this century, and is principally
       responsible for the tremendous illiteracy problem that India
       faces. This book analyzes various aspects of the contradic-
       tion between these and other official myths and goals, and
       the Sisyphean realities of Indian elementary education. The
       fundamental thesis, delineated in a historical and
       comparative perspective, is that the system was destined to
       fail and will continue to fail, as its workings, as well as
       the perspectives of the educational establishment, are based
       on a theoretically deficient and utopian model of mass
       elementary education, out of touch with the realities of the
       Indian situation.

328.   Lindsey, J. K. Primary Education in Bombay: Introduction to
       a Social Study. Oxford: Pergamon, 1978.

       This study examines how mass universal education, as an
       integral part of an advanced capitalist society, is
       fundamental to the reproduction of such a society, and has
       been and is still being introduced into an under-developed
       society making the transition to capitalism under the
       constraining influence of imperialism. How does the school
       perform when capitalist social relations must be produced and
       not simply reproduced and maintained?   The elements of
       'traditional' and capitalist social relations are isolated
       and their inter-relationship explored. Subsequently, these
       elements are related to a few key factors in the process of
       primary education in an attempt to determine if the existing
       mixture of social relations is being reproduced or if the
       school is helping to displace 'traditional' relations by
       capitalist ones.

329.   Mali, M. G. Social Benefits and Economics of Single-Teacher
        Schools. Gargoti: AJAM Postgraduate College of Education,
        1979.

        A study of single-teacher schools (which comprise almost
        forty percent of all Indian schools) based on a sample of a
        hundred schools in three talukas in Maharashtra, data gath-
        ered through interviews and questionnaires administered to
        teachers, educational officers and concerned persons, and
        observations. These schools are found to be an integral part
        of education devoted to illiterate and poor communities.
        Presently neglected, the schools could be significant units
        for community development in small villages.

330.   Mehdi, Bager and J. D. Virmani. The Arts and the Primary
        School Curriculum. New Delhi: The Curriculum Group,
        National Council of Educational Research and Training,
        1980.

        In many present-day schools, the arts are being given an
        important place in the curriculum, as the subjects help to
        overcome the imbalances resulting from the undue emphasis
        being given to the study of the three R's. Art is seen to
        take an important role in the development of the whole child.
        This publication explores the various ways of integrating the
        arts in the school curriculum.

331.   Naik, J. P. Elementary Education in India: The Unfinished
        Business. Bombay: Asia, 1966.

        The progress of elementary education in India has been
        unsatisfactory even in the post-independence period despite
        constitutional provisions and an awareness of the importance
        of education to the country's economic growth. This book
        analyzes the reasons for this situation and suggests
        practical remedies. According to the author there are two
        controllable factors responsible for this problem: (1)
        failure to adopt the right strategy; and (2) failure to
        accord adequate priority to elementary education. While
        making a plea to the educated classes to accord the highest
        priority to elementary education, the author cautions against
        the conflicting pulls of quality and quantity. The author's
        solution in this context would be to mount a crash program of
        quantitative expansion followed by a centrally-sponsored
        scheme for qualitative improvement.

332.   Nair, P. R. G. Educational Reforms in India: Universaliza-
        tion of Primary Education in Kerala. Trivandrum: Centre
        for Development Studies, 1983.

333.   Nayana, Tara S. Education in a Rural Environment. New
        Delhi: Ashish, 1985.

        An empirical study of certain problem areas in primary
        education in Tumkur district, Karnataka. Non-enrollment,
        irregular attendance, premature withdrawal of children from
        schools, and detention are discussed in the context of the
        universalization of primary education. Suggests a system of
        non-formal education to complement the formal.

334.   Primary Education in Rural India: Participation and Wastage.
        Bombay: Tata McGraw-Hill, 1971.

335.   Venkatasubramanian, K. Wastage in Primary Education.
        Bombay: Orient Longman, 1983.

        Presents a detailed study of the limitations of the
        conventional school system, with its problems of wastage and
        dropouts, in Tamil Nadu, India. Argues that conventional
        school systems have become a barrier to social development,
        and raises the key question of 'What should Education be
        for?'

        Articles

336.   Chatterjee, B. B. "Pattern of School Achievement in Primary
        Grades." Indian Educational Review 12 (April 1977): 29-
        67.

        The National Council of Educational Research and Training
        had carried out a large-scale research project in
        developmental psychology in collaboration with a number of
        university departments of psychology and education in order
        to have a wide regional coverage. This study was entitled
        'Developmental norms project for children of two and a half
        years to five years of age'. Encouraged by the experience of
        conducting such a collaborative study, the NCERT decided to
        extend it to cover school-going children between five and a
        half to eleven years of age, studying in classes one to five.

337.   Garg, V. P. "Universalization of Elementary Education in
        India: Past Experiences, Future Strategies." Education
        Quarterly 36 (April 1984): 1-10.

338.   Kumar, K. "Primary Education: Problems and Purpose, a
        Comment." Economic and Political Weekly 15 (April 26,
        1980): 794-95.

339. Kurrien, John. "Towards Universal Elementary Education:
      Promise and Performance." Economic and Political Weekly 16
      (October 1981): 1608-18.

      Official claims and estimates about the prospect of
      universalization of elementary education in the near future
      appear reasonably optimistic and credible and there has even
      been mention of various target dates, the farthermost being
      1991.
      This article disputes these claims and shows that official
      enrollment statistics bear little relation to actual
      attendance of students in the classrooms; that enrollment
      figures are often inflated because there is so much more
      money for a state making vast enrollment claims.
      The article presents, after making the necessary
      statistical corrections, the actual progress in education
      registered since Independence and concludes that even
      universal primary education--five years of compulsory
      schooling--would be a remarkable achievement if it were to be
      attained by the turn of the century.

340. Mehta, Prayag. "Motivating Primary Education: A
      Psychological Strategy for Eliminating Wastage." Indian
      Educational Review 9 (July 1974): 1-24.

      The following assumptions relating to the problems of young
      children in primary schools, particularly in rural areas,
      have been tested in the experiment reported in this article:
      (i) the motivation program will increase the pupil's desire
      to 'belong' to his instructional group; (ii) the classroom
      motivation development curriculum will enhance the pupil's
      'interest' in the school, and strengthen his school-going
      tendency; (iii) it will enhance the pupil's sense of self-
      worth (self-esteem) leading to greater involvement in school
      and home activities; and (iv) it will accelerate his sense of
      responsibility.

341. Nair, P. R. G. "Effective Cost of Primary Education in
      India." Economic and Political Weekly 11 (September 18,
      1976): 1536-40.

342. Rao, T. V. and Others. "Pattern of Adjustment of Fifth Grade
      Children from Delhi, Coimbatore and Calcutta." Indian
      Educational Review 7 (January 1972): 91-113.

      The authors discuss an investigation undertaken to compare
      the adjustment patterns of fifth grade children from the
      cities of Delhi, Calcutta and Coimbatore. The tool used was

the Pre-Adolescent Adjustment Scale (Pareek, et al., 1970) and the sample comprised 1427 fifth grade children from Delhi, 558 children from South Delhi, 418 from Calcutta and 486 from Coimbatore. The authors found significant differences between the adjustment patterns of the children from these cities. Although a general trend of moderately high adjustment was found among all subjects, children from Calcutta showed better adjustment than the children from Delhi, followed by the children from Coimbatore.

343.   "Wastage and Stagnation in Primary Education; Nine Articles on the Theme." Education Quarterly 20, no. 3 (1968): 1-46.

NEPAL

344.   Nepal. Ministry of Education. Programme for the Improvement and Strengthening of Primary Education Over the Period 1982-88. Kathmandu: Ministry of Education, 1981.

        This paper reports some findings of a programme prepared by the Ministry of Education for the overall development and improvement of primary education in Nepal for the period 1982-88. (Nepal had reverted from a three-year to a five-year primary cycle in 1980.) The program is designed to gradually improve primary education in a comprehensive, systematic, and integrated fashion so that it becomes more effective.

PAKISTAN

        Books

345.   Asberg, Rodney. Primary Education and National Development: A Case Study of the Conditions for Expanding Primary Education in West Pakistan with an Introductory Discussion of Educational Planning in Relation to Different Aspects of National Development and Education. Stockholm: Almquist and Wiksell, 1973.

346.   Eastmond, Jefferson N. A Strategy for Upgrading Primary Education in Pakistan. Islamabad: Ministry of Education, 1977.

This study suggests that upgrading education requires a systematic effort to resolve its problems, expand its impact, and improve its quality by (1) acquiring commitment, (2) determining the present status, (3) setting goals and establishing a plan, (4) executing the plan, and (5) monitoring and evaluating progress. In Pakistan, a national commitment is needed to solve the problems of primary education. In all districts, school mapping and current pupil participation studies should be conducted followed by a planning exercise to provide guidelines and a sequence for completion of specific school projects. This would culminate in a national plan for the systematic development of primary education. Evaluation (via the Gross Product of Education) of the goals for primary education should be considered in the context of total education development. Spending more money will not provide measurable improvements in pupil attendance, but solutions to educational problems can be provided through empirical research such as that conducted in 1976-77 in the areas of female education and pupil attendance, participatory planning, village attitudes and environments, education management and supervision, learning environments, teacher personnel, and school buildings. Future research in these areas should focus on how best to channel resources to fulfill district plans, adult education, school health programs, and the more effective use of staff.

347. Shah, Saeedullah. A Feasibility Study of Achieving Universal Primary Education in Pakistan. Berkeley: University of California, Program in International Education Finance, 1975.

This report describes a mathematical model used to test the feasibility of achieving universal primary education in Pakistan. Background information is given on proposals from the Pakistani Commission on National Education that attempted to increase the percentage of children in primary schools, the most recent of these aimed at 100 percent enrollment by 1979 for boys and 1984 for girls. The model sets up equations that project school age population, school enrollment, the number of teachers required, and cost. Results are graphed and discussed with full computer printouts given in the appendices. It is proposed that universal education is unrealistic under the present policy of expanding the existing education system. Social and economic factors such as cost and resistance to coeducational schools are cited. Suggestions for alternative approaches to achieving universal primary education are given.

Articles

348.   Bray, Mark. "Universal Primary Education in Pakistan: A
        Perpetually Elusive Goal?" International Review of
        Education 29, no. 2 (1983): 167-78.

349.   Qureshi, M. H. "Universalization of Primary Education in
        Pakistan: Pilot Primary Project." Education Review 1, no.
        5 (1980): 93-101.

SRI LANKA

350.   Peiri, Kamala. Tiny Sapling, Sturdy Tree: The Inside Story
        of Primary Education Reforms of the 1970s in Sri Lanka.
        Oslo: Universitetsforlaget, 1983.

        A lively account of the implementation of a project to
        change primary schools in Sri Lanka into places where
        children could learn actively in settings of freedom and
        responsibility. Analyzes the social, political and cultural
        factors in Sri Lanka to be taken into consideration when
        planning.

351.   Vickery, D. J. A Primary School Design Workbook for Hot Dry
        Asia. Colombo: Asian Regional Institute for School
        Building Research, 1969.

CHAPTER 9

SECONDARY EDUCATION

BANGLADESH

352.   UNESCO.   Regional Office for Education in Asia and the
        Pacific. Bangladesh: Secondary Schools Science Education
        Project, Final Report. Bangkok: UNESCO, 1983.

        Volume One described the project, its objectives,
        components, costs, and implementation. Volume Two describes
        science education in Bangladesh and Volume Three discusses
        the utilization of science rooms and labs and gives costs,
        designs, and science equipment needed.

INDIA

        Books

353.   Mansukhani, G. S. and G. S. Dhillon, eds. Whither
        Secondary Education. New Delhi: Oxford and IBH, 1973.

354.   Mukerji, S. N. Secondary Education in India. New Delhi:
        Orient Longmans, 1972.

355.   Mukhopadhyay, M. Barriers to Change in Secondary Education:
        Some Case Studies. Howrah: Education Books, 1981.

        Adopts a systematic view to identify the barriers to the
        process of change at various levels of the educational
        structure. Case studies from a district each in Gujarat and
        West Bengal are presented and discussed at the levels of the
        resource system, the communication system and the adopter
        system. The roles of the District Educational Officer and of
        other organizations working as resources systems for
        innovations are analyzed in their communication with the
        schools, and in their relation with social organization of
        the schools and the innovation management process. Major

barriers to change in secondary education are found to be the
inadequacy of management of innovations and the lack of a
planned effort.

356.   Saiyidain, K. G., ed. The Fourth Indian Year Book of
        Education: Secondary Education. New Delhi: National
        Council of Education Research and Training, 1973.

357.   Verma, G. K., Christopher Bagley and Kanka Mallick. Illusion
        and Reality in Indian Secondary Education. London: Saxon
        House, 1980.

        Articles

358.   Ahluwalia, S. P. "Secondary Education in India, 1947-1961:
        Some Discernible Trends." Pedagogica Historica 6 (No. 2,
        1966):   343-63.

359.   Aikara, Jacob. "The Higher Secondary in the 10+2+3 Pattern."
        New Frontiers in Education 8 (October-December 1978):   22-47.

360.   Anand, C. L. "Social Structure and Processes in a High
        School in South India." Indian Educational Review 11
        (January 1976):   33-42.

        This report presents an account of an informal study
        undertaken by the author with regard to the social structure
        and processes of an aided high school in the capacity of a
        participant-observer. An opportunity for this came when the
        author was required to work with the B.Ed. trainees as a
        full-time internship (teaching practice) supervisor for a
        period of over two months at the Canara Boys' High School,
        Mangalore, Karnataka State (India).   .

361.   Sapra, C. L. "A Study of Relationship between Size, Costs
        and Efficiency of Secondary Schools." Indian Educational
        Review 8 (January 1973):   181-200.

        Efficiency of a school is defined as performance of pupils
        in the examinations of the Central Board of Secondary
        Education and such aspects of pupils' development as work-
        experience, citizenship training, etc., which are not
        evaluated in external examination and for the training of
        which the school is not exclusively responsible, have been
        left out. A systematically selected random sample of 51 of
        the 256 government higher secondary schools of Delhi studied
        here shows negative but statistically an insignificant

relationship between size of school and educational efficiency both raw and adjusted for factors like class size, teachers' qualifications, status of school building etc. Teaching costs per pupil show an inverse relationship with school size upto and between 750 and 850 pupils.

362.   Zachariah, Mathew. "The Durability of Academic Secondary Education in India." Comparative Education Review 14 (June 1970): 152-62.

Deals with the state of Indian secondary education during the period between 1952 to 1964. From 1952, the Federal Government of India and the State governments in India initiated several attempts to change the character and structure of academic secondary education. These attempts met with indifferent success. The academic orientation and emphasis of secondary education proved to be quite resilient in the face of reform attempts. This is usually explained in terms of the inadequacies of administering newly initiated reforms, but the position of this paper is that conflict over educational goals and differences of opportunities among the castes and classes are more important. The social class approach sheds new light on many of the educational theories and practices in India and exposes the crucial "failure of will" in implementing reforms.

NEPAL

363.   Butler, Lucius.   "Secondary Education in Nepal." International Education 3 (Fall 1973): 14-20.

This article describes the development of education in Nepal from its beginnings in indigenous education associated with Hindu and Buddhist religions to the present democratic period, which began in 1971 and entails a reform in curriculum and school organization.

CHAPTER 10

TERTIARY AND HIGHER EDUCATION

BANGLADESH

Books

364. Bangladesh. University Grants Commission. Overviews on
     University Education and Research in Science in Bangladesh.
     Dhaka: UGC, 1977.

365. Choudhury, A. H. Economic Aspects of Higher Education and
     Student Unrest in Pakistan. Dhaka: Society for Pakistan
     Studies, 1971.

     Attempts to trace the origins of student unrest and analyze
     its causes, and then discusses the problem within historical,
     economic and social frameworks. The first part of the book
     deals with general trends in higher education and the second
     part investigates the causes of student unrest which include
     political reasons such as universities being used by national
     parties to support or oppose national government; academic
     reasons such as increases in student fees, unpopular
     curriculum changes and admissions policies, inadequately
     experienced staff and inadequate living conditions, economic
     concerns like unemployment of college graduates, unfavorable
     positions (low pay, overwork) as teachers which many are
     forced into, and lastly student unrest can be contributed to
     social factors such as government and university corruption
     and favoritism.

366. Huq, Muhammad Shamsul. Higher Education and the Dilemmas of
     Poor Countries: A Search for New Path in Bangladesh.
     Dhaka: Foundation for Research on Educational Planning and
     Development, 1975.

367.   Islam, Taherul. An analysis of Public Recurring Expenditure
       of Higher Education in Bangladesh. Dhaka: University
       Grants Commission, 1975.

       The higher educational institutions in Bangladesh fall
       between two--the universities and the Degree colleges. In
       1972-73 total enrollment in the universities of Bangladesh
       stood at 29,534 of which 85 percent were in general
       universities and 15 percent in the Technical universities (9
       percent in the Agricultural and 6 percent in the Engineering
       university). About three-fourths of all enrolled students
       attended Dhaka University (52 percent) and Rajshahi
       University (24 percent) in 1972-73.
       Since independence there has been remarkable growth in
       general university enrollment. 85-95 percent of the current
       expenditure of the universities is financed through
       Government Grants in Aid and the entire recurring expenditure
       of the Government colleges is entirely financed through
       public budget. This study examines the allocative efficiency
       and equity aspects of the use of public funds at higher
       levels of education. The resource-use pattern at higher
       levels of education, the pattern and problems of financing
       current expenditure at university and college levels have
       been examined. Some projections of the future growth of
       demand for public funds at the universities have been made
       and alternative sources for financing higher education have
       been explored. The social and private costs of university
       education in Bangladesh have been estimated.

368.   Jilani, Ghulam. From College to University: A Study Based
       on the Findings of a Research Project on High Percentage of
       Failures in Examinations in East Pakistan. Lahore: Uni-
       versity of Punjab, 1968.

369.   Overviews on University Education and Research in Science in
       Bangladesh. Dhaka: University Grants Commission, 1977.

370.   Stock, A. G. Memoirs of Dacca University, 1947-51. Dhaka:
       Green Book House, 1973.

INDIA

       Books

371.   Aikara, Jacob, ed. Innovations in Higher Education in
       India. Pune: Dastane Ramchandra, 1984.

Discusses the structural and functional aspects of innovations in higher education, presenting five major innovations of the post-independence period--correspondence education, national service scheme, internal assessment, vocationalization at the "+2" stage, and autonomous colleges. Analyzes them in their historical context and evaluates their impact.

372.   Airan, J. W., ed. College in Education. Bombay: Manaktala, 1967.

In this volume the aims and purpose of higher education and to some extent of education in general is dealt with. The suggestions made in the report are about the proper selection of students, provision of educational guidance, improving the quality of teaching personnel, devising imaginative curricula and formulation of sound administrative practices. It also discusses a number of other current problems, such as the place of general education, medium of instruction, evaluation, and the imparting of religious and moral instruction.

373.   Altbach, P. G. The University in Transition: An Indian Case Study. Bombay: Sindhu, 1972.

A study of the organization and functioning of the University of Bombay, with stress on the affiliated colleges and the interaction of the colleges with the University and with society. Chapters dealing with college teachers and with the political context of the university are included.

374.   Ashby, Eric. Universities: British, Indian, African. Cambridge, Mass.: Harvard University Press, 1966.

375.   Basu, A. N. University Education in India. Calcutta: Book Emporium, 1944.

376.   Bose, P. K. Calcutta University: Some Problems and their Remedies. Calcutta: Calcutta University, 1973.

377.   Bose, P. K. Higher Education at Cross-Roads. Calcutta: World Press, 1977.

A discussion of trends in higher education in India and in West Bengal, in particular, based in part on data from the third National Survey on Higher Education, 1976. The forebodings of the Education Commission with respect to falling standards are found to be justified. A plan of action is suggested, with required structural, organizational

and managerial changes, as well as in methods of teaching and
assessment. Also contains a discussion of the views of the
University Grants Commission, the problems of educated
unemployed and the new pattern as implemented in West Bengal.

378.   Desai, D. M. Some Critical Issues in Higher Education in
        India. Bombay: A. R. Sethi, 1970.

379.   Dibona, Joseph. Change and Conflict in the Indian
        University. Bombay: Lalvani, 1973.

380.   Dickinson, Richard D. The Christian College in Developing
        India: A Sociological Inquiry. London: Oxford
        University Press, 1971.

        Provides an overall picture of the Christian higher
        educational effort in India. Describes the Christian
        colleges in India today--where they are, who sponsors them,
        why they were established and what are their current
        objectives, the religious policy of the institutions, their
        involvement in nation building, their participation in
        community affairs, etc. Outlines trends, problems, and
        possibilities which could assist in planning for the
        development of scarce material and human resources in the
        future.

381.   Dongerkery, S. R. University Autonomy in India. Bombay:
        Lalvani, 1967.

        This book is the first of its kind on a subject that has
        attracted considerable attention in the country in the last
        few years, especially since the amending legislation passed
        by the Andhra Pradesh Government, imposing curbs on the
        autonomy of the Osmania University, the Andhra University and
        the Sri Venkateswara University. Chapters V and VI of the
        book contain a graphic and detailed account of Osmania's
        historic fight in defense of its autonomy, the outcome of
        which was watched with the greatest interest, not only by the
        Indian academic world but also by the Indian parliament, the
        Press and the public of the country, involving, as it did,
        the issues of academic and intellectual freedom that are of
        the utmost importance for a healthy national life.

382.   Gandhi, Kishore. Issues and Choices in Higher Education:
        A Sociological Analysis. Delhi: B. R., 1978.

383.   Garg, V. P. The Cost Analysis in Higher Education. New
        Delhi: Metropolitan, 1985.

384. Gaudino, Robert L. The Indian University. Bombay: Popular Prakashan, 1965.

Elaborately discusses the origin of the university from the setting of the Indian universities: how it begins by an act of establishment, which is a creation of the legislative authority to medium of instruction. It discusses how the universities are given authorities, bodies, boards to control its work, what are relationships between universities and the colleges and the specific characteristics of the colleges, the relationship between the government and the universities, university decision making and administration who the teachers and the students within the university and the quality of learning.

385. Gautam, G. Crisis in the Temples of Learning. New Delhi: S. Chand, 1972.

386. Haggerty, William. Higher and Professional Education in India. Washington, D.C.: U. S. Department of Health, Education and Welfare, 1969.

Although the book title indicates the subject higher and professional education, it discusses geographical setting, historical background, present conditions of India: cultural diversity, Governmental structure, population, economic, and planning and goals. Education system in general and national policies and goals are also discussed. Finally it provides the background of higher education, where education before 1857, during 1857 to Independence in 1947 and during post-independence period are discussed.

In 1857, modern Indian university education came into being with the founding of the three affiliating Universities of Bombay, Calcutta, and Madras. By 1969, the Federal or State Governments had authorized 93 institutions to grant degrees. The number of higher education students has increased in each decade since 1936 at a rate of over 100 percent. In 1967-68, 2,218,972 students were enrolled in higher education courses. Of these, 84.6% were working toward the B. A., B. Comm., or B. Sc. degree, and less than 6% toward a postgraduate degree. The total number of colleges has almost doubled in this decade, increasing from 1,537 in 1960-61 to 2,942 in 1968-69. Since 1959, five Indian Institutes of Technology, each receiving international aid, have been established to develop engineering and technical courses based on modern discoveries and methods. Since 1960, six States have each established an agricultural university that combines education, research, and extension services in program similar to that of the land-grant colleges in the United States.

387.   Heredia, Rudolph C. Structure and Performance of College
        Education: Organizational Analysis of Arts and Science
        College in Bombay. Bombay: Somaiya, 1981.

        Analyzes the internal organizational structure of the
        college as an academic social system and evaluates the
        functional efficiency of the affiliating university. The
        survey covers the population of Bombay city arts and science
        colleges affiliated to Bombay University, with reference to
        the period 1970 to 1976. The study stresses the real issues
        for policy decisions: resource concentration, academic
        professionalization and decentralization of the system, with
        the university playing a supportive rather than a controlling
        and standardizing role.

388.   Hudson, Yeager. Profile of a College: A Self-Study of
        Ahmednagar College, Ahmednagar, Maharashtra. Bombay:
        Nachiketa, 1972.

389.   India, Ministry of Education, and Youth Services. Growth in
        Higher Education, 1966-67 to 1970-71. New Delhi: 1972.

390.   John, V. V. Freedom to Learn: The Challenge of the
        Autonomous College. Delhi: Vikas, 1976.

391.   John, V. V. The Great Classroom Hoax and Other Recollections
        on India's Education. New Delhi: Vikas, 1978.

392.   John, V. V. Misadventures in Higher Education. Delhi:
        Young Asia, 1973.

393.   Joshi, K. L. Higher Education: Historical and Other
        Problems. Bombay: Popular Prakashan, 1981.

        Analyzes problems of higher education in their historical
        context. Some of the issues discussed are increasing
        government control, bureaucratic regulation, the indifference
        of academicians, scarcity of funds, educational expansion,
        educated unemployment and lack of systematic policy
        formulation. Discusses present problems of modernization,
        the constraints of a legacy from 1857 to 1947 and the
        relation between educational expansion and economic growth.

394.   Joshi, K. L. Problems of Higher Education in India.
        Bombay: Popular Prakashan, 1976.

395.   Kamat, A. R. Cost Studies in Higher Education. Poona:
        Gokhale Institute of Politics and Economics, 1965.

396.   Kamat, A. R. Unit Cost in Higher Education: Two Studies
       in Education. Bombay: Asia, 1968.

397.   Kapur, J. N. Current Issues in Higher Education in India.
       New Delhi: S. Chand, 1975.

398.   Kaul, J. N. Higher Education in India: 1951-71 - Two
       Decades of Planned Drift. Simla: Indian Institute of
       Advanced Study, 1974.

       Analyzes the digeneration of the higher educational system.
       Views it as a situation of 'planned drift', with growth but
       negligible development along the lines of the intentions of
       policy makers and national requirements. Lack of perspective
       of priorities and the fact of an alien implementation are
       considered as important reasons for the crisis. Hope is seen
       in a possible cultural revolution from within the academic
       community. Presents a detailed analysis of statistical data
       and policy documents.

399.   Kaul, J. N., ed. Higher Education, Social Change and
       National Development. Simla: Indian Institute of Advanced
       Study, 1975.

       This book deals with the following topics: growth and
       development of higher education in India--its problems and
       perspectives, higher education and social change in India,
       higher education as an instrument of social change and
       national development, reorientation of First and Second
       degree courses, need for selective admission, the role of
       colleges in advanced teaching and research, financing higher
       education in India, governance and decision-making process in
       the universities and colleges, and coordination and
       improvement in standards of higher education.

400.   Kochhar, S. K. Guidance and Counseling in Colleges and
       Universities. New Delhi: Sterling, 1984.

       Suggests that guidance and counseling should be woven into
       the fabric of higher education. Provides the guidance
       workers in college and universities with a handy book to
       direct their course of action. Discusses different aspects
       of a guidance and counseling program, types and
       characteristics of psychological tests and suggests measures
       to be taken by government bodies.

401.   Malik, S. C., ed. Management and Organisation of Indian
       Universities. Simla: Indian Institute of Advanced Study,
       1971.

402.   Mansukani, G. S., ed. Crises in Indian Universities. New
       Delhi: Oxford and IBH, 1972.

       The book deals with the complex problems facing the Indian
       universities today and throws light on important issues like
       University Autonomy, Examination Reform, Science Education
       and Research, Relations Between College and the Community,
       Student violence, Student Participation and Problems of Girl
       students.   The contributions have been made by specialists
       who have made specific studies of their topics.

403.   Matthai, Ravi, J. The Rural University. Bombay: Popular
       Prakashan, 1985.

404.   Mohan, Madan.   Problems of University Education in India.
       Meerut: Meenakshi Prakashan, 1972.

405.   Mukherjee, S. K.   Challenges in the Management of Higher
       Education in India.   New Delhi: Zaheer Science Foundation,
       1978.

       A Foundation lecture on the role of higher education in
       development; the issues involved and the problems faced are
       discussed.

406.   Mukherji, S. N. Higher Education and Rural India.   Baroda:
       Acharya Book Depot, 1956.

407.   National Board of Christian Higher Education.   Challenges and
       Opportunities in Indian Higher Education.   Delhi: National
       Board of Christian Higher Education in India, 1970.

408.   Parikh, G. D., ed.   The Crisis in Higher Education.
       Bombay: Leslie Sawhny Centre, 1972.

409.   Patil, V. T. The Semester System: Substance and Problems.
       New Delhi: Sterling, 1984.

410.   Pillay, S.   Rise and Growth of the Rural University.
       Bombay: Bombay University, 1966.

411.   Raghavan, J. Veera, ed.   Higher Education in the Eighties:
       Opportunities and Objectives.   New Delhi: Lancer
       International, 1985.

       A collection of ten seminar papers on the subject.   Covers
       definitions of the role of university as an agent of change,
       education and employment, a survey of higher education since

Independence indicating trends and problems, specific issues in higher education such as autonomy, centers of excellence and bilingual education of tribals. Includes a summary of discussions and extracts from relevant reports.

412. Ramacharuan Nair, K. R. The Emerging Spectrum: Essays on Indian Higher Education, Bombay: Himalaya, 1986.

413. Ramakrishnan, Ganapati. A Community College for India. Madras: Institute for Development Education, 1980.

Presents the community college as an alternative in education. Discusses the role of education in development and the need for community colleges. Presents a profile of potential students, the American experience, the experiment in Salurtaluka with a profile of that taluka. Sees the need for developing such colleges on a national scale and presents an agenda for action.

414. Rao, M. L. and T. V. Rao. Higher Education in India: Trends and Bibliography. Ahmedabad: Indian Institute of Management, 1976.

415. Reddy, D. J. Challenges in Higher Education. Tirupati: Sri Venkateswara University, 1972.

416. Reddy, D. Jaganatha. Issues in Higher Education. Madras: Seshachalam, 1973.

417. Reddy, P. Jaganmohan. Perspectives on Education and Culture. Hyderabad: Osmania Graduates Association, 1983.

A collection of essays and speeches by a former Vice-Chancellor of Osmania University, Andhra Pradesh, discussing a range of problems and issues in higher education.

418. Review Committee on Post-Graduate Education and Research in Engineering and Technology. Report. New Delhi: 1980.

The Review Committee appointed by the Government of India in 1978 was given the task of evaluating present post-graduate courses and their contributions to national development. Patterns of assistance to the graduate programs and co-operation with major engineering schemes were also considered. The finds of the study indicate that the capacity for generating technological growth within the country has to be strengthened. Investment in scientific and technological education and research has to be increased many-fold to meet the growing needs of the country. Ways have to be sought to attract bright people into post-graduate education. Recommendations are made for improving admission and scholarship policies, restructuring courses, providing part-time continuing education programs, studying the employment situation, improving the teaching faculty and other related aspects of graduate and research programs.

419.   Samuel, N. Koshy. The Organization and Administration of Higher Education in India Since Independence. Lanham, Maryland: University Press of America, 1983.

Analyzes the administration and organizational structure of Indian institutions of higher learning after independence. This book consists of a descriptive and analytical study of the above topic, examining the present role as well as the future of higher education in India.

420.   Shah, A. B. The Controversy Over Aligarh. Pune: New Quest, 1978.

421.   Shah, A. B., ed. Higher Education in India. Bombay: Lalvani, 1967.

The volume is a symposium that defines the major problems of higher education in contemporary India and suggests radical and constructive solutions to them. It gives critical insight into crucial problems of higher learning and prompts a second look at the Education Commission's recommendations.

422.   Shah, A. B., ed. Modernization of University Teaching: Natural and Social Sciences. Bombay: Nachiketa, 1969.

423.   Sharma, G. D. Enrollment in Higher Education: A Trend Analysis. New Delhi: Association of Indian Universities, 1977.

Examines the trends in enrollment in higher education over a period of 15 years from 1961-75. From about the mid-fifties to the late sixties, India had an unprecedented rate of expansion at the college and university level. Sometimes it was as high as 13-14% per year. However, during the period the declining rates of growth in enrollment is observed. Therefore, the study examines the factor associated with the variation in enrollment during 1961-73. Quantifiable factors, namely, expenditure on higher education, students' fees, per capita net domestic product

and growth in employment among degree holders, have been
regressed on enrollment data. Some of the non-quantifiable
factors, namely, government policies, new developments in
education that might have influenced trend in enrollment have
also examined. Some policy suggestions are provided.

424.   Shrimali, K. L. The Myth of University Autonomy and Other
        Essays. New Delhi: Kalamkar Prakashan, 1980.

        Essays relating to the perceived relation between the
university and society. The topics covered are the degree of
government control; student political activity; the social
functions of teaching, research and community work; the
extent to which universities reflect and perpetuate an
inegalitarian society and the problem of unemployed
graduates. The topics are presented with a historical
background.

425.   Singh, Amrik. Redeeming Higher Education: Essays in
        Educational Policy. Delhi: Ajanta, 1985.

        A wide-ranging discussion of key policy questions in higher
education by a former Vice Chancellor. Among the topics
considered are the role of the academic profession, teachers'
strikes, economic aspects of higher education, autonomy
versus accountability, and university reform,.

426.   Singh, Amrik. Asking for Trouble: What it Means to be a
        Vice-Chancellor Today. New Delhi: Vikas, 1984.

        An account of the author's experience as Vice-Chancellor of
Punjab University, Patiala, during 1977 to 1979, placed in
the context of the working of higher education in India.
Discusses student and teacher organizations, the role of
politicians and the state, academic autonomy and
accountability and details of university functioning. Views
the experience of a Vice-Chancellor in his relations with
government, academics and students and in the context of
national crisis, as significant in understanding the role of
education in society.

427.   Singh, Amrik and Philip G. Altbach, ed. The Higher
        Learning in India. Delhi: Vikas, 1974.

        Compiles twenty-two articles on various issues, such as,
structure and governance, financial aspects, education as
investment, students and teachers, language, examinations,

reform, science and higher education. Also provides two case
studies and bibliography on Indian Higher Education.

The authors of these articles have underscored two issues:
one is the ineffectiveness and irrelevance of the Indian
university; the second related to the difficulty of
overcoming these two weaknesses in the context of the current
social and economic situation. More specifically attention
is devoted to student politics, women's higher education, the
academic profession, the place of English in Indian
education, the strategy of change in examinations and the
brain drain crisis.

428.   Singh, C. D. Graduate Education in Commerce. Calcutta:
        Nay Prakashan, 1979.

429.   Srivastava, Anand P. Pathology of Higher Education: Some
        Challenges before University Faculty. Kanpur: Reprint,
        1979.

        A collection of articles by the author, that reflect on
        current problems of university education. Aspects covered
        are a general evaluation of higher education, the faculty
        component, students, curriculum and quality of instruction,
        libraries and information systems. Also contains a
        commentary on the Draft National Policy on Education in India
        (1979) and an appendix that presents the Policy Frame adopted
        by the University Grants Commission for the development of
        higher education.

430.   Suri, M. Shahnaz. American Influence on Higher Education
        in India: A Study of Post-Independence Era. New Delhi:
        Sterling, 1979.

        Explores American interest in and influence on Indian
        higher education. Contains a historical review of American
        aid; the role of U.S. government agencies and programs,
        private agencies, university and church organizations; forms
        of aid through finance, personnel and books and the Indian
        response. Views the wide ranging influence as generally
        positive, with major U.S. contributions in the field of
        science, technology and the use of technology in the
        classroom to assist the learning process.

        Articles

431.   Ahmed, Rias. "Universities: Perspectives and Problems."
        Journal of Higher Education 7 (Spring 1982): 177-87.

Discusses various means of putting universities securely on
the path to change in teaching, research, extension and
management; also discusses the role of universities and
university education and research, university administration
and management. Comments on various administrative,
financial and social problems and also on the issue that
extension activities improves quality.

432. Altbach, Philip G. "Bombay Colleges." Minerva 8 (October
      1970): 520-40.

433. Altbach, P. G. "Higher Education in India." Higher
      Education in Nine Countries: A Comparative Study of
      Colleges and Universities Abroad. By B. B. Burn, pp. 317-
      43, New York: McGraw-Hill Book Co., 1971.

434. Altbach, Philip G. "India and the World University Crisis."
      The Student Revolution. Edited by Philip G. Altbach, pp.
      1-26, Bombay: Lalvani, 1968.

435. Altbach, Philip G. "The University as Centre and Periphery."
      Journal of Higher Education 4 (Autumn 1978): 157-70.

436. Anant, Santokh Singh. "Segregation of Sexes in Indian
      Universities." Crisis in Indian Universities. Edited by
      G. S. Mansukhani, pp. 150-61, New Delhi: Oxford and IBH,
      1972.

      Argues that sex segregation in universities and elsewhere
      throughout Indian society impedes social development and
      mature adult relationships.

437. Beteille, Andre. "The Indian University: Academic Standards
      and the Pursuit of Equality." Minerva 19 (Summer 1981):
      282-310.

      This article discusses the power of the Indian
      universities, which become caught in the tension between the
      ideal of equality and facts of inequality. The Indian
      university is situated in a field of conflicting forces. The
      conflicting forces are, on one side, the inequal social
      order; on the other side, the commitment to equality which is
      contained in the Indian Constitution and which is often
      invoked by politicians of all political persuations, by
      publicists and by academics. The universities are expected
      to reduce the constraints of inequality; their very survival
      is endangered by the rising tide of populist demand. This
      article examines whether they can do anything to resolve it.

438.   Brass, Paul R. "The Politics of Ayurvedic Education: A Case
         study of Revivalism and Modernization in India." Education
         and Politics in India. Edited by S. H. Rudolph and L. I.
         Rudolph, pp. 342-71. Delhi: Oxford University Press,
         1972.

439.   Chandra, Satish. "Higher Education in India: Plans and
         Prospects." Journal of Higher Education 1, no. 1 (1975):
         5-14.

         Takes a historical perspective on the socioeconomic milieu
         in which higher education has developed in India. Comments
         on the need for regulation of the Rapid and unplanned growth
         of higher education. Talks about the role of the UGC in
         planning and developing colleges, questions the relevance of
         higher education and suggests reforms--special mention is
         made about students amenities.

440.   Chitnis, S. "Urban Concentration of Higher Education."
         Economic and Political Weekly 4 (July 1979): 1235-38.

441.   Dabholkar, Devadatta. "Striving for Height in Higher
         Education." Journal of Higher Education 6 (1980-81): 41-
         50.

442.   Deva, Indra. "Latent Function of Higher Education in India."
         Journal of Higher Education 7 (Spring 1982): 211-17.

         Comments that the growth of higher education is
         disconnected with the well-known objectives of learning and
         that one begins to suspect that it serves some latent
         function for the existing socioeconomic system. Enumerates
         reasons behind the increase in the number of educational
         institutions and its consequences dampening effect on
         research endeavor, race for employment and costs of the
         present arrangement. Also suggests some measures to improve
         the situation.

443.   Dhawle, Anand S. and Amitabha Ghose. "A Study of the Image
         of Indian Journals on Management and Social Sciences in the
         International Academic Community." Journal of Higher
         Education 4 (Spring 1980): 313-26.

444.   Eisemon, Thomas Owen. "Autonomy and Authority in an Indian
         University: A Study of the University of Bombay." Compare
         14, no. 1 (1984): 59-68.

445.   Filella, J.   "College Climates: A Psycho-Social Matrix
       Model."   New Frontiers in Education 13 (January-March
       1983):   1-12.

446.   Ganesh, S. R. and D. Sarupira.   "Explorations in Helplessness
       of Higher Education Institute in the Third World."   Higher
       Education 12 (April 1983):   191-204.

       After independence, the Education Commission called for the
       creation of new institutions to undertake the task of higher
       education in technology, agriculture and management.
       Three models of higher education were imported.   In the
       field of technology the "MIT model" was advocated by the
       Sarkar Committee.   The five Indian Institutes of Technology
       (IITs) were the results of this thinking.   The "Land-grant
       University Model" provided the basis for development of
       agricultural universities.   The "Business School Model" was
       instrumental in the creation of the Indian Institutes of
       Management (IIMs) at Ahmedabad and Calcutta.   In this
       article, we explore the implications of importing the "MIT
       model" in the case of ITTs and venture some possible
       explanations of the feelings of institutional helplessness
       through in-depth data collected in one IIT.   We believe that
       the "sorting" process implicit in the MIT and the Business
       school models, in particular, when imposed on the Indian
       socioeconomic milieu has aggravated the isolation of the
       elites from the realities of the country as well as increased
       dependence of the West.   This, has in turn, resulted in
       mediocrity and irrelevances even in these islands of intended
       excellence.   The IIT experience serves to illustrate this ar-
       gument.   Our argument is developed through: 1) understanding
       the phenomenon of sorting and how this distances the IIT
       graduate, in particular, from the rest of the engineering
       graduates, among others;   2) placing the argument in the
       perspective of transfer of intellectual technology from the
       West.

447.   Heredia, Rudolf.   "Religious and Social Behaviour among
       Academics: Some Findings of a Survey."   New Frontiers in
       Education 14 (July-September 1984):   36-46.

448.   Ilchman, W. F. and T. N. Dhar.   "Optional Ignorance and
       Excessive Education: Educational Inflation in India."
       Asian Survey 11, no. 6 (1971):   523-43.

449.   Jayaram, N.   "Higher Education, Inequality and Social Change
       in India."   Sociological Bulletin 28 (March and September
       1979):   46-58.

450.   John, V. V. "India's Challenge: Education for Social
        Justice." New Frontiers in Education 14 (April-June 1984):
        17-25.

451.   John, V. V. "Towards a Meaningful First Degree." Journal
        of Higher Education, 1 (Monsoon 1975): 51-60.

        A critique of the existing first degree courses in our
        universities. Stresses the need for a change in
        undergraduate curriculum and makes certain policy
        recommendations. Comments on the capacities of teachers,
        their ability to take up new responsibilities in view of a
        change in curriculum and, on the teacher-student ratio.

452.   Kamat, A. R. "Higher Education: Kothari Commission and
        After." Journal of Higher Education 8 (Autumn 1982): 141-
        54.

453.   Kamat, A. R. "Higher Education: Myth--Old and New--Comments
        on the Education Commission's Report." Economic and
        Political Weekly 2 (April 15, 1967): 715-22.

454.   Kamat, R. V. "The Case for Autonomy." Journal of Higher
        Education 1 (Monsoon 1978): 91-98.

455.   Karve, D. D. "The Universities and the Public in India."
        Minerva 1 (Spring 1963): 263-284.

        This article deals with some of the ways in which public
        policy, political practice and public opinion in India affect
        the functioning of the Indian universities. It also
        describes some of the peculiarities of the Indian university
        system.

456.   Kaul, J. N. "Development of Indian Higher Education."
        Economic and Political Weekly 7 (August 1972): 1645-52.

        This article reviews the process of this linear growth in
        enrollments and compares it with conditions of higher
        education as they exist in some of the other countries whose
        example may be relevant for India.
        It recommends deliberate curbing of the present
        expansionary process, selection of students for higher
        education strictly on merit, incorporation of a multiplicity
        of relevant professional courses including correspondence
        courses, and a reorientation of the university courses to
        remove the present accent on academic trivia and theory and
        underpin the academic curriculum with direct work and
        production experience. It is emphasized that illiteracy is a

far more important target for educational planning than has
been recognized or provided for till now.

Provisions for education have to be much more guided by
assessments of manpower requirements, and the content of
education has to be much more determined by considerations of
relevance and usefullness in the overall development of the
country.

457.   Khader, M. A. and Sushila Singhal. "Institutional Quality,
        Student Input and Output: Analysis of Six Indian
        Universities." Journal of Higher Education 9 (Monsoon
        1983): 35-46.

Studies the growth in demand for education and the linear
expansion of educational institutions in post-independent
India. Comments that the qualitative differentation among
colleges and universities is a result of an inadequate
increase in inputs, the existing institutional environment,
student characteristics and student output. The analysis
uses samples (both at institutional and individual level) to
conclude that the level of selectivity of able students is
with a favorable socioeconomic background. Academic
willingness to bear the responsibility of improving the
performance of average students is responsible for the
concentration of academically talented students in a few
elite institutions. These factors affect the input and
output of students, their quality and thus determine the differentiation in quality among colleges and universities. It
is suggested that some factors that affect selectivity be
identified and controlled through reallocation of a resource
using appropriate policy measures.

458.   King, A. D. "Elite Education and the Economy ITT Entrance:
        1965-70." Economic and Political Weekly 5, no. 35 (1970):
        1463-71.

459.   Kurrien, John. "Salvaging Higher Education: Limiting the
        Importance of Degrees." Journal of Higher Education 9
        (Autumn 1983): 207-16.

A proposal to delink degrees from job selection and further
education has been suggested. This follows from the growing
lack of faith of both employers and university officials in
degrees, which is further compounded by the fact of varying
standards. Describes the unfairness of evaluation
procedures, the unawareness of university officials and
employers regarding the existence of many universities in our
country. The possible objections to delinking, viz.,
administrative difficulties, corruption and lowering

efficiency are discussed and suggestions regarding a delinked higher education scenario are put forward.

460.   Mahmood, M. "Language Politics and Higher Education in India." Indian Journal of Political Science 35, no. 3 (1973): 277-78.

461.   Malhotra, Ashok and Sushanta Banerjee. "Higher Education: Frames of Reference in Existing Literature." Journal of Higher Education 3 (Spring 1978): 301-14.

        Reviews the ways of studying the institutions and processes of higher learning in India as reflected in the existing literature. Refers to the following books: (1) Gaudino, R. L. "The Indian University," (2) Dibona, J. E., "Change and Conflict in the Indian University," (3) John, V. V. "Misadventures in Higher Education," (4) Malik, S. C. "Management and Organization of Indian Universities," and (5) Shah, A. B., ed. "Higher Education in India." Describes the content, methodology and flavor of these books.

462.   Mehrotra, R. C. "Industry - University Interaction." Journal of Higher Education 8 (Monsoon 1982): 19-28.

463.   Mehrotra, R. C. "Science, Technology Development and the Universities." Journal of Higher Education 6 (1980-81): 25-40.

464.   Morehouse, Ward. "Myth and Reality: Animadversions on Science, Technology, and Society in India." Knowledge 6 (June 1985): 406-36.

        Describes India's recent development of science and technology in terms of social change, economic progress and national power. Explores the causal links between science and technology and the role public policy has had in the attainment of technological autonomy. Examines myths of science associated with Third World countries like India.

465.   Narayan, D. S. "Higher Education in India." Bulletin of the UNESCO Regional Office for Education in Asia. 7 (September 1972): 46-63.

466.   Rabindranathan, M. R. "Regional Imbalance in the Growth of Higher Education in India." Journal of Higher Education 4 (Monsoon 1978): 33-40.

467.   Rajaraman, R. "Higher Education To Set House in Order." Economic and Political Weekly 7 (March 4, 1972): 554-557.

468. Ramakrishna, G. "Higher Education: A Perspective from the
      Periphery." Journal of Higher Education 7 (Monsoon 1981):
      51-8.

      Comments on the K. N. Raj Committee report on the three
      universities in Karnataka State. Refers to the "social
      freedom of higher education," commenting on the elicit nature
      of the education system and the role of the Planning Commis-
      sion and the UGC in this context. Discusses some aspects of
      post-graduate education and research and finally, the
      problems of colleges and college improvement programs.

469. Raman, Vasanthi. "Some Notes on the Intelligentsia."
      Journal of Higher Education 1 (Autumn 1975): 211-22.

470. Rao, V. Bhaskara. "Teaching and Research in Higher
      Education: Some Problems." Journal of Higher Education 4
      (Monsoon 1978): 11-22.

471. Rao, V. K. R. V. "Some Thoughts on Higher Education."
      Journal of Higher Education 6 (1980-81): 1-8.

472. Ray, Anil Baran. "Parochialism vs. Cosmopolitanism in Indian
      Higher Education." Journal of Higher Education 3 (Monsoon
      1977): 55-64.

473. Rudolph, Lloyd I. and Susanne Rudolph. "Standards in
      Democratised Higher Education." Economic and Political
      Weekly 5 (January 1970): 209-18.

      The alleged decline in the standards of education as a
      consequence of the vast expansion in education since
      Independence has been loudly and frequently lamented but less
      frequently analyzed empirically.
      This power stresses the importance of disaggregating the
      field of education regionally and sectorally as a preliminary
      to generalization about educational standards. This method
      yields a differentiated view of the fate of standards.
      It is suggested that, at least statistically speaking, the
      expansion of higher education has not resulted in a swamping
      of the post-graduate-graduate sector by the first degree or
      pre-university levels. On the contrary, so far as the
      structure of higher education is concerned, there has been
      some upgrading. The proportion accounted for by the BA level
      has increased at the expense of the proportion accounted for
      by the intermediate and PUC levels and the post-graduate
      level has made a modest proportionate advance.
      Statistics also suggest a shift from arts to science,
      technology and the professions while the founding of new

technological and scientific institutions of high quality suggest the upgrading of leading sectors for economic development.

In the social sciences, new fields have been added and old ones strengthened since Independence and a few outstanding men in a variety of fields are, and are perceived to be, the peers of internationally outstanding professionals.

474.   Sahoo, P. K. "Higher Education in India - Certain Issues." New Frontiers in Education 13 (October-December 1983): 62-8.

Reviews the expansion of university education in India and discusses some issues relating to higher education, viz., demand for education, rate of enrollment, research efficiency, etc. Uses data concerning stagewise and facultywise growth of enrollment.

475.   Siddey, S. C. and R. K. Gupta. "Determinants of Levels of Higher Education in States." Journal of Higher Education 9 (Monsoon, 1983): 133-44.

Comments that the level of development of higher education has not been uniform within the country, for example, some of the states/union territories such as Delhi, Chandigarh, Punjab, Gujarat, Haryana, Maharashtra, West Bengal, Pondicherry, U.P., depict a much better picture as compared with Bihar, Orissa, Andhra Pradesh, Assam and Himachal Pradesh. An attempt has been made to analyze the statewise position and to identify the variables--socioeconomic and political--which are responsible for the development of higher education in a state. A popular and common belief that literacy alone is responsible for the level of higher education in a state is disproved.

476.   Singh, Amrik. "Foundation and Role of UGC." Journal of Higher Education 7 (Monsoon 1981): 31-44.

Comments on the unique combination of powers vested with the UGC in regards to provision of funds and determination and coordination of standards. The focus of discussion is on how the UGC came to be established and how it was decided to vest it with the power it commands today. Various regulations, Bills and Acts are examined in this context.

477.   Singh, Amrik. "The Indian University Grant Commission." Higher Education 13 (October 1984): 517-33.

The Indian University Grants Commission (UGC), established
shortly after Independence, has vested in its powers the
responsibility of regulating academic standards as well as
disbursing funds provided by central government.
Unfortunately, in spite of such responsibilities being
entrenched by statute, the UGC has chosen not to exercise
them which has had serious consequence for academic standards
in Indian universities. The Indian university structure was
modeled on the collegiate structure of the University of
London with the result that the vast expansion of student
numbers in the 1950s and 1960s led to an uncontrolled
increase in the number and size of the colleges which themselves came to dominate the university system. Again the UGC
chose not to intervene and did not attempt to co-ordinate the
growth of the colleges. Bearing in mind the public pressures
for an expansion of university education, it would have been
unrealistic to expect the UGC to have tried to prevent
expansion but it could have sought to moderate it and to
impose co-ordination. One result has been the growth of
research institutes and high caliber teaching institutes
outside the established university system. The UGC is now
attempting to remedy the situation but it is clear that this
will be a long and uphill task.

478.   Sreenivasan, Sheilu. "Foreign-Aided IIT Education."
       Journal of Higher Education 4 (Autumn 1978): 187-200.

479.   Yadav, R. C. and H. P. Singh. "Wastage at the Ph.D. level."
       New Frontiers in Education 12 (October-December 1982):
       43-8.

       An investigation of an Indian university to find out how
       many Ph.D. scholars enrolled in five of its faculties during
       the period 1970-74, completed their work and submitted their
       theses. Mentions the procedures followed, the analyses of
       data collected and draws conclusions from the same.

480.   Zachariah, Mathew. "Fair Access to Higher Education:
       Reflections on India's and China's Experience of the Past
       Thirty Years." Journal of Higher Education 8 (Spring
       1983): 311-20.

NEPAL

Book

481.   Shrestha, Kedar N. Higher Education in Nepal. Bhaktapur:
           1980.

           This is a study of Tribhuvan University, the only
        university of the country. The National Education System
        Plan (1971-1976) recommended revamping the higher education
        system to meet manpower requirements of the country, and
        integrating all institutions of higher education under the
        University. The present problems of structure, financing,
        curriculum and evaluation of student achievement as analyzed
        in this study point to the need for reorganization of the
        higher education system.

   Article

482.   Vir, D. "Higher Education and Modernization in Nepal."
           Eastern Anthropologist 34, no. 4 (1981): 317-21.

PAKISTAN

    Books

483.   Siddiqui, M. Raziuddin. Establishing a New University in a
           Developing Country: Policies and Procedures. Islamabad:
           UGC, 1977.

484.   University Grants Commission. Statistics on Higher Education
           in Pakistan. Islamabad: The Commission, 1976.

485.   University Grants Commission. Study Group on Improvement of
           Education and Research in the Universities--Report.
           Islamabad: The Commission, 1975.

Article

486.   Ziring, Lawrence. "Dilemmas of Higher Education in Pakistan:
        A Political Perspective." *Asian Affairs* 5 (May-June 1978):
        307-24.

        Relates problems of higher education in Pakistan since the
        1950s. Intense student involvement in politics and conflict
        between traditional and modern versions of Islamic society
        have continually promoted turmoil in university life and
        government response to student unrest.

SRI LANKA

    Books

487.   Kintzer, Frederick C. *Junior University College Movement in
        Ceylon*. Washington: International Educational and
        Cultural Exchange, 1980.

        This document describes the developing Junior University
        College system in Ceylon. Six institutions, resembling
        American community or junior colleges, were established in
        1969 to fill Ceylon's manpower needs not met by her
        universities, technical colleges, and teachers' colleges.
        The Junior University College's three-fold aim includes
        imparting essential knowledge, supplying vocational skills,
        and encouraging the intellectual enrichment of citizens.
        Two-year diploma programs included traditional academics, as
        well as programs for filling manpower shortages in crucial
        industries. Personal development is stressed, with emphasis
        on preparation for "manhood as well as manpower." The
        document includes consideration of the language problem
        (staff members translate books and materials into Sinhala and
        Tamil, while students' English improves via voluntary speech
        classes and peer tutoring); student services, emphasizing
        educational and career counseling; teaching methods, which
        include demonstrations, discussions, role play, and tours, as
        well as more traditional methods; and community services.

488.   *Post-Graduate Education in Sri Lanka*. 2 Volumes. Colombo:
        Materials and Manpower Resources Division, Ministry of
        Finance and Planning, 1982.

Articles

489.   Abeywickrama, B. A.   "Higher Education in Ceylon."   Bulletin
         of the UNESCO Regional Office for Education in Asia 7
         (September 1972):   34-45.

490.   DeSilva, C. R.   "Weightage in University Admissions:
         Standardisation and District Quotas in Sri Lanka, 1970-75."
         Modern Ceylon Studies 5, no. 2 (1974):   151-78.

491.   De Silva, K. M.   "A University Grants Commission in South
         Asian Setting: The Sri Lanka Experience."   Higher
         Education 13 (October 1984): 553-68.

         University education in Sri Lanka in modern times has a
         short history of just over six decades.   From 1921 to 1959
         there was one University College (1921-1942) or University on
         the island.   With the establishment of two other universities
         in 1959, the need for co-ordination of higher education
         activity though a University Grants Commission (UGC) or
         similar body arose.
             The establishment of the National Council of Higher
         Education (NCHE) in 1966 was part of a policy of bringing
         greater government influence to bear on universities and was
         therefore resented and resisted by the latter.   However, the
         new body, while it lasted, served as a very effective buffer
         against undue government interference in university affairs.
         The six year period beginning in 1972 saw a process of
         centralization of university education under strong
         government control.   The UGC established in 1979 has much the
         same powers as the NCHE, a wider range in fact than those
         enjoyed by the British UGC, and much greater influence in
         university education than the British prototype.
             Universities in Sri Lanka have always depended on the state
         for almost all their funds.   While this has naturally given
         government much influence in shaping the structure and
         expansion of universities, the principle of university
         autonomy was strongly entrenched between 1942 and 1966.
         There was a departure from this in 1966, but more
         particularly between 1972 and 1978.   The Universities Act No.
         16 of 1978 re-introduced the concept of autonomous
         universities.   The one area in which state influenced has
         been the predominant factor is university admissions and this
         influence began in the mid-1950s long before the concept of
         university autonomy came under systematic attack from the
         government's Ministry of Education.

492.   Gamage, D. T. "A Review of the Problems, Issues and
       Government Policies on Higher Education in Sri Lanka."
       Perspectives in Education 1 (April 1985):   75-90.

493.   Gamage, D. T. "The Struggle for Control of Higher Education
       in a Developing Economy: Sri Lanka." Comparative
       Education 19, no. 3 (1983):   325-39.

       Argues that in Sri Lanka the development of higher
       education has reflected a struggle for power and control.
       The country which has inherited a British educational system
       as a result of its colonial past, has not been able to modify
       the goals of the colonial system significantly to meet local
       needs and aspirations, even after a period of 34 years of
       independent rule.

494.   Gunawardena, Chandra. "Ethnic Representation, Regional
       Imbalance and University Admissions in Sri Lanka."
       Comparative Education 15 (October 1979):   301-12.

       This paper discusses the regional imbalances and
       representation of four ethnic groups: Sinhalese, Tamils, the
       Moors/Malays and the Burghers who constitute 72.0%, 20.5%,
       07.1% and 0.3% of the population respectively, to the
       university.   Earlier (1942), the author examines, the Tamils
       and the Burghers were over-represented in the university
       population.   By 1963, Sinhalese predominance at the
       university was striking.   Their proportion has risen to a
       percentage of 81.8%.   This increase had come about at the
       expense of the other ethnic groups.

495.   Jayasuriya, D. L. "Developments in University Education:
       The Growth of the University of Ceylon (1942-65)."
       University of Ceylon Review 23 (1965):   83-153.

496.   Kintzer, Frederick C. "Junior University College Movement in
       Ceylon." International Education and Cultural Exchange 6
       (Fall 1970):   76-85.

497.   Pieris, R. "Universities, Politics and Public Opinion in
       Ceylon." Minerva 2 (1964):   435-54.

498.   Uswatte-Aratchi, G. "University Admissions in Ceylon: Their
       Economic and Social Background and Employment
       Expectations." Modern Asian Studies 8, no. 3 (1974):   289-
       318.

CHAPTER 11

SPECIALIZED EDUCATION: AGRICULTURAL, VOCATIONAL,

TECHNOLOGICAL AND TEACHER TRAINING

BANGLADESH

Book

499.   Muyeed, Abdul. School Works Programme, Comilla Kotwali
       Thana, 1963-1964. Comilla: Pakistan Academy for Rural
       Development, 1965.

Article

500.   Dove, Linda. "Mobile Teacher Trainers for UPE: An
       Experiment Programme in Rural Bangladesh." Community
       Development Journal 20 (January 1985): 41-48.

       The importance of teacher training is examined,
       specifically, the concept of mobile teacher trainers in
       Bangladesh. Discusses primary education in Bangladesh,
       primary school teachers, development of teacher training,
       Assistant Thana Education Officers (ATEOs), cluster training,
       teacher leaflets, and ATEOs as field officers and as mobile
       teacher trainers.

INDIA

Books

501.   Bhalerao, Usha. Educated Blind of Urban Madhya Pradesh: A
        Sociological Study. New Delhi: Sterling, 1983.

        Based on a doctoral study of a sample of educated blind and
        in-depth case studies, by a person, herself blind. Covers
        several sociological factors, i.e., family and marriage,
        education, socio-religious condition, occupations and
        economic condition, bio-medical history, recreation and
        social activities. About half the sample are found to be
        employed and the majority of these as teachers of music.
        While noting the improved status of the blind, the author
        stresses the need for placement in remunerative employment.

502.   Chandrakant, L. S. Polytechnic Education in India.
        Bombay: Taraporevala, 1971.

        This study explores the phenomenal expansion of technical
        education which took place in India since 1947 at the
        polytechnic Diploma level. In 1947, only fifty-three
        institutions conducted Diploma courses and they admitted only
        3670 students each year. The number of Diploma holders
        trained each year were less than 1500 a year. At present,
        India has 279 institutions capable of admitting about 50,000
        students a year. The number of Diploma-holders trained each
        year has jumped to about 23,500. This book also describes
        the types of technician courses, polytechnic curriculum,
        reorganization of polytechnic courses, curriculum
        development, the polytechnic students and the polytechnic
        faculty in India, and also provides an engineer-technician
        ratio.

503.   Desai, M. M., ed. Creative Literature and Social Work
        Education. Bombay: Somaiya, 1979.

        Presents the proceedings of a workshop held in Bombay in
        April 1978. The workshop concentrated on the themes of
        family life and social deprivation in its attempt to
        sensitise the inter-disciplinary participants to the use of
        creative literature in teaching social work as part of a
        process of indigenising social work education by linking it
        to the struggles and aspirations of the community, as
        mirrored in creative literature. Contains papers on the

value of creative literature, their selection, attempts to link Marathi, Gujarati and English literature to the themes of the workshop, guidelines on teaching, and reports of group discussions on specific items of literature. The appendices contain papers illustrating the use of literary pieces, students' perceptions of the subject as seen in assignments and documentation of English, Marathi and Gujarati language literary material.

504. Environmental Education at the School Level. New Delhi: National Council of Educational Research and Training, 1981.

This publication deals with the emerging trends and status of environmental education in the Indian context. Definitions of environmental education, guiding principles, alternative models for patterning environmental education curriculum and formulating teaching/learning strategies both information and non-formal education are discussed.

505. Jain, R. K. Higher Education for Business in India; A Critique of Commerce Education in Indian Universities. Nagpur: Vishwa Bharati Prakashan, 1966.

506. Kakkar, N. K. Workers' Education in India. New Delhi: Sterling, 1973.

507. Kaul, M., S. S. Kuchaal and K. Chowdhry. Study of the Framework Structure and Funding of Technical Education Systems in India. Ahmedabad: Indian Institute of Management, 1977.

508. Kochhar, S. K. Educational and Vocational Guidance in Secondary Schools. New Delhi: Sterling, 1978.

509. Kuppuswamy, B. Advanced Educational Psychology. New York: Apt Books, 1984.

The rapid advance in Secondary Education in the last two decades has led to a tremendous increase in the number of teachers' colleges in the country. This has created a demand for those with Master's degree in Education. In recent years many universities have started M.Ed. courses. Consequently, the need for textbooks and additional reading material for this level of teacher training is growing. It is to meet this need that this book on "Advanced Educational Psychology" has been prepared.

510.   Longer, V. Youth in Step: History of the National Cadet
        Corps. New Delhi: Lancer International, 1983.

        A history of the birth and development of the National
        Cadet Corps--youth military training programs--in its
        relation to the national mainstream. The sources are
        official papers, government orders, minutes of meetings, and
        interviews.

511.   Mandke, Vijay V. BITS Practice School: A Case Study in
        Industry - University Collaboration. Pilani: Birla
        Institute of Technology and Science, 1980.

        A case study of the practice school system evolved by the
        Dirla Institute of Science and Technology, early efforts
        between 1964 and 1970 and the functioning from 1973:
        planning, educational contents, manpower development,
        facilities, finances and administration. Indicates
        directions for the future, such as post-graduate and post-
        doctoral programs in research, consultancy and involvement in
        rural development.

512.   Mathur, Ashok; Moonis Raza and G. S. Bhalla. Vocationalism
        of Education in India: A Regional Perspective. New Delhi:
        J. N. U. Centre for the Study of Regional Development, n.
        d.

        This study deals with vocational education plans for the
        terminal state of school education at the district level in
        India in 300 districts. Chapter One gives a picture of the
        development of vocational education in India. Chapter Two
        deals with a methodology for framing micro-regional
        vocational plans. Chapter Three classifies the districts
        into typologies on the basis of similarity of occupational
        characteristics and efforts made to evolve a uniform pattern
        of vocational courses for districts falling within each
        occupational typology. Chapter Four outlines the trends of
        occupational change and its vocational implications during
        1961-1971 in the districts of Haryana, Gurgaon, Karnal and
        Mahendragarh. Chapter Five gives a report of the vocational
        survey undertaken in the Gurgaon district. Statistical
        tables are contained in Volume II.

513.   Pareek, Uday. Education and Rural Development in Asia.
        New Delhi: Oxford and IBH.

        Describes the successes and failures of experiments
        undertaken in different countries of Asia towards organizing
        educational innovation in the service of rural development.

Gives detailed discussion of the different concepts and frameworks underlying education and rural development. Discusses the goals and the strategies used to help education perform its role in rural development.

514.   Prasad, C. Elements of the Structure and Terminology of Agricultural Education in India. Paris: UNESCO, 1981.

Studies the relationship between agricultural education and general education, especially the role of agricultural education institutions in non-formal education in India before and after independence. The various levels of agricultural education are defined as: basic and multi-purpose schools, non-degree programs, and higher education. It also describes the pedagogy of teacher training in agriculture and strategy of agricultural training for development.

515.   Rao, S. V. Education and Rural Development. New Delhi: Sage, 1985.

516.   Shanker, Uday and Lakshmi Shanker. Sex Education. New Delhi: Sterling, 1978.

Presents an exhaustive treatment of the subject in its relation to population control. Stresses the need for imparting sex education in schools and colleges, and discusses the mode of doing so.

517.   Sharma, R. C. Environmental Education. New Delhi: Metropolitan Books, 1981.

Contains chapters on the meanings, scope, background, principles and problems of environmental education. The author discusses how environment may be used as a medium of learning and how activities in conserving the environment may be used in making educational programs interesting and relevant.

518.   Singh, Tribhuwan. Diffusion of Innovations among Training Colleges of India. Varanasi: Bharat Bharati Prakashan, 1978.

Classifies into ten areas the innovations for teacher education programs, recommended by various committees and organizations between 1947 and 1974. Studies the process and extent of diffusion of these innovations, through data collected from 209 teacher training colleges and interviews and observations conducted in forty of these colleges. Some of the conclusions are that innovations have been accepted in institutions where teacher educators have had a wider exposure and that the generally distorted implementation of innovations has been due to inadequate care as to their relevance to the needs of particular institutions.

519.   Singh, Y. P., U. Pareek and D. R. Arora. Diffusion of an Interdiscipline: Social Sciences in Agricultural Education. Delhi: New Heights, 1974.

520.   Sinha, P. R. and N. V. Kolte. Adult Education in Relation to Agricultural Development. Hyderabad: National Institute of Community Development, 1974.

521.   Srivastava, A. P., and A. Srivastava. On Bringing up Weak and Slow Learning Children: Research Findings and Knowhow. New Delhi: The Learning Laboratory, 1983.

Points out the disadvantages faced by weak and slow learning children in the present educational system and environment. Illustrates techniques for developing various facilities of the slow learners in keeping with their needs and abilities during the formative years. The book is directed at parents, in particular, and teachers.

522.   Timmaiah, G. and others. Vocational Education - Problems and Prospects: A Case Study of Karnataka State. Bombay: Himalaya, 1982.

An evaluation of the vocational courses introduced in Karnataka state at the +2 pre-university stage, to train students for middle level jobs anticipated in industry and service sectors and for self-employment. Seeks to assess the demand for vocational skills in relation to their supply, to give an account and an evolution of the experiment, with its problems, prospects and policy implications. The study is based on interviews with students, ex-students, teachers and administrators in these vocational education institutions.

Articles

523.   Aswathanarayana, U. "Towards Excellence in the Teaching of Geological Science at the Post-graduate Level." Journal of Higher Education 1 (Spring 1976): 387-96.

524. Bandyopadhyay, S. and S. Kumar. "Application of Management
      Concepts in a College: A Study in Feasibility." Economic
      and Political Weekly 10 (September 6, 1975):   95-98.

525. Banerji, D. "Social Orientation of Medical Education in
      India." Economic and Political Weekly 8 (March 1973):
      485-88.

      Even in the industrialized countries, medical educators
      have been compelled to bring about changes in their system of
      education to suit the rapidly changing conditions.
      Additionally, for India the existing system of medical
      education had two fundamental shortcomings: (a) it was
      evolved to serve a very small privileged section of the
      society; and (b) along with the natural science essentials,
      it carried with it the cultural accretions of the West.
      To bring about social orientation of medical education in
      the country, departments of preventive and social medicine
      were established in medical colleges. The teachers of
      preventive and social medicine have, however, conspicuously
      failed in meeting the challenge. At best they have ended up
      by putting in the old wine of hygiene and public health in
      the new bottle of preventive and social medicine.

526. Bhambhari, C. P. "Political Science in India: Academic
      Colonialism and Lessons for the Third World." Economic and
      Political Weekly 10 (May 3, 1975):   730-35.

527. Biswas, A. K. "Teaching of Economics in India." Economic
      and Political Weekly 7 Annual Number, (February 1972):
      345-50.

528. Chaturvedi, Vipula and Mahesh C. Chaturvedi. "International
      Perspectives of Collaboration in Higher Technical
      Education." Education Quarterly 35 (October 1983):   1-8.

529. Dayal, Maheswar. "Strategies for Development of Appropriate
      Rural Technologies and their Extension." New Frontiers in
      Education 14 (October-December 1984):   10-17.

      Comments on development policy and its reflection on
      economic and social growth with justice. Reviews the
      policies of developing countries like India to increase
      agricultural output and productivity, increase in access of
      the rural poor to social services, facilities, literacy,
      etc., which contribute to overall rural development.
      Discusses appropriate technology and its meaning within the
      Indian context, energy usage and the extension of improved
      technologies in the rural areas.

530.   Desai, A. S. "The Foundations of Social Work Education in
        India and Some Issues." Indian Journal of Social Work 46,
        no. 1 (1985): 41-57.

531.   Dubey, V. K. and C. Prasad. "Teaching, Research and
        Extension in Indian Agricultural Universities." Journal of
        Higher Education 2 (Spring 1977): 393-400.

        Suggests a blend between teaching, research and extension
        so as to contribute towards agricultural production, and
        designs a conceptual framework for the same. Comments on the
        confusion and problems arising from the differentiation in
        quality between agricultural universities. Summarizes a
        pilot study which puts forward the author's categories of
        conceptual perception regarding the integration of teaching
        research and extension. Reports the research findings,
        resulting from a discussion of these concept with university
        administrators.

532.   Ganesh, S. R. "Performance of Management Education
        Institutions: An Indian Sampler." Higher Education 9 (May
        1980): 239-54.

        In the 1950s and 1960s, several institutions were created
        in India to cater to the needs of management education and to
        assist in the process of national development. To date,
        there has been very little systematic comparative analysis of
        the experience of creating these institutions and examining
        their performance. To present paper reports the results of
        an attempt to assess the performance of six management
        education institutions in India which were established in the
        1950s and 1960s and equally divided between post-graduate and
        post-experience education. Being an exploratory study, the
        emphasis has been on developing a methodology for assessment
        of performance and applying this to the area of management
        education. Basically, performance on both system survival
        and system effectiveness dimensions has been incorporated
        into the performance measurement attempt. System survival
        has been operationalized through a series of indicators on
        capability development; the system effectiveness dimension
        has been operationalized through a series of indicators on
        innovative thrust and penetration for these six institutions.
        An attempt has also been made to relate various process
        mechanisms of institution building to the different aspects
        of performance. Thus, the paper also explores the
        relationship of institution building processes with
        performance.

533.   Ganguli, Prabuddha. "Science Teaching in Rural India--an
        Experiment." Journal of Higher Education 1 (Autumn 1975):
        266-68.

534.   Gurumurthy, K. G. "University Education and Rural
        Development." Journal of Higher Education 4 (Spring 1980):
        353-64.

535.   Hone, A. "Economics of Improving Technical Education."
        Economic and Political Weekly 3 (January 1968):   119-26.

536.   Jayaram, N. "Social Implications of Medical Education in
        India." Journal of Higher Education 3, no. 2 (1977):   207-
        220.

537.   Joshi, B. C. "Problems of Chemical Education and Research."
        Journal of Higher Education 2 (Spring 1977):   367-76.

        Enumerates the problems of chemical training and research
        in universities which are the result of the rapid expansion
        of universities, unmatched by an equal increase in inputs and
        facilities. Discusses the objectives of chemists, teaching
        of chemistry, chemical research, areas of work, newer sources
        of energy and food, with a view to solving relevant problems
        of social significance.

538.   Mandle, Vijay V. "Management Education and Development."
        Journal of Higher Education 1 (Spring 1976):   349-57.

        Discusses the nature of development and its problems.
        Surveys management education during the pre- and post-
        independence periods. Observes that management schools have
        been contributing to national development by training
        manpower and also notes some shortcomings. Provides an
        alternate model which can rectify them. Discusses "the five-
        year integrated MMS program with practice" and comments on
        the feedback from it.

539.   Mathai, Ravi J. "The Organisation and the Institution: Man-
        agement Education in India." Economic and Political Weekly
        15 (May 31, 1980): 69-72.

        Argues that institutions in the field of management
        education in India, rather than reacting to short-term
        demands and being drawn into problems in many sectors, need a
        vision so as to view the nation's operating system as an
        integrated whole. The vision should guide organizational
        objectives and choices for spheres of work.

540.   Mohan, P. and R. Evanson. "The Indian Agricultural Research
        System." Economic and Political Weekly 8 (March 31, 1973):
        A-21-26.

541.   Mukerji, S. K. "Developing Colleges of Basic Sciences and
        Humanities in Agricultural Universities." Journal of
        Higher Education 5 (Autumn, 1979): 195-202.

        A study of the objectives and key programs of colleges of
        basic sciences and humanities (BSH) within existing
        conditions of the agricultural universities. Reviews the
        problems of BSH with reference to curriculum and promotion of
        growth in each subject. Suggests encouragement of research
        inter-university workshops, etc. for further development in
        BSH.

542.   Nayar, D. P. "Problems of Technical Education." Economic
        and Political Weekly 5 (March 21, 1970): 533-39.

543.   Paul, S. "Management Education: Social Costs and Returns."
        Economic and Political Weekly 5 (May 30, 1970): M-46-52.

544.   Prasad, C. "Agricultural Extension Curriculum and Change
        Agendas - Some New Guidelines." Journal of Higher
        Education 5 (Monsoon 1979): 75-88.

        Emphasizes the need and importance of extension activity
        and its role in agricultural development. Defines extension
        education and the interaction between agriculture, extension
        and social science. Criticizes the academic programs of
        extension education with a view to assess whether the exten-
        sion profession has been serving the cause of community
        development. Discusses the academic curriculum in
        agricultural extension, guidelines on curriculum and the
        extension role of agricultural universities.

545.   Rangaswami, G. "Self Improvement of Agricultural
        Universities." Journal of Higher Education 2 (Spring
        1977): 317-92.

        Comments on the objectives with which agricultural
        universities have been set up, and the Indian Council of
        Agricultural Research model act and its purpose. Suggests
        means of improving two aspects, viz., (i) technical component
        and (ii) managerial component for improving agricultural
        universities which can then serve the rural community
        effectively.

546.   Rao, C. N. R. "Materials Science Education." Journal of
        Higher Education 7 (Monsoon 1981):   83-91.

547.   Rao, J. S. "Science and Technology in India." Science 229
        (July 1985):   30-34.

        Assesses the current status of science and technology in
        India, focusing on developments in agriculture, energy,
        medicine, space, basic sciences, and engineering. Indicates
        that although India has benefited from many fields from
        international collaboration during the last 30 years, the
        country's leaders have also placed particularly strong
        emphasis on self-reliance.

548.   Rudra, K. K. and S. P. Rastogi. "Regional Distribution of
        Selected Technical Educational Facilities in India."
        Journal of Higher Education 4 (Monsoon 1978):   23-32.

549.   Saran, Yogendra. "India: A Strategy to Improve Technical
        Education." Prospects 6, no. 2 (1976):   245-53.

        Discusses the efforts of the Ministry of Education and
        Social Welfare, Government of India, in improving the
        condition of polytechnic education. Efforts in curriculum
        development, human resource development, examination reforms
        and their impact are discussed. The article concludes that
        the process of improving a system of education is very
        complex. Innovations are generally looked at with a lot of
        suspicion in the initial stages. Traditions are the toughest
        barrier to cross and have to be overcome cautiously. The
        problem of management of innovations and co-ordination of
        various efforts with limited financial resources is another
        major problem. Changing the attitudes of senior
        administrators and principals through short courses and
        reinforcing their efforts through better management
        techniques proved to be very helpful. Mass-scale teacher
        involvement in the entire process was another factor
        responsible for success.

550.   Singh, B. "Impact of Education on Farm Production."
        Economic and Political Weekly 9 (September 28, 1974):   A-
        92-96.

551.   Vedanayagam, E. G. "Remedial Education: With Reference to
        Reading." New Frontiers in Education 13 (October-December
        1983):   17-27.

552.   Von Mehren, A. T. "Law and Legal Education in India: Some
        Observations." Harvard Law Review 78 (1965):   1180-89.

PAKISTAN

Books

553.   Ghani, M. A., ed. Training for Higher Productivity: Papers
        Contributed in a Seminar Organised by the Society for the
        Advancement of Training, Pakistan, Sept. 8, 9 and 10, 1970.
        Karachi: The Society, (1970).

554.   Mir, Mohammad. Technical Education in Pakistan, A Study of
        Issues and Strategies. Islamabad: National Book Founda-
        tion, 1980.

        Technical education in its present form, started in 1955.
        Since then there was a recommendation to have a massive shift
        from general to agro-technical education, to vocationalize
        the secondary school program, and to upgrade the technician
        training program.

555.   Report to the Government of Pakistan on Co-operative
        Education. Geneva: International Labour Office, 1966.

NEPAL

Books

556.   Pradhananga, Upendra. Management Education in the Tribuhavan
        University. Kathmandu: Research and Management Forum,
        1982.

557.   Sharma, Suresh Raj. Education for Work. Kathmandu:
        Research Center for Educational Innovation and Development
        (CERID), Tribhuvan University, 1983.

        This is a completion of articles, papers and abstracts of
        study reports written essentially on various aspects of
        technical education.

Articles

558.   Belbase, Lekh Nath, and Loren B. Jung.   "Some Issues
        Influencing the Planning and Implementation of Vocational
        Education in Nepal." International Review of Education 30,
        no. 2 (1984): 171-82.

559.   Blackwell, James E. "Fundamental Education and Village
        Development in Nepal." Community Development Journal 4
        (October 1969): 175-85.

        The Village Development Project, in operation in Nepal from
        1952 until 1959, was less than successful in its total effect
        because of competition between U.S. and Indian foreign aid
        programs and the unfamiliarity of village development workers
        with rural life.

SRI LANKA

560.   Mathew, Walter. "Special Education in Sri Lanka."
        Australian Journal of Mental Retardation 5 (March 1979):
        8-11.

        Sections address the ascertainment of handicap, estimates
        of the need, statutory provisions, the National Education
        Commission's influence, the special residential school
        program, the integrated program, post-school provision, and
        teacher training.

CHAPTER 12

PRIVATE EDUCATION

(INCLUDING RELIGIOUS EDUCATION)

INDIA

Books

561. Ahmad, Zulficar and Munawar Mirza. The Financing of Privately - Managed Schools in the Punjab. Paris: UNESCO-IIEP, 1975

562. Mathias, T. A., ed. Education and Social Concern: Report of the JEA Seminar on the Social Mission of the Jesuit School and College. Delhi: Jesuit Educational Association of India, 1968.

Report of a seminar held during May 15-21, 1968. Presents then position papers and eleven reports of discussions, the conclusions of discussion groups and the general conclusion of the seminar.

563. Murickan, J. Catholic Colleges in India: A Study. Mangalore: Xavier Board of Higher Education in India, 1981.

An empirical analysis of forty Catholic colleges based on questionnaires sent out to knowledgeable persons within and outside the institutions. Discusses the position of Catholic colleges in the national context of the church and government. Presents an analysis of the internal structure of the institutions, their relation with and impact on the external milieu and the expectations from and of the participants in the institutions.

564.   Singh, Nirmal. Education Under Siege: A Sociological Study
        of Private Colleges. New Delhi: Concept, 1983.

        Analyzes the conditions and consequences of private control
        of public education.   Presents a macro-perspective on
        education and society in India from the nineteenth century to
        the present, for a micro-level study of seven private
        colleges in Kanpur. Holds that there is a dual system of
        education, one that supplies professionals for various
        privileged positions, and the other which supplies lower
        level personnel, giving the impression of an open-door
        educational system which is in fact of poor quality.
        Concludes that the siege of higher education by the private
        control of college managements, subverts national values and
        is opposed to education.

565.   Singh, R. P. The Indian Public Schools. New Delhi:
        Sterling, 1972.

        Article

566.   Singh, Nirmal. "A Perspective on Higher Education in India -
        the Case for Private Control." Journal of Higher Education
        5 (Monsoon 1979):   21-32.

        A historical analysis of the development of education in
        India. Studies the state and society and its effect on the
        educational system after independence. Comments on the dual
        system of education as reflected in the parallel existence of
        private fee-charging better schools, and public schools of
        poor standard. Discusses how this is sustained by policy
        decisions and the merits and demerits of private control of
        education.

CHAPTER 13

CURRICULUM, METHODS, EVALUATION

AND EDUCATIONAL TECHNOLOGY

BANGLADESH

Books

567.   Academy for Fundamental Education. Primary Training
       Institutes in Bangladesh: A Study on Facilities,
       Achievements and Drawbacks. Mymensingh: 1981.

       This report revealed that many of the PTIs have inadequate
       physical facilities. One of the recommendations is the
       setting up of a well-designed evaluation system to assess the
       performance of trainees, the content of curriculum and in
       total the achievement of the goal of the entire PTI program.

568.   Haq, A. K. Bazlul. Progress of Rural Education in Comilla
       Kotivali Thana (1968-1973). Comilla: Bangladesh Academy
       for Rural Development, (1975).

569.   Haque, Mazharul and Robert W. Schmeding, eds. The Education
       in East Pakistan: Research Project. Dhaka: Institute of
       Education and Research, 1970.

       This comprehensive research project on Education in East
       Pakistan (now Bangladesh) provides vital data and statistics
       for educational planning. Particular attention was given to
       the identification of the major educational goals with which
       universal education in Bangladesh has to be concerned. The
       book involved the study of the following areas: enrollment,
       teaching profession, consultative services, curriculum
       testing and measurement practices in primary and secondary
       education, guidance, adult education, physical facilities,
       and educational finance.

570.   University of Dhaka. Institute of Education and Research.
        An Evaluation of the Curricula of Teacher Education
        Programmes of Bangladesh: Research Report. Dhaka: The
        Institute, 1976.

        Articles

571.   Rasmussen, Poul Erik. "The Mass Educational Programme of the
        IRDP/DANIDA Project, Noakhali, Bangladesh: A Success Story
        So Far." International Journal of Educational Development
        5, no. 1 (1985): 27-39.

        Outlines the history, the basic idea, and the structure of
        the mass educational program and gives a brief account of the
        results attained so far. The results are evaluated with
        reference to their significance in achieving the desired
        objectives and on the basis of self-reliance and lasting
        development effects.

572.   Sharfuddin, S. M. "Change in Mathematics Education Since the
        late 1950's -- Ideas and Realisation: Bangladesh."
        Educational Studies in Mathematics, 9 (May 1978): 159-170.

        This article reports on two changes: in 1960 a Mathematics
        Curriculum Committee was appointed to introduce a uniform
        curriculum throughout the country; in 1975, a National
        Curriculum Committee was formed to prepare curricula in the
        light of modern knowledge.

INDIA

        Books

573.   Bhimasankaram, C. V. Mathematics Education. Bombay: Book
        Field Centre, 1979 (2nd edition).

        Discusses the points of view for and against 'new'
        mathematics and presents solutions to the problems connected
        with the learning/teaching of the subject through practical
        techniques. Major aspects discussed are the foundation of
        mathematics in historical perspective, schools of
        mathematical thought, a comparative view of 'old' and 'new'
        mathematics and research trends.

574.   Buck, M. P. and P. A. Patel. Towards Work-Centered
        Education; A Programme of Socially Useful Productive Work
        in Education. Ahmedabad: Injarat Vidyapith, 1979.

        The aims and objectives of the concept of socially useful
        productive work are explained and guidelines are provided for
        the implementation of the concept in schools and for teacher-
        training.

575.   Chandra, Arvindra. Curriculum Development and Evaluation
        in Education. New Delhi: Sterling, 1977.

576.   Chatterjee, K. K. English Education in India: Issues and
        Opinions. New Delhi: Macmillan, 1973.

577.   Chauhan, S. S. Innovations in Teaching-Learning Process.
        New Delhi: Vikas, 1979.

        Discusses innovations in teaching technology, such as, the
        use of computers and programmed instruction; methods of
        improving the teaching-learning process, such as team
        teaching and micro-teaching; and, norm-referenced and
        criterion-referenced evaluation of teaching-learning
        outcomes. Identifies problems in implementation.

578.   Chickermane, D. V. Experiments in Rural Education.
        Gokarn: Research Centre in Rural Education, 1978.

        Describes experiments in rural education such as the single
        teacher school, the ungraded school unit, continuing
        education, adult literacy through projected visual aids, and
        bilingualism in rural primary schools.

579.   Chickermane, D. V. The Single-Teacher School in Rural
        Education and Development. New Delhi: National Council of
        Education Research and Training, 1979.

        The introductory pages of the book describes the situation
        of schools in the rural areas and report that of the total
        number of schools in the Indian Union, forty percent are
        single-teacher schools or multiple class teaching schools.
        Problems of these schools in dealing with mass delivery of
        teaching, irregular attendance of pupils, lack of physical
        facilities, residential accommodation of teachers and other
        aspects are discussed with practical advice as to how a
        teacher may handle the situation. The last chapter describes
        the role a single-teacher school can play in rural
        reconstruction.

580.   Dandekar, V. M. Evaluation in Schools. Poona: Shri Vidya
        Prakashan, 1971.

581.   Dandekar, V. M. Psychological Foundations of Education.
        New Delhi: Macmillan, 1976.

        An introduction to the principles of psychology and their
        use in teaching. Covers the learning process at different
        stages of development, factors influencing learning and the
        situational use of psychology. Memory, motivation,
        perceptions, intelligence, personality and testing are some
        of the other topics treated in relation to education.

582.   Deo, Pratibha. Revaluation in University Examinations.
        Agra: National Psychological Corporation, 1983.

        Investigates the quantitative and qualitative effects of
        re-evaluation on the results of candidates appearing for
        examinations in universities in India where the re-evaluation
        facility exists. The data is subjected to statistical
        analysis. Data obtained through questionnaires sent to
        different universities, regarding their opinion on and
        functioning of the re-evaluation system, is also analyzed.

583.   Desai, Daulatbhai and Ameeta Govind. Studies in Achievement
        Motivation: Towards Psychological Education. Baroda:
        Faculty of Education and Psychology, M.S. University of
        Baroda, 1979.

        Presents the results of studies on achievement motivation
        in India and includes a discussion of psychological education
        and research in the area.

584.   Dhar, Niranjan. Fundamentals of Social Education.
        Calcutta: Minerva, 1971.

        The document records the results of an investigation of the
        types of programs and operational methods that were organized
        in the schools of the Delhi Administration "for inculcating
        moral, social, and spiritual values" in the pupils.

585.   Goyal, B. R. Moral Education in Delhi Schools. New Delhi:
        National Council of Educational Research and Training,
        1979.

        The document records the results of an investigation of the
        types of programs and operational methods that were organized
        in the schools of the Delhi Administration "for inculcating
        moral, social, and spiritual values" in the pupils.

586.   Gupta, Arun K. A Study of Classroom Teaching Behaviour and
        Creativity. New Delhi: Light and Life, 1980.

        Studies the relation between institutional climate,
        teachers' verbal behaviour, and students' activity, on the
        basis of a sample of ninth standard boys and girls studying
        science in Jammu. One of the major conclusions is that
        democratic behaviour on the part of teachers and informal
        open functioning of schools promotes creativity. The present
        situation is found not to generally meet this need.

587.   Gupta, S. K. Teaching Physical Sciences in Secondary
        Schools. New York: Apt Books, 1984.

        This book is an endeavor to meet the requirements of B.Ed.
        and M.Ed. courses of Indian universities keeping in view
        modern trends and practices useful for making physical
        sciences interesting and understandable to secondary school
        students.

588.   Harper, A. E. and Vidya Sagar Misra. Research on
        Examinations in India. New Delhi: National Council of
        Educational Research and Training, 1976.

        Contains a review of research on examinations in India and
        abroad, and a report of two studies on the reliability of
        examinations in India. The results of the studies are
        presented at three levels to meet different interests: a
        brief statement of findings, the major findings, highlighted
        and a detailed report of the results. Traditional essay type
        examinations are found to be unreliable and recommendations
        for improvement in the system are made.

589.   Kochhar, S. K. Teaching of Social Studies. New Delhi:
        Sterling, 1983.

        Attempts to provide the social studies teacher with new
        concepts and latest teaching procedures and techniques for
        teaching the subject. Deals with almost all aspects of
        teaching social studies.

590.   Kulshrestha, S. P. and D. N. Pahinwal, eds. Recent Advances
        in Educational and Psychological Testing in India. Dehra
        Dun: Dugal Kishore & Co., 1984.

591.   Mahanti, Jagannatha. Educational Broadcasting: A Radio
        and Television in Education. New Delhi: Sterling, 1984.

592.   Maikap, S. C. Cadet Corps in India: Its Evolution and
        Impact. Calcutta: Darbari Udyog, 1979.

        A history of the National Cadet Corps movement in India
        based on government records and interviews of cadets and
        officers. Holds that one of the major reasons for its
        deterioration is poor financing. Similar schemes in the U.
        K., U. S. A., U. S. S. R., Australia and China are evaluated.

593.   Mamidi, M. R. and S. Ravishankar. Curriculum Development
        and Educational Technology. New Delhi: Sterling, 1984.

        A collection of papers on the subject from educationists in
        the field. Covers types of educational technology for the
        different stages of education in a general perspective that
        suggests the integration of curriculum development with
        innovative technology for the improvement of the quality of
        education. Aimed primarily at students, teachers and
        researchers in the subject.

594.   Mehdi, Baqer and B. P. Gupta. Psychology of the Child and
        the Curriculum. Delhi: National Council of Educational
        Research and Training, Curriculum Group, 1979.

595.   Ministry of Education and Social Welfare. Working Group on
        Educational Technology. Report. New Delhi: Ministry of
        Education and Social Welfare, 1978.

        This is the report of a Working Group which was set up to:
        (1) Identify the role of educational technology in education;
        (2) determine the priority areas in using educational
        technology; (3) work out detailed schemes for development of
        educational technology programs, and (4) indicate their
        financial implications. The report carries a critical review
        of the following problems: lack of staff for implementing
        educational technology programs; inadequate physical
        facilities; absence of a co-ordinating mechanism between
        media agencies and departments or education; unsatisfactory
        pattern of assistance; and lack of acceptance of a concept of
        educational technology.

596.   Mohanty, J. Educational Broadcasting: Radio and
        Television in Education. New Delhi: Sterling, 1984.

        Contains twenty chapters on educational broadcasting, i.e.,
        radio and television, covering five overlapping areas:
        historical perspective, planning, production, utilization,
        and, evaluation and research. An introductory chapter,
        'Educational Broadcasting: National Perspective and

Priorities', discusses the efforts made by national and international agencies in policy formulation, management and production of educational radio and television programs. Also contains chapters evaluating the experiences of BBC and the Open University and their relevance to the Indian context.

597.   Narang, S. K. Academic Performance: Some Personality and Perception Variables. New Delhi: S. Chand, 1981.

Studies the relationship between the academic performance of eleventh standard boys and girls and of a sample of extreme academic achievers, on the one hand, and the intelligence, adjustment, achievement motivation and perceptions by self, peers, teachers and the father, on the other hand. Academic performance appears to be significantly related to intelligence, achievement, motivation, and the perceptions of those concerned.

598.   Narayan, R. Falling Education Standards. Agra: Lakshmi Narain Agarwal, 1970.

599.   National Workshop on Computer Literacy Curriculum, NCERT, 26-27 March 1984. Class: Computer Literacy and Studies in Schools, Report. New Delhi: National Council of Educational Research and Training, 1984.

Anybody who grows up in the world of tomorrow, not knowing computers, not understanding computers, not being able to use them, will be lost, and that country which does not prepare its citizens to be fully familiar and conversant with computers, their technologies and their applications would not be able to keep its place in the industrial hierarchy in the community of nations.

600.   Padmini, T. Fostering Cognitive Development in Primary School Entrants. New Delhi: Bahri, 1983.

Documentation of a program to develop cognitive abilities in controlled situations in five school environments among children aged five to seven. Attempts to reconcile Piaget's approach with the psychometric approach. Contains a review of relevant theories and research, and suggests a teaching strategy.

601.   Passi, B. K. and others. Creativity in Education: Its Correlates. Agra: National Psychological Corporation, 1982.

A trend report covering 160 studies and a presentation of
abstracts of some of these empirical researchers carried out
on the correlational aspects of creativity in the Indian
context. The trend report discusses the studies grouped
under demographic, affective and cognitive aspects. The
abstracts certain details in regards to objectives, design,
sample, tools, and major findings.

602.   Patel, R. N. Educational Evaluation: Theory and Practice.
        Bombay: Himalaya, 1978.

        Discusses theoretical and practical aspects of the subject,
        covering evaluation and the role of objectives, listing
        methods, qualitative testing and internal assessment. Part
        two presents elementary testing methods useful to the
        evaluator.

603.   Patil, V. T. The Semester System: Substance and Problems.
        New Delhi: Sterling, 1984.

        Takes a look at the structure and substance of the semester
        system, its relevance and drawbacks in a period of transition
        from tradition to modernity. Policy changes are suggested
        with a view to improving the quality and relevance of
        education. Questions of grading and provision of question
        banks are discussed in the related context of internal
        assessment.

604.   Rai, Kamala. Diffusion Process of Educational Innovations.
        Agra: National Psychological Corporation, 1982.

        Discusses concepts and processes involved in the diffusion
        of innovations, on the basis of related studies. Includes an
        empirical study of a diffusion process related to examination
        reform, based on responses from a sample of school teachers
        in Gujarat state. Covers four elements of the process:
        awareness, adoption, internalization, and self-perceived
        change orientation. One of the conclusions is that adoption
        depends on those who implement, the teachers, being properly
        informed and convinced.

605.   Raina, M. K. Education of the Left and the Right:
        Implications of Hemispheric Specialization. New Delhi:
        Allied, 1984.

        Details the inadequacy of traditional patterns of education
        in the light of developments in 'split-brain' research and
        information processing. Holds that present education
        concentrates on developing certain areas of the brain to the

neglect of others. Suggests a teaching system for neurological symmetry and includes contributions from educationists, psychologists, and neurologists.

606. Rao, B. A. and S. Ravishankar, eds. Readings in Educational Technology. Bombay: Himalaya, 1982.

A collection of papers on educational technology covering a wide range of topics relating to conceptual clarification and research in the field. Aimed primarily at graduate and post-graduate level students and teachers in the area. The contributions are from leading educationists in India and abroad.

607. Sali, V. Z. Principles and Techniques of Unit Testing. New Delhi: National, 1982.

An introduction to a tool that is considered to gauge the student's comprehension of specific topics. Directed at secondary school teachers and covers theoretical aspects and the construction, administering and analysis of such tests.

608. Sampath, K. and others. Introduction to Educational Technology. New Delhi: Sterling, 1984.

A summary of the principles and techniques of educational technology, covering theory and methods of communication, teaching aids, the systems approach, reprographic equipment, the use of projected, non-projected and aural aids, field experiences, programmed instruction, and teaching machines.

609. Sandeep, Ponnala. Schools and Mental Abilities. New Delhi: Light and Life, 1981.

Using the theoretical model of Piaget for cognitive development, the study based on schools in and around Hyderabad, Andhra Pradesh state, analyzes the complexities of learning situations and their influence on the cognitive abilities of the students of different age groups. While broadly confirming the developmental stages of Piaget's theory, the study emphasizes the importance of home, culture, and socioeconomic background as influences on development. Central schools are found to be more effective than other schools.

610. Sharma, Radha R. Enhancing Academic Achievement: Role of Some Personality Factors. New Delhi: Concept, 1985.

Repudiates the belief that academic performance is
exclusively a function of intelligence and analyzes other
factors that have recently assumed a special significance.
Examines the role of three vital personality factors, viz.
self concept, level of aspiration and mental health, in
academic achievement on a sample of 1060 higher secondary
students, both boys and girls, between the ages of 13+ and
18+ years with the help of standardized tools. Suggests
recommendations for enhancing academic achievement.

611.   Singh, Amrik. Commonsense About Examinations. Delhi:
        Oxford, 1984

        The university examination system in India has been the
        source of considerable criticism, but it has remained
        basically unchanged. Singh examines the nature of the
        controversy and presents some proposals for reform. He is
        critical of the usual reform proposal, internal assessment
        and indicates that this will not work in the Indian context.
        He proposes an alternative approach which includes changes in
        the syllabi, new and more imaginative ways of setting
        question papers and new means of grading.

612.   Singh, A. and H. S. Singhal, eds. The Management of
        Examinations. New Delhi: Association of Indian
        Universities, 1977.

613.   Singh, Pritam. Evaluating Students in Elementary Schools:
        Theory Into Practice. New Delhi: Department of
        Measurement and Evaluation, National Council of Educational
        Research and Training, 1983.

        In this innovative effort in evaluating students'
        performance in the elementary schools in India, emphasis is
        not laid on measurement of students' learning but on
        improvement of their achievement. It is essential that
        evaluation be treated as an inseparable part of the
        teaching/learning process and the evaluation data be used
        more as a diagnostic device so that proper remedial
        instruction could be undertaken to improve students'
        learning. The comparison of students' performance with
        respect to the pre-determined criteria or expected level of
        performance is considered more important than determining the
        extent of deviation of a student from the class norm. For
        proper feedback, the other components like analysis,
        interpretation and use of results are also incorporated.
        Some guidelines have been provided for development of a plan
        of action for reforming evaluation at the elementary stage.

614.   Singh, Pritam. A Monograph on Improving Practical
        Examinations in Science. New Delhi: National Council of
        Educational Research and Training, 1983.

        The existing system of examining students for practical
        work in science is far from satisfactory. Emphasis on
        functional understanding rather than skills, on product
        rather than processes of performance, impressionistic marking
        rather than objective scoring, etc., are the two obvious and
        glaring deficiencies. It is, therefore, necessary that the
        genesis of practical work be understood by teachers,
        practical examiners and paper setters so that they can
        appreciate the role of psycho-motor objectives in development
        and assessment of practical skills. A number of issues
        peculiar to evaluation of practical work are involved
        relating to the designing of question papers, development of
        making schemes and conduct of examinations. These have been
        discussed in this compendium along with the sample question
        papers in physics, chemistry and biology.

615.   Singha, H. S. Public Examinations: A Critique. New
        Delhi: Vikas, 1984.

        A critical perspective on the public examination system,
        highlighting its disfunctionality. Contends that research on
        examinations is focused on psychometric aspects, not on an
        evaluation of their benefits. Points out the contradictions
        arising out of these examinations, using a historico-
        philosophical approach and supported by the opinions of
        authorities.

616.   Sinha, Subodh Kumar. Examination Today: Problems and
        Reforms. New Delhi: Classical, 1984.

        Suggests that an effective improvement in the system of
        examination needs to be based on a socio-psychological study
        of the examination system, together with a study of the
        academic and administrative aspects of education.
        Accordingly, the author surveys research in the area and
        presents an attitudinal study of stratified sample of under-
        graduate and post-graduate students of arts, science, and
        commerce courses at Ranchi University. Attitudes of teachers
        and guardians towards the examination system are also
        discussed. Students are found to express dissatisfaction
        with the examination system. Its basis is not the written
        examination in itself, but in its implementation by teachers
        and students. Essay examinations are found to be reliable
        and relevant.

617.   Srivastava, H. S.   Examination Reforms in India.   Paris:
        UNESCO, 1979.

        Deals with external examinations at the school stage of
        education, particular emphasis is devoted on secondary level
        of education.   The book is divided into eight sections which
        discuss the historical background out of which the
        examination reform program developed, an overview of the
        program's goals, areas and directions of work, reforms in
        written and oral examinations.   It also introduces the
        concept of 'Prep Index' (the Index of proficiency in
        Educational Practice)--a procedure for quantitative
        assessment of qualitatively conceived situations.   It
        advocated the ultimate abolition of external examinations and
        their replacement by assessments undertaken by the teachers.
        Some innovations aimed at the qualitative improvement of
        examination procedure and practices are described.   It also
        looks at objectives in relation to curriculum, which have
        been set for examination reform programs in the ten-years
        primary and lower secondary school, and in classes XI and XII
        of higher secondary education.

618.   Varshney, Uma.   Education for Political Socialization.
        Meerut: Meenakshi Prakashan, 1983.

        Assesses the extent to which civic education fosters the
        assimilation of the political culture of the country and
        promotes political socialization.   The performance of urban
        and rural Intermediate College, i.e., twelfth class, students
        were examined with the help of a citizenship scale covering
        the areas: Political knowledge, political interest--
        participation, political efficacy--cynicism, civil sense and
        democracy.   A content analysis of the civics course
        prescribed by the U. P. Board of High School and Intermediate
        Education was carried out and opinions as regards the
        curriculum was sought from the concerned teachers.
        The study carried out in institutions located in and around
        Varanasi finds that students who have read civics are ahead
        of those who did not offer the subject, in specific
        components of citizenship: political knowledge, political
        interest--participation, political efficacy--cynicism and
        democracy.   The course appears to have no impact in
        inculcating a civic sense, so that the author concludes that
        'no conscious and systematic effort is made in the
        educational system, nor perhaps by any other agency to
        develop civic sense among the pupils' (p. 155).   The author
        compares the responses of urban and non-urban male and female
        students.   The content of textbooks is found to be unrelated
        to issues and problems actually faced.   The priorities of the

textbook authors show no correspondence with those of the teachers.

619. Vilanilam, J. V. Education and Communication. Trivandrum:
      Kairali Books International, 1985.

Articles

620. Anand, C. L. and P. N. Dave. "An Analytical Study of Some
      Major Objectives of Teaching Social Studies and ways of
      Attaining Them." Indian Educational Review 6 (July 1971):
      238-49.

      This study of the teaching of social studies at the
      secondary level in four Indian States was undertaken to
      determine (i) whether the teachers properly understood the
      integrated approach to social studies as envisaged by the
      experts; (ii) whether the teaching was done in accordance
      with the principles of modern curriculum planning. The
      findings suggest that while there is a good deal of
      understanding of what should be done, the picture of what is
      being done in actual practice is not very encouraging.

621. Anand, Rishi and V. Shankaran. "An Endeavour Towards Anatomy
      of Science Education." Journal of Higher Education 2
      (Autumn 1976): 197-202.

622. Ananthakrishnan, M. V. "Place of Laboratory Work in
      Science/Engineering Education." Journal of Higher
      Education 7 (Spring 1982): 243-51.

623. Ananthakrishnan, M. V. "Purposeful Physics Curricula: A
      Systems Model." Journal of Higher Education 8, (Monsoon
      1982): 41-52.

624. Barnabas, Manorama. "Undergraduate Education under the
      Semester System." Journal of Higher Education 3 (Spring
      1977): 329-40.

625. Bose, Arun. "Undergraduate Curricula in Social Sciences."
      Journal of Higher Education, 1 (Monsoon 1975): 61-75.

      Attempts to define the functions of undergraduate curricula
      and the problems caused by the existence of rival schools.
      Deals with issues like nationalization and internalization of
      courses, vocationalization of undergraduate curricula, and
      makes certain proposals for changing them.

626.   Chatterjee, Partha and others. "Teaching Political Science:
        The Debate on New Orientations." _Journal_ _of_ _Higher_
        Education 2 (Monsoon 1976):   5-12.

        Comments on the present standard of education in political
        science departments. Emphasizes the need for updating the
        course, forging suitable linkages between different levels of
        syllabi, introducing a theoretical-cum-evaluative orientation
        of study, methodological orientation, introducing an inter-
        disciplinary component and securing a regional and
        ideological balance.

627.   Chaurasia, G. and G. K. Kaul. "Recent Trends and Development
        in Primary and Secondary Education in India."
        International _Review_ _of_ _Education_ 13, no. 13 (1967):   345-
        54.

        This article describes some of the measures and programs in
        education adopted in India to improve the qualitative aspects
        of education at the primary and secondary levels.

628.   Chossudoosky, M. "Dependence and Transfer of Intellectual
        Technology: The Case of Social Sciences." _Economic_ _and_
        Political _Weekly_ 12 (September 3, 1977):   1579-83.

629.   Chowdhury, K. "Organizational Innovation in Universities:
        Relevance of Industrial Experience." _Economic_ _and_
        Political _Weekly_ (August 30, 1969):   M-97-100.

630.   Das, J. P. and P. S. Singha. "Caste, Class and Cognitive
        Competence." _Indian_ _Educational_ _Review_ 10 (January 1975):
        1-18.

        In the first part of the paper, some issues relating to
        cognitive competence in culturally different sub-populations
        have been considered. One of these is concerned with the
        possibility of assortative mating in the high caste Brahmins,
        whereas random mating among the Harijans. Results of an
        experiment involving the cognitive competence of four caste-
        class samples have been reported in the second part of the
        paper. The samples consisted of Class V children who were
        compared with each other on personality and cognitive test
        scores, and were drawn from (a) the orthodox Brahmin caste
        living in the village, (b) non-orthodox Brahmin living in an
        urban area, (c) urban Harijans. All of them were
        economically poor, unlike the last sample, (d) the rich
        Brahmin from an urban area. The performance of the Harijan
        and Brahmin children who were of low socioeconomic class was
        not different in the cognitive tests. However, the rich

Brahmin children were invariably superior to all other
children in most of these tests. The implication of the
results has been discussed.

631. Dave, Ravindra and Walker Hill. "Educational and Social
      Dynamics of an Examination System: A Case Study of India."
      Comparative Education Review 18 (February 1974): 24-38.

      The paper analyzes the educational and social aspects of
      the Indian examination system. In India, like other Asian
      countries the examinations have a central importance in the
      educational program and their impact is felt throughout the
      society as well as in the schools. With particular reference
      to examinations for secondary education, the study highlights
      the multidimensional character of the problems to be faced
      when a comprehensive reform of an examination system is to be
      planned.

632. Deb, B. M. and others. "Teaching Innovation and Assessment
      in University Chemical Education." Journal of Higher
      Education 2 (Monsoon 1976): 19-32.

633. Deo, Pratibha. "Revaluation at the University Examination:
      Its Effects on the Results of Candidates." Journal of
      Higher Education 6, nos. 1-3 (1980-81): 83-104.

634. Dhaliwal, A. S. and B. S. Sainai. "A Study of the Prevalence
      of Academic Underachievement among High School Students."
      Indian Educational Review 10 (January 1975): 90-109.

      The present study was carried out with three purposes in
      view. First, it was designed to test the adequacy of the
      operations to be employed in the computation of indices of
      over- and under-achievement; second, it proposed to ascertain
      to what degree under-achievement was prevalent among high
      school students and, third, it aimed at investigating into
      the relationships of indices of over- and under-achievement
      pertaining to different subjects of curriculum.
      Operationally, the phenomena of over- and under-achievement
      have been defined in terms of the discrepancy between the
      measure of intelligence used as a predictor and that of
      achievement used as a criterion, and before working out such
      a discrepancy, the former measure was regressed according to
      the degree of empirically discovered functional relationship
      between the two variables. The findings of the present study
      confirm that the thus worked out indices of over- and under-
      achievement are independent of the predictor variable but are
      related to the criterion variable. These two qualities of
      the indices of over- and under-achievement are,

experimentally speaking, the test of adequacy of the
operations to be employed in computing such indices.

635.   Ezekiel, N. "Modernization and Education: The Role of
        Secondary School Curriculum." Indian Educational Review 13
        (October 1978): 74-81.

        Examines modernization and education by ascertaining
        conditions and describing situations which make education
        change the traditional society into a modern one, and also
        what modernization means in the context of this society.
        Determines the role of secondary school curriculum (new) in
        making a "new generation" of modern men and women with a new
        set of skills, value attitudes, and the cultivation of a new
        set of norms.

636.   Filella, J. "Values and the Teaching-Learning Process: An
        Integrated Approach." New Frontiers in Education 14
        (January-March 1984): 1-18.

637.   Ganeshan, D. Raja. "Making Philosophy Utility-oriented."
        Journal of Higher Education 2 (Spring 1977): 357-66.

638.   Ghose, A. M. "Modernisation of our Courses and Syllabi in
        the Humanistics and Social Sciences." Journal of Higher
        Education 4 (Monsoon 1978): 75-80.

639.   Goel, S. C. "Examination Reforms: A New Perspective."
        Journal of Higher Education 2 (Monsoon 1976): 49-58.

640.   Gurpal, Singh Jarial and Sansanwal, B. N. "Effect of a
        Training Programme on the Development of Verbal and Non-
        Verbal Creative Thinking Ability of Students." Indian
        Education Review 19 (July 1984): 1-12.

641.   Haq, Ehsanul. "Sociology of Curriculum: The Role of School
        Textbooks in Nation Building." Indian Educational Review
        11 (January 1976): 1-16.

        In this study, an attempt has been made to examine the
        relevance of school textbooks to the process of nation-
        building in the light of some of the Constitutional values.
        The author has done a comparative study of prescribed
        textbooks. The study highlights the extent to which
        constitutional values are incorporated into the textbooks as
        necessary condition to accelerate the level of political
        awareness and responsiveness which are some of the features
        of a modern polity.

642. Iyer, T. S. K. V. and V. Krishnamurthy. "Examination Reform:
      Innovations in Teaching and Learning." _Journal_ _of_ _Higher_
      Education 2 (Monsoon 1976):   83-94.

643. Jayagopal, R.   "University and Emerging Educational
      Technologies for Adult and Continuing Education." _Journal_
      _of_ _Higher_ _Education_ 4 (Spring 1980):   365-72.

644. Joshi, Kireet.   "Reflections on 'New Education'." _New_
      Frontiers _in_ _Education_ 13 (January-March 1985):   13-50.

645. Kalra, R. M. and Matthew H. Bruce.   "Examination and
      Evaluation in Science Education in India: A New Approach."
      Indian _Educational_ _Review_ 8 (January 1973):   37-56.

      Since Bloom's initial study of the examination system in
      India, studies and practical experience have further
      confirmed the need for adopting a new approach in evaluation.
      Evaluation requirements of proper system of science education
      lie in stressing other objectives than the achievement of the
      right answer alone.   Necessary for this is decentralization
      of responsibility for program development down to the level
      of state, district, and classrooms.   The implications of this
      for pretesting, science instruction, examinations, etc., are
      elaborated.   The authors have reported the results of a study
      of "culturally different" pupils in Canada to show the
      efficacy of the proposed scheme of evaluation.

646. Kohli, Tehal and J.N. Joshi.   "Behavioural and Environmental
      Correlates of Academic Achievement and Over and Under
      Achievements: A Multivariate Correlational Approach."
      Indian _Educational_ _Review_ 19, no. 3 (1984):   24-39.

647. Koul, Lokesh. "Scaling of Some Significant Innovations in
      Examination System: Views of University Teachers and
      Students." _Indian_ _Educational_ _Review_ 14 (July 1979):   18-
      33.

      This study makes an investigation into the views of
      university teachers and students separately, regarding the
      relative scale positions of significant innovations in Indian
      examination system at the university and college levels.
      Thirteen innovations were arranged in different pair
      combinations in the form of a check-list.   The check-list
      blanks were administered to the groups of eighty university
      teachers and 250 students.   Thurstone's Pair Comparison
      Method was applied separately to the responses of the groups
      of teachers and students to determine the relative scale
      positions of the innovations.

648.   Kundu, M.   "Teaching in a Poly-Cultural Context."   Journal
        of Higher Education 8 (Autumn 1982):   191-98.

649.   Mahajan, H. N.   "Question Banks and Construction of Tests and
        Reporting of Results for Internal Assessment and External
        Examination."   Journal of Higher Education 9 (Autumn 1983):
        235-44.

650.   Mehrotra, R. C.   "New Educational Technology and the   and
        the Teaching of Chemistry."   Journal of Higher Education 1
        (Monsoon 1975):   31-42.

651.   Misra, R. G. and O. P. Arora.   "Direct Grading vs. Grading
        via Analytical Marking."   Journal of Higher Education 3
        (Monsoon 1975):   95-106.

652.   Misra, V. S.   "A Follow-up Study of Examination Reforms in
        the Gauhati University."   Indian Educational Review 7
        (January 1972):   53-66.

        In 1963, the Gauhati University introduced certain reforms
        in its examination system.   The study discussed here is a
        preliminary attempt to find out to what extent these measures
        have improved the accuracy of examination marks.   This has
        been investigated under two heads: chance errors and
        constant errors.   The study suggests that the chance errors
        are smaller in the reformed examination.   Under the head
        'constant errors' the influence of scaling has been studied
        and it is inferred that the examination reforms in the
        Gauhati University have improved the accuracy of marks.   The
        author also discusses the limitations faced by researchers
        who attempt to investigate the influence of the examination
        reforms.

653.   Natarajan, V.   "Introduction of Examination Reform."   New
        Frontiers in Education 13 (July-September 1983):   24-37.

654.   Palsane, M. N. and H. G. Desai.   "Grading in the
        Examinations: An Illusory Reform."   Journal of Higher
        Education 2, no. 1 (Monsoon 1976):   59-68.

655.   Pareek, Udai and T. V. Rao.   "Behaviour Modification in
        Teachers by Feedback Using Interaction Analysis."   Indian
        Educational Review 6 (July 1971):   11-46.

        The authors report the results of a ten-day training
        program conducted with a group of teachers, using feedback on
        Flanders' Interaction analysis.   The results show that as a
        result of this short training in interaction analysis and

feedback on the same, the teachers started using more of indirect patterns of interaction, i.e., praising, encouraging, accepting and clarifying ideas, etc., with their students. The authors also discuss some implications of these results.

656. Patel, G. S. and S. R. Patel. "A Survey Study of Semester System." Indian Education Review 13, No. 3 (1984): 49-58.

657. Quraishi, Z. N. "On Curriculum and Teaching in Higher Education." Journal of Higher Education 1 (Spring 1976): 403-407.

A critique of the Indian educational system. Comments on the 10+2+3 system, the vocationalization of education, medium of education, curricula, case for college autonomy and on education and social revolution.

658. Ramasubban, Radhika. "The Teaching of Sociology." Journal of Higher Education 1 (Monsoon 1975): 77-86.

Reviews the basic problems faced while teaching sociology at the undergraduate level with a special emphasis on curricula. Comments on teaching methods and makes certain recommendations for improvement.

659. Rao, S. N. "A Prognostic Study of Achievement in Relation to Academic Adjustment." Indian Educational Review 6 (July 1971): 196-213.

In this study, the investigator, employing four predictor variables, predicted achievement at graduation for each of 1642 randomly chosen degree class students. Subjects achieving above the predicted level plus one standard error of estimate were identified as overachievers and those achieving below the predicted level less one standard error of estimate were designated as underachievers. The investigator then studied the patterns of academic adjustment of the Ss thus selected, some personality variables, and some of the factors affecting the academic adjustmental patterns of overachievers and underachievers, employing relevant instruments. The results indicate that academic achievement is significantly related to academic adjustment, that the academic adjustment of overachievers is significantly related to the aspects of personality which were studied, and that the academic adjustmental patterns of overachievers and underachievers differ significantly. The study highlights the importance of the need for counseling and guidance for students found to be inappropriately adjusted to the academic situation.

660.   Rastogi, K. G. and L. C. Singh.   "Influence of Language and Script on Affective Meaning."   Indian Educational Review 11 (January 1976):   61-9.

Whether languages are to be taught as curricular subjects or as media of instruction as various stages of education has long been a source of controversy.   Linguists and educationists extend their arguments for and against one or the other language in the Indian situation.   It is interesting to know the effect of (i) language (mother tongue and medium of instruction) and (ii) the script on the effective meaning of selected concepts.

Twelve sample concepts were selected so that they were similar both in pronunciation and meaning in two languages: Hindi and Kannada.   These concepts represent political, literary, artistic, scientific, social, educational and religious aspects of Indian life.   Two groups of bilingual and one group of trilingual subjects were selected from the high schools in Bangalore city.   Each group consisted of fifteen-twenty boys of ages fourteen-seventeen who were studying in Class X.   A set of 12 Semantic Differential Scales in Hindi, Kannada, and English were used to measure the effective meaning of concepts.   The analysis of variance was computed to examine various hypotheses.

The study shows that by and large the mother-tongue and its script affect the meaning of concepts in any situation--educational or social more than a foreign language and its script.   In other words, there is a tendency on the part of subjects to rate concepts more towards the positive side when presented in mother tongue with its script than when presented in the second and third languages with different scripts.

661.   Ratna, Ved.   "An Investigation into some Factors Affecting the Achievement of National Science Talent Search Scholars in University Courses."   Indian Educational Review 9 (July 1974):   143-55.

The sample for the investigation reported here comprised 120 NSTS awards attending summer schools after having taken the B.Sc. second year examinations of their respective universities.   The study reveals, among other things, that higher motivation and better study habits are one characteristic of awards from 'low status' schools.

662.   Raza, Moonis and Amitabh Kundu. "Evaluations in Higher
        Education". Journal of Higher Education 5 (Spring 1980):
        359-69.

663.   Reddy, Venkala Rami A. "Attitude of Postgraduate Students
        towards Internal Assessment." Indian Educational Review 13
        (July 1978): 16-32.

        An attitude scale designed by the author to measure the
        attitude of students towards internal assessment was
        administered to a group of 240 postgraduate students of a
        university where internal assessment is being tried as an
        experiment. The sample of students was selected by a three-
        stage stratified random sampling procedure. It was found
        that the second (final) year students who had undergone the
        system for one year had a significantly lower mean score than
        the first years. Male students favored internal assessment
        more than females. Generally, students of the science
        faculty had a more favorable attitude towards the system than
        their counterparts in the arts faculty. Nearly seventy
        percent of the students expressed that internal assessment
        should be retained. But very few of them preferred complete
        internal assessment. As many as fifty percent wanted
        internal assessment for fifty percent of marks only.
        Different aspects of the problem have been discussed.

664.   Reddy, Venkala Rami A. "A 700 Year Follow Up Study on
        Internal Assessment." Journal of Higher Education 4
        (Monsoon 1978):   47-56.

665.   Seshadri, C. "The Concept of Moral Education: Indian and
        Western - A Comparative Study." Comparative Education 17,
        no. 3 (1981): 293-310.

        Presents a critical account of the Indian conception of
        moral education as indicated in the thoughts expressed on the
        various aspects of this problem by modern Indian education
        thinkers, in the references to this problem by the various
        Committees and Commissions on education set up during the
        last three decades and in the syllabi of 'moral education'
        courses offered in Indian Schools. The comparative study of
        Indian and contemporary Western views on the different
        aspects of moral education reveals that the Indian view of
        moral education differs from its Western counterpart in its
        conception, objectives, content and methodology, and the
        interpretations of the role of the teacher.

666.   Shahare, M. L. and T. Ramasami. "Examinations of Union
        Public Service Commission vis-a-vis Higher Education."
        Journal of Higher Education 7 (Monsoon 1981): 45-50

667.   Sharma, Atmanande and K. P. Garg. "Predicting Higher
        Secondary School Success." Indian Educational Review 6
        (January 1971): 183-95.

        The authors report a study undertaken to investigate the
        prognostic value of middle school examination marks for
        success at the higher secondary examination. Other purposes
        were to obtain a prediction formula for streaming students
        entering the secondary stage, and to establish multiple cut-
        off scores in meaningful subjects for the three streams. The
        sample comprised 255 students from Class VIII (1963-64) and
        the criterion was their higher secondary examination marks
        (1967). The critical score for predictors was determined by
        calculating tetrachoric r's for different values of a
        predictor. The investigators found that the middle school
        examination marks have no predictive value for the commerce
        and humanities streams; for science, they are useful to some
        extent though not very efficient. The authors have worked
        out a key profile based on achievement scores in the subjects
        for various streams, which can readily help in the streaming
        of students.

668.   Sharma, Sagar. "Self-Acceptance and Academic Achievement: A
        Review of Research." Indian Journal of Education 6
        (January 1971): 118-25.

        Studies conducted in the last two decades to establish the
        relationship between self-acceptance and academic achievement
        provide contradictory findings. Some report a linear
        relationship between these two variables and others present a
        zero relationship, while two studies recently conducted in
        India provide evidence of a curvilinear relationship. In
        this paper the author critically examines all these studies
        and offers suggestions for further research in the area. He
        also stresses the importance of more cross-cultural research
        for making reliable generalizations.

669.   Shukla, Snehlata. "Achievement of Indian Children in Mother
        Tongue (hindi) and Science." Comparative Education Review
        18 (June 1974): 237-47.

        India participated in the measurement of achievement in two
        subjects, mother tongue (Hindi) and Science, a study
        conducted by the International Association for Evaluation of
        Educational Achievement. The result of the test score was

very low for Indian children. Also, the variables contributing to total variance in achievement scores were different from those in developed countries. This article tries to explain the possible reasons for these two situations. From the analysis, it is concluded that by revision of curricula, production of good textbooks and teacher's guidance and intensive in-service training for teachers, improvement of cognitive achievement of Indian children can be possible.

670.   Singha, H. S. "Public Examinations in 2001." Journal of Higher Education 9 (Spring 1984): 315-22.

671.   Tharu, Jacob. "Examination Reform: Towards an Integrated Perspective." New Frontiers in Education 14 (April-June 1984): 30-35.

672.   Tharu, J. "Towards a Meaningful System of Grades." Journal of Higher Education 2, (Monsoon 1976): 73-82.

NEPAL

Book

673.   Tribhuvan University. Achievement Study of Primary School Children. Kathmandu: Research Center for Educational Innovation and Development, 1982.

This research analyzes the marks secured by the pupils in the literacy test in reading, writing, and arithmetic. Tools used for the study are the Literacy Test Battery and the educational interview form. Some of the findings of the evaluative study on the effectiveness of primary education show that the measure of variability is much wider in writing and in arithmetic than in reading. The literacy test did not indicate a wide variation in the achievement level of Nepali speakers and non-Nepali speakers. Boys perform better than girls in arithmetic, though not in reading and writing. In general, the students were found to be backward in arithmetic as compared to their performance in reading and writing. The results of the literacy test did not indicate any great difference in the performance level of the students in the Terai and in the hills.

PAKISTAN

Books

674. Allama Iqbal Open University. The Effectiveness of Radio and
      Television in the Distance Teaching Programme of Allama
      Iqbal Open University. Islamabad: Institute of Education
      and Research Cell and Institute of Educational Technology,
      Allama Iqbal Open University, 1982.

      The recommendations call for particular consideration of
      the individual needs of students when planning the timing of
      programmes, with radio being more frequently used than
      television, greater attention should be paid to the quality
      of the programs.   An evaluation of radio and television
      should be made at the end.

675. Cooperation in Curriculum Explorations: Report of a High-
      Level Personnel Exchange Workshop (Pakistan, 1-10 November
      1975). Bangkok: Unesco Regional Office for Education in
      Asia, 1976.

676. Klitgaard, Robert E. and others.   Cognitive Equality and
      Educational Policies: An Example from Pakistan.
      Washington, D.C.:   Educational Resources Information Center
      (ERIC), 1979.

      It was concluded, in an empirical study of distributions of
      examination scores within secondary schools in Karachi,
      Pakistan, that intraschool inequalities in student
      achievement were relatively large;   that variables for
      socioeconomic background and school policy did not explain
      the intraschool variations across schools; and that a school
      which was particularly equal on one test was not particularly
      equal on another.   Data were gathered from a stratified
      random sample of 207 secondary schools, based on neighborhood
      socioeconomic status, type of school, including government,
      nationalized, or private; and the mix of male and female
      students.   Results were analyzed from scores on tenth grade
      essay tests in the humanities and sciences.   Data on teacher
      characteristics were used to calculate student-teacher ratio
      and teacher experience.   Schools were classified according to
      the median income of students' households.   Based on results
      of the study, it was hypothesized that Karachi school
      personnel were indifferent to the intraschool variations or
      did not have effective means for closing the gap.   Further
      research, using longitudinal data, was recommended.

677.   Pakistan. Ministry of Education. <u>Achievement in Education,</u>
        <u>1958-1964).</u> Karachi: Central Bureau of Education, 1965.

678.   People's Open University. Integrated Functional Education
        Project. <u>Needs Assessment Report (NAR):</u> <u>Based on Findings</u>
        <u>of Needs Assessment Interviews Conducted in and Contacts</u>
        <u>Established with the Target Villages in Daultana Markaz.</u>
        Islamabad: The University, 1976.

679.   Rauf, Abdul. <u>Dynamic Educational Psychology.</u> Lahore:
        Ferozsons, 1975.

        Articles

680.   Hayes, L. D. "Islamization and Education in Pakistan."
        <u>Asia Pacific Community</u> no. 23 (1984): 96-105.

SRI LANKA

        Book

681.   Sub-regional Curriculum Workshop (1976: Colombo).
        <u>Curriculum for Development:</u> <u>Analysis and Review of</u>
        <u>Processes, Products and Outcomes:</u> <u>Final Report, Sub-</u>
        <u>regional curriculum Workshop, Colombo, Sri Lanka, 1-30</u>
        <u>October 1976.</u> Bangkok: Unesco Regional Office for
        Education in Asia, 1976.

        Articles

682.   Dore, R. P. "Pre-Vocational Studies in Sri Lanka."
        <u>Literacy Discussion</u> 6 (Fall 1975): 1-19.

        An examination of problems in pre-vocational studies in Sri
        Lanka leads to the conclusion they are largely due to
        educator and administrator attitudes regarding the role of
        pre-vocational education. Success of the new program (which
        contains its own problems) depends upon changing student
        attitudes towards employment.

683.   Fernando, T. O. P.   "Pre-vocational Education in Sri
        Lanka." Prospects 4 (Spring 1974):   72-76.

        A Proposal for the introduction to pre-vocational subjects
        into the general secondary curriculum hopes to partially
        solve the employment problems of those entering the job
        market after completing secondary education.

684.   Gunawardena, A. J.   "Changes in Mathematics Education since
        the Late 1950's -- Ideas and Realisation: Sri Lanka."
        Educational Studies in Mathematics 9 (August 1978):   303-
        16.

        Four major events and their impacts are discussed: in
        1961, the government took over all schools; a new curriculum
        program was implemented in 1965; a 1971 rebellion of the
        youth resulted in drastic changes in education; and a new
        government in 1977 changed many aspects of the education
        program.

685.   Perera, L. S. and S. Rupasinghe. "Some Observations on the
        Feasibility of the White Paper Recommendations for a New
        Scheme of Measurement and Evaluation in the School System
        in Sri Lanka." International Journal of Education
        Development 3, no. 2 (1983):   183-92.

686.   Ranaweera, A. Mahinda.   "Sri Lanka: Science Teaching in the
        National Languages." Prospects 6, no. 3 (1976):   416-23.

        Presents a history of the use of national languages as the
        medium of instruction in math and science education in Sri
        Lanka.   Concludes that the transition from English to the
        national languages as the medium of instruction helped
        destroy class barriers.

CHAPTER 14

TEXTBOOKS

INDIA

Books

687.   Nischol, K. Women and Girls as Portrayed in Hindi
       Textbooks. New Delhi: National Council of Educational
       Research and Training, 1976.

688.   Nomani, Rashid. Textbooks for Secular India. New Delhi:
       Sampradayikta Virodhi Committee, 1970.

689.   Rastogi, K. G. Preparation and Evaluation of Textbooks in
       Mother Tongue: Principles and Procedures. New Delhi:
       National Council of Educational Research and Training, 1976.

       Articles

690.   Elder, Joseph W. "The Decolonization of Educational Culture:
       The Case of India." Comparative Education Review 15
       (October 1971): 288-95.

       This article focuses on two aspects of the decolonization
       of educational culture: 1) How does India present to its
       young its experiences under Western colonialism? 2) How does
       such a nation define for its young its post-independence
       relations with the West?
       The findings reported are based on a content analysis of
       744 lessons in the language textbooks from two sections of
       India--Lucknow, the capital of the Hindi speaking state of
       Uttar Prades, and the city of Madurai, the cultural capital
       of the state of Tamil Nadu. The material analyzed was the
       1962-63 and 1970-71 texts for grades two through ten.
       Reveals that in some respects the Tamil and Hindi textbooks
       indicate an impressive amount of decolonization. They stress
       the cultural glories of India prior to her colonization, pass

lightly over the period of colonial rule, and focus on the
challenges and accomplishments of Independent India. But, in
a more subtle way, beneath the decolonized surface, the
Indian textbooks transmit to their students an awareness of a
West that is still technologically superior, still to be
blamed, still to be emulated, and still to be sought for
approval.

691.   Kalia, Narendra Nath. "Images of Men and Women in Indian
          Textbooks." Comparative Education Review 24 (June 1980):
          S209-S223.

        In 1965, the Government of India proposed to create a
        curriculum conducive to sex-role equality. This commitment
        was reiterated a decade later in a proposed amendment to the
        Indian Constitution which, among other fundamental duties,
        called upon Indian citizens to "... to remove any practice
        derogatory to the dignity of women." However, a content
        analysis of Indian textbooks shows that the government has
        not utilized its control to produce textbooks conducive to
        its promise of sex-role equality in education. This article
        demonstrates that Indian school textbooks promote an ideology
        which refuses females equal access to opportunities and
        rewards even in areas where the sex of a person is totally
        irrelevant. More subtly, Indian textbooks prepare males for
        a bustling world of excitement and decision making while
        conditioning the females to seek fulfillment in the
        background where servitude and support are the only
        requirements.

692.   Kalia, Narendra Nath. "Why I Would be Ashamed to be a Woman
          in Today's India: A Content Analysis of Sex Role Model in
          Indian School Text Books." Indian Journal of Social
          Research 19 (April-December 1978): 64-75.

693.   Kumar, Krishna. "The Textbook as Curriculum." Bulletin of
          the Indian Institute of Education 2 (1981): 75-84.

694.   Nischol, K. "The Invisible Woman: Images of Women and Girls
          in School Textbooks." Social Action 26, no. 3 (1976):
          267-81.

        This is a report of a study of selected English language
        textbooks used in Indian schools. Examines images of women
        and girls in textual material and illustrations. Females
        portrayed were found to be "invisible," having no names and
        playing few (largely familial) roles. Girls are portrayed as
        relatively passive and are mentioned less frequently than

boys. They lack intellectual interests and resourcefulness. Sexes are usually separated.

NEPAL

Article

695. Yadunandan, K. C. "Nepal: For Better Planning of Textbook Production." Prospects 13, no. 3 (1983): 361-69.

While Nepal no longer needs to purchase textbooks from India, the development of a national textbook publishing industry has not been problem-free. High costs, shortages of qualified editors, and problems with finding competent printers, storing printed books and distributing texts have all complicated textbook production.

CHAPTER 15

LANGUAGE

INDIA

Books

696.   Annamalai, E., ed. <u>Bilingualism</u> <u>and</u> <u>Achievement</u> <u>in</u> <u>School</u>.
       Mysore: Central Institute of Indian Languages, 1980.

       Three studies on the effects of bilingualism on the
       learning process: the relation between home bilingualism on
       student achievement in all subjects at school, the effect on
       bilingual medium on two subjects and the performance of
       students studying through the medium of mother-tongue.

697.   Chaturvedi, M. G. and B. V. Mohale. <u>Position</u> <u>of</u> <u>Languages</u> <u>in</u>
       <u>School</u> <u>Curriculum</u> <u>in</u> <u>India</u>. New Delhi: NCERT, 1976.

698.   Goel, B. S. and S. K. Saini.   <u>Mother</u> <u>Tongue</u> <u>and</u> <u>Equality</u> <u>of</u>
       <u>Opportunity</u> <u>in</u> <u>Education</u>. New Delhi: NCERT, 1972.

699.   John, V. V.   <u>Education</u> <u>and</u> <u>Language</u> <u>Policy</u>.   Bombay:
       Nachiketa, 1969.

       This is an examination of Indian language policies from an
       educational point of view.   Among the more notable things in
       the book is the author's closely-argued thesis that a well
       designed curriculum in the mother tongue should be made the
       basis of the transformation in the quality of Indian
       education, for it will help the pupil to cultivate
       "intellectual self-confidence, a vantage point whence he can
       advance to the study of other languages and subjects without
       the timidity and fear that characterize so much of school and
       college studies amongst us today."

700.   Pattanayak, D. P.   Language Curriculum: An Approach to the
        Structure of Curriculum in Indian Languages.   Mysore:
        Central Institute of Indian Languages, 1977, 2nd edition.

        An attempt to devise curricula for language teaching in a
        multilingual society where, as a result of inadequate policy,
        the student is often found to remain illiterate in mother
        tongue and handicapped in the medium of instruction.   The
        essays cover mother tongue teaching and sample curriculum,
        bilingual elementary education, Indian languages as second
        and foreign languages, Hindi as mother tongue and second
        language; curricula for Sanskrit, English and non-formal
        education.   Discussed in the context of different levels of
        education.

701.   Pattanayak, D. P.   Multilingualism and Mother Tongue
        Education.   Delhi: Oxford, 1981.

        A collection of essays that deals with the problem of
        language and education, in a situation where there are 1652
        dialects as mother tongues and 15 major recognized languages.
        Discusses problems such as the elitist structure of
        education, the authoritarianism reflected in the choice of
        the medium of instruction, education for the minorities,
        tribal and adult education, planning of scripts, formal and
        non-formal education.   The author points out the weakness of
        the formal system of education, while searching for
        alternatives to it and enquiring into the effective use of
        language as a medium of instruction and communication.   Also
        contains a foreword and essay by Ivan Illich.

        Articles

702.   Acharya, Poromesh.   "Abolition of English at Primary Level in
        West Bengal."   Economic and Political Weekly 17 (January
        23, 1982):   124-26.

        Examines issues relating to pedagogy and equal opportunity
        in the context of the agitation over the Left Front
        Governments' move to abolish the teaching of English at the
        primary level of education.   Concludes that abolition would
        be in the interests of mass education and hence the
        opposition from affluent classes.

703.   Das Gupta, J.   "Language, Education and Development
        Planning."   Prospects 6, no. 3 (1976):   382-87.

704.   Datta, Bhabatosh. "Storm over English in West Bengal."
        Economic and Political Weekly 16 (April 4, 1981): 619-22.

        Points out the neglect of questions relating to teaching
        facilities, textbooks, standard of teachers and teaching
        during the language controversy in West Bengal. A positive
        approach to education at various stages is needed.

705.   Ekka, Francis. "Status of Minority Languages in the Schools
        of India." International Education Journal 1, no. 1
        (1984): 1-20.

706.   "English, Hindi, and the Medium of Instruction." Minerva 6
        (Autumn 1967): 123-30.

        The article describes chronologically the political debate
        on the issue of medium of instruction in India.

707.   "Further Steps Towards the Displacement of English." Minerva
        7 (Autumn-Winter 1968-69): 179-234.

        Discusses chronologically the political controversies and
        conflict between different states and central government and
        students over the issue of English as an official language
        during late 1960s. It also describes student unrest that
        took place over medium of instruction issue during the period
        in different states.

708.   Gajendragadkar, P. B. "The Medium of Instruction in Indian
        Higher Education: The Language Question." Minerva 6, no.
        2 (1968): 257-67.

709.   Magarajari, S. "Some Historical Notes on the Decline of
        English." Journal of Higher Education 2 (Spring 1977):
        341-50.

NEPAL

    Books

710.   Chand, Geeta and others. Studies in Bilingualism in Nepal:
        A Survey of Bilingualism and Primary Education in Bara and
        Chitwan Districts of Narayani Zone, Nepal: Report on Pilot
        Project No. 2. Kathmandu: Institute of Nepal and Asian
        Studies, Tribhuvan University, 1975.

711.   Malla, Kamal Prakash. English in Nepalese Education.
        Kathmandu: Ratna Pustak Bhandar, 1977.

SRI LANKA

    Book

712.   Walatara, D. The Teaching of English as a Complementary
        Language in Ceylon. Colombo: Lake House Investments,
        1965.

        Deals with the problem of the decline in the quality of
        English language teaching in Ceylon in which the author
        states that presently the attitude to English is inadequate
        and mechanistic. This can in part be attributed to the
        general idea that language teaching aims at mechanistic
        control of the skills and structures. The book is divided
        into Aims, Theory and Practice and contains numerous
        appendices and a bibliography.

CHAPTER 16

LITERACY AND BASIC EDUCATION

BANGLADESH

Books

713.   Adult Literacy Motivation: A Survey on Adult Education in
       Bangladesh. Dhaka: Foundation for Research on Educational
       Planning and Development.

       This survey was conducted to ascertain, examine, and
       evaluate the factors which motivate students, teachers and
       organizers of adult literacy programs. Factors which stand
       in the way of adult learners becoming literate are also
       identified. The study is based on data collected from six
       adult education centers.

714.   Bangladesh Literacy Situation. Bangkok: UNESCO, 1984.

       Provides information and insights about: the dimensions of
       the problem of illiteracy and its effect on development;
       programs undertaken; national literacy policies and plans;
       strategies being developed to eradicate illiteracy. Also
       assesses the likely future of literacy programs in the
       country.

715.   Khan, M. F. Literacy and Bangladesh. Dhaka: Association
       for Community Education, 1979.

       Article

716.   Dove, Linda A. "How the World Bank can Contribute to Basic
       Education Given Formal Schooling Will Not Go Away."
       Comparative Education 17, no. 2 (1981): 173-83.

       Examines the potential of the World Bank scheme, outlined
       in its 1980 Education Sector Policy Paper, for helping

Bangladesh achieve universal basic education.   Considers such
issues as formal vs. non-formal schooling, costs, and teacher
training.   Part of a theme issue on the World Bank Paper and
Third World educational development.

INDIA

Books

717.   Bhatia, S. C., ed.   Eradication Illiteracy through Students:
        Proceedings of the Jammu Workshop, 1982.   New Delhi:
        Indian University for Continuing Education, 1982.

        Report of a regional workshop held on August 17, 1982, to
        promote and plan action for the eradication of illiteracy
        with the involvement of students.   The paper covers a review
        of existing programs with suggestions for alternate models
        involving students and teachers.

718.   Gandhi, Mohandas K.   Basic Education.   Ahmedabad: Navajivan,
        1951.

        A brief essay setting forth Mahatma Gandhi's views on the
        problems of education in India.

719.   Goyal, Bhagat Ram and Prativa Das Gupta.   Study of Basic
        Education Institutions, Search for Relevance.   New Delhi:
        National Council of Educational Research and Training,
        1981.

        The focus of the study is to identify programs and
        strategies adopted in basic education institutions which have
        relevance for the much needed reform.

720.   Gupta, R. K.   Readings in Basic Education.   New Delhi:
        NCERT,   1968.

721.   Jayagopal, R.   Village Case Studies in Literacy Programmes.
        Madras: Department of Adult and Continuing Education,
        University of Madras, 1981.

        The purpose in compiling these case studies in literacy at
        some of the villages in Tamilnadu, is to illustrate a cross
        section of de-facto teaching/learning situations prevailing
        at the micro level, for example, the literacy centres.   The
        case studies are presented with real episodes with brief

descriptions of the socioeconomic and other demographic
descriptions followed by some relevant issues arising out of
the same.

722. Joshua, Alexander. Rural Primary Education and Adult
      Literacy in Tamilnadu. Madras: Sangam, 1978.

      Highlights the significance of primary education and the
      role of adult literacy, with special reference to the rural
      areas of Tamil Nadu. The quantitative and qualitative
      characteristics of Rural Primary Education and Adult Literacy
      are summarized in the study.

723. Rao, G. Sambasiva, ed. Problems of Women's Literacy.
      Mysore: Central Institute of Indian Languages, 1979.

      A collection of papers presented at a national seminar held
      in 1975, on the causes of illiteracy among women and means to
      eradicate it. The areas covered are functional literacy,
      motivation for education, vocational training, role of
      voluntary organizations, and the community in women's
      literacy and the role of women's education in development.
      Emerging themes are the need for: efforts to enroll girls in
      school and to provide non-formal education to the drop-outs
      and "stay-at homes", utilizing the capacities of married
      educated women, encouragement for women's participation in
      decision making at home and in society.

724. Roy, P. and J. M. Kapoor. The Retention of Literacy. Delhi:
      Macmillan, 1975.

725. Saraf, S. N. Literacy in a Non-Literacy Milieu: The Indian
      Scenario. Paris: UNESCO, International Institute for
      Educational Planning, 1980.

726. Shrivastava, Om. Literacy Work among Small Farmers and
      Tribals. New Delhi: Marwah, 1981.

      An evaluation of an adult literacy project of the Seva
      Mandir in Badgaon taluka, Udaipur district, Rajasthan State.
      The focus is on the effectiveness of specific components used
      in the project--participation of adults in planning and of
      village youth as teachers, use of local dialect, examination
      procedures, follow-up. The study is based on a sample of 14
      centers, with interviews of students, teachers, supervisors,
      and analysis of records. Suggests that adult literacy
      projects require the participation of the community at all
      stages.

727.   Verma, I. B. Basic Education; a Reinterpretation. Agra:
        Sri Ram Mehra, 1969.

    Articles

728.   Miller, Josef. "Literacy for Integrated Rural Development."
        Indian Education 30 (1984): 99-115.

729.   Tilak, Jandhyala B. "Literacy, Education and Agricultural
        Productivity in India." Indian Educational Review 14 (July
        1979): 1-17.

        In this paper an attempt is made to focus light on the
        problem of agricultural productivity and the impact of
        literacy and education on it. The study finds that literacy
        and education do enter into the agricultural production
        function and they are not less significant variables than the
        traditional factors. The study also examines the importance
        given to and the problems involved in the growth of education
        in rural India. The author opines that there is a large
        scope for reforming the curriculum towards productivity-
        orientation without much radical reforms.

PAKISTAN

    Books

730.   Hesser, Florence E. Village Literacy Programming in
        Pakistan: A Comparative ABE Study with Guidelines.
        Vancouver: British Columbia University Center for
        Continuing Education; International Council for Adult
        Education, 1978.

        Ten literacy pilot programs developed by the Adult Basic
        Education Society (ABES) of Pakistan in Gujranwala, Pakistan,
        between 1963 and 1973 were analyzed and evaluated to evolve a
        series of adult literacy program development guidelines. The
        programs were evaluated on the basis of an eleven-category
        evaluation system developed by Cyril Houle in his study "The
        Design of Education". After evaluation with respect to
        materials, teaching method, student participation, teacher
        participation, location planning, support, supervision and
        follow-up, three other approaches to adult literacy program
        design were similarly evaluated: (1) Laubach's religiously

oriented approach, (2) Paulo Freire's psycho-socially oriented approach, and (3) that approach revolving around aspects
of functional literacy which is espoused by the United
Nations. After a comparison of the effectiveness of these
approaches to that of the ABES programs, fifty-seven
guidelines were developed for program planning; creating and
using materials; facilitating student and teacher program
participation; selecting a program location; and program
support, supervision and follow-up. (A discussion of ABES
aims and purposes, ABES objectives, and an outline of the ten
pilot projects are appended.)

731.   Ibne, Insha. Developing Reading Habits in Asian Conditions.
       Karachi: National Book Centre of Pakistan, 1967.

732.   Kazi, Syed Firasat Ali, ed. Literacy Profile of Pakistan,
       1951-81. Islamabad: Literacy and Mass Education
       Commission, 1984.

       Detailed and compact information about the literacy rate in
       the country at the national, provincial and district level
       are analyzed by sex and by urban and rural areas.

       Articles

733.   Hussain, Ghulam. "Pakistan: The Role of the Agricultural
       University in Promoting Adult Literacy." Literacy Work 4
       (April/June 1975): 69-82.

       The article reviews new approaches to develop and organize
       adult literacy programs for the rural population. The entire
       program of teaching covered neo-literates, functional
       literacy, and vocational training. Curriculum development,
       teacher training, reading materials, and education of rural
       women are discussed.

734.   "Pakistan: Lifelong Literacy Project." Literacy Work 3, no.
       4 (April 1974): 93-106.

       The article reports on progress towards lifelong literacy
       education in Pakistan, covering the project's introduction in
       1972 and reviewing current activities in brief but concrete
       sketches of such topics as materials, operation of projects,
       and student drop-outs. Appendices include a map and
       occupational breakdowns of teachers and students.

735.   Uz-Zaman, Rafe. "Functional Literacy through Television in
        Pakistan." _Prospects_ 12, no. 2 (1982): 233-41.

        The Pakastani Adult Functional Literacy Project (AFL)
        produced educational television programs which were shown at
        community viewing centers. Evaluation results are
        encouraging.

736.   Uz-Zaman, Rafe. "Pakistan: Five Cycles of the Adult
        Functional Literacy Project, 1975-80." _Education in Asia
        and the Pacific: Reviews, Reports and Notes_. 18
        (September 1981): 1-8.

        This is a description of a pilot project to see how
        television might make a significant contribution in the
        campaign to eradicate illiteracy. The project aimed at
        making adults functionally literate in six months. The
        content, administration, short-comings, and achievements of
        tele-lessons are described.

CHAPTER 17

NON-FORMAL EDUCATION

(INCLUDING DISTANCE EDUCATION)

BANGLADESH

Book

737. Foundation for Research on Educational Planning and
Development. A Pilot Research Project on Nonformal
Education: A Micro Study. Dhaka: FREPD, 1979.

Articles

738. Iman, T. "Functional Education -- A Developmental Structure
of Learning in Bangladesh." International Review of
Education 28, no. 2 (1982): 267-70.

739. "Non-Formal Education in Bangladesh." Indian Journal of
Adult Education 40 (June 1979): 9-17.

Describes many ecological, social, and economic problems of
Bangladesh in order to show the need for development of
nonformal education to increase productivity in agriculture
and related industries. Describes nine nonformal education
projects in various areas of rural development, cooperatives,
extension services, and adult education.

INDIA

Books

740.   Anand, Satyapal. University without Walls: The Indian
        Perspective in Correspondence Education. New Delhi:
        Vikas, 1979.

        Deals with distance teaching/learning. The first section
        underlines the failure of the system of university education
        and makes a case for correspondence education. Also surveys
        the Indian and international context of correspondence
        education and the socioeconomic background of the Indian
        alumni. The second section illustrates Indian and Western
        skills, tools and practices in distance education.

741.   Asian Institute for Rural Development, Bangalore. Formal and
        Non-Formal Education in Rural Development; A Sample Survey
        in the State of Kanataka. Paris: UNESCO, 1980.

        Information collected from the survey makes it possible to
        review the situation of formal and non-formal education in
        India. With regard to formal education, the country has to
        fulfill Article Forty-five of the Indian Constitution by
        providing ten years education at least by the end of the
        century. Non-formal eduation is to be deemed as a system for
        assisting in the universalization of education; to work, the
        system should be designed after a thorough study of the needs
        and problems of the people in the area.

742.   Gupta, Daljit et al. Non-Formal Education in Action. New
        Delhi: National Council of Educational Research and
        Training, 1980.

743.   Jesudason, V. and others, eds. Non-Formal Education for
        Rural Women to Promote the Development of the Young Child.
        New Delhi: Allied, 1981.

        An evaluation report of an experimental action-cum-research
        project integrating maternal and child health, nutrition,
        child care, and family planning through functional literacy
        programs and Mother Child Centres during the period August
        1972-August 1975 in Mehbubnagar, Andhra Pradesh. The Mother
        Child Centres are found to be effective as regards to gains
        in knowledge among the target groups, resulting in improved
        attitudes and adoption of sensible practices. Modest
        reduction in nutritional deficiencies are found in both women

and children. The package of services is found to be transferable to Auxiliary Nurse Midwives in peripheral villages, when accompanied by suitable support measures.

744. Naik, Chitra. Growing up at Kosbad Hill: A Study of the Vikaswadi Experiment. Kosbad: Gram Bal Shikshan Kendra, 1978.

An account of the experiment in pre-school and primary education conducted by the Centre for the Education of Rural Children (Gram Bal Shiksha Kendra). Describes the approach of non-directive child education of tribal children, where learning is conducted in their natural milieu so as to encourage freedom and creativity. Narrates the different phases of this project, its attempts to respond to new challenges and to assimilate the relevant ideas of Gandhi, Froebel and Montessori.

745. Naik, J. P. Some Perspectives on Non-Formal Education. Bombay: Allied, 1977.

Conceptually distinguishes between incidental, non-formal and formal education in a historical perspective. Discusses possible methods of non-formal education, in its links and impact on the formal. The relation between the three types is seen as part of a larger process of evolving a comprehensive and radical 'educational system for society' in India. A concluding chapter discusses programs with suggestions for their organization and implementation.

746. Parmaji, S., ed. Distance Education. New Delhi: Sterling, 1984.

A collection of papers by authors from professional fields like engineering, law, journalism, and teacher education, who discuss the role of science and technology in distance education through correspondence, radio, film, and television. Contributes to the debate on the capacity of distance education to compliment general and professional education and to meet the requirements of continuing and adult education.

747. Reddy, A., ed. Life Long Learning: Operational Concepts. Hyderabad: Osmania University, State Resource Centre for Adult Education, 1983.

Papers presented at a symposium to discuss the concept of life long learning, and the assumptions and methodologies that underlie it. The contributors are from different disciplines in the social sciences and bring their particular perspectives to the subject.

748.   Shah, A. B. and Susheela Bhan, eds. Non-Formal Education and the NAEP. Delhi: Oxford, 1980.

A collection of thirteen papers dealing with two themes: non-formal education in India discussed in its socio-economic, political, cultural and formal educational context; and the National Adult Education Programme, launched in 1978 to educate about a hundred million in the age-group of fifteen to thirty-five within five years. The assumptions and targets of the program are questioned on the basis of the Policy Statement and the Program Outline. The editors hold that socio-cultural factors influence the success of the program more than the funds and manpower invested in it.

749.   Singh, R. P. and Neerja Shukla. Non-Formal Education: An Alternative to Formal System. Chandigarh: Bahri, 1979.

Discusses theoretical aspects and field practices in non-formal education, the concept and its scope, the role of the state and voluntary organizations, the philosophy underlying it, experiences in non-formal education in India and abroad. Contains a review of studies on the subject.

Articles

750.   Ahmed, Rias. "INSAT-IB and Higher Education". Journal of Higher Education 9 (Spring 1984): 301-303.

Talks about the problems in higher education related to finance, development, and employment. Emphasizes the role of audio-visual aids in enhancing the quality of higher education and reviews the attempts made by the UGC in this context.

751.   Chaudhary, P. N. and K. G. Agrawal. "Professional Obsolescence and the Role of Continuing Education." Journal of Higher Education 3 (Monsoon 1977): 73-88.

752.   Datt, Ruddar. "Planning and Development of Distance Education." Journal of Higher Education 9 (Spring 1984): 305-14.

Reviews the extent of development of correspondence education in India. Enumerates several reasons for the lack of development of correspondence institutes and lists several issues which deserve attention in this context. Suggests some measures for improvement.

753.   Gupta, M. L.   "Productivity Trends in Correspondence Education." Journal of Higher Education 8 (Spring 1983): 349-56.

Concentrates on "The Centre of Correspondence Education-- University of Rajasthan, Jaipur", and covers the period 1968-69 to 1976-77. Discusses the extent of productivity trends in correspondence education with reference to undergraduate and post-graduate courses.

754.   Hussain, M. A. "Continuing Education and its Role in Human Resource Development in India." Journal of Higher Education 7 (Monsoon 1981):   123-32.

Comments on the need for continuing education with reference to changes in the socioeconomic infrastructure and its role in socio-economic development. Defines 'continuing education' and discusses the role of the UGC in the context. Finally, analyzes the programs of various institutions in different states and comments about the inadequacy of efforts made.

755.   Iredale, Roger. "Non-Formal Education in India: Dilemmas and Initiatives." Comparative Education 14 (October 1978): 267-75.

Various problems of non-formal education are discussed in this article, especially its power in solving the problems which formal education has failed to do and some problems of its implementation.   The author argues that the State Planning Commission's document of 1972 was not consciously planning for major innovation in teaching styles or curriculum in its out-of-school programs, but was staying fairly close to the ethos and methods of the existing educational structure.   It discusses the initiatives of some non-formal approaches and problems of separating them from traditional educational structure.

756.   Koilpillai, Victor. "Leadership Training through Non-formal Education: The RUHSA Experience." New Frontiers in Education 13 (January-March 1983):   31-41.

A study of the disciplinary program of health care and socioeconomic development, started by the Christian Medical College and Hospital, Vellore, and its Rural Unit for Health and Social Affairs (RUHSA). Studies the emergence of youth

clubs, the identifying of leaders and the training programs
in the context. Evaluates the efforts made by RUHSA and
enumerates its results.

757.   Kurrien, John. "Non-Formal Education for Rural Dropouts: A
        Critique of the Bhumiadhar Model." Indian Journal of
        Social Work 39 (January 1979): 409-24.

758.   Lenbart, Volker. "Education Alternatives in the Third
        World." Indian Education, 30 (1984): 7-20.

759.   Palsane, M. N. "Continuing and Non-Formal Education:
        Universities Introduction with and Contribution to
        Continuing Education. Journal of Higher Education 4
        (Spring 1980): 343-52.

760.   Sharan, Girja. "Non-Formal Education among Workmen: An
        Experiment in Ahmedabad." Economic and Political Weekly 15
        (August 30, 1980): M74-M84.

        Takes the position that gross enrollment, expansion of
        physical facilities and increased allocations are
        insufficient indications of the progress of education. There
        is a need for innovative experimentation in pedagogy.
        Describes an attempt at education of adult workers in small
        industries in Ahmedabad. Recognizes that co-learning and
        initiative by workers and volunteers need, at some stage, to
        go beyond the confines of the worker's immediate work and
        life experience and to include elements of social knowledge,
        history, and technology.

NEPAL

    Books

761.   Nepal, Ministry of Education. Non-Formal Education in Nepal:
        A Report of a Seminar. Kathmandu: Ministry of Educaiton,
        1981.

        Deals with the development of non-formal education and
        functional literacy programs, government agencies, college
        industry, and welfare and service agencies monitor the non-
        formal education programs.

PAKISTAN

Books

762. Kaye, A. R. A Case Study in Distance Learning Systems: The
      Allama Iqbal Open University, Pakistan. Milton Keynes,
      England: Centre for International Cooperation and
      Services, Open University, 1978.

763. Khan, K. A. The Mosque Schools in Pakistan: An Experiment
      in Integrating Nonformal and Formal Education. Paris:
      UNESCO, 1981.

      A wide-ranging study of the centrality of the mosque to
      Islamic education in Pakistan emphasizing Islamic educational
      traditions, the historical background of such education, the
      obstacles to educational improvement in Pakistan, and the
      attempt to provide universal primary education.
      Traditionally, the Prophet Mohammad and the Holy Quran have
      been sources of knowledge, inspiration to further education,
      and Islamic principles. They thus provide a foundation for
      traditional Islamic educational institutions such as the
      Kuttab (for elementary education), the mosque, and private
      scholars. Conventional schools, however, have proved
      incapable of resolving such representative problems as
      illiteracy, low enrollments, and high costs and dropout
      rates. To remedy these ills, Pakistan's New Education Policy
      of 1978 proposes the exploitation of the mosque's traditional
      educational role. Though more research is needed, the
      enduring centrality of the mosque in education suggests its
      importance as an instrument for eduational improvement and
      the spread of literacy in Pakistan. Three tables present
      literacy rates in Pakistan (1972), estimated 1982 enrollments
      in Punjab Province, and comparative expenditures for
      conventional and mosque schools. Appendices provide a
      statement of national eduational aims, extracts from
      religious books, a map of Pakistan, and an account of
      traditional Islamic education in other countries.

SRI LANKA

Books

764.   Kaye, A. R. A Case Study In Distance Learning Systems -- The
       Sri Lanka Institute of Distance Education (SLIDE). Milton
       Keynes: Center for International Co-Operation and
       Services, Open University, 1979.

       Outlines the function and structure of the Sri Lanka
       Institute for Distance Education (SLIDE), created in 1977.
       Teaching is conducted via printed materials, weekend
       tutorials, and laboratory and practical experience during
       school vacations.   The course covers certficates in
       mathematics and in technology, (electrical, electronics,
       telecommunications, mechanical and civil engineering).

765.   Marga Institute.   Non-Formal Education in Sri Lanka: A
       Study. Colombo: Marga Institute, 1974.

766.   Marga Institute.   The Sinhala Reading Public: A Study.
       Colombo: Marga Institute, 1974.

       Article

767.   Colletta, N J. et al.   "Cultural Revitalization,
       Participatory Non-formal Education and Village Development
       in Sri Lanka: The Sarvodaya Shramadana Movement."
       Comparative Education Review 26 (June 1982): 271-85.

       Reports on the result of a study of the Sarvodaya
       Shramadana Movement in Sri Lanka. The basic philosophy of
       the Sarvodaya that has emerged is the universal awakening of
       villages through the sharing of labor in projects vital to
       them. An integral part of the philosophy is the important
       principle of self-reliance. The study indicates that the
       movement has certainly created the proper social-
       psychological climate of awareness and change and has also
       successfully mobilized various peer groups into self-help
       development projects.   While this social-psychological
       infrastructure is a necessary factor for the third stage of
       sustained economic development it is not sufficient. The
       mobilization of human resources may need to be complemented
       by the allocation of financial, managerial, and technical
       resources from other levels.

CHAPTER 18

ADULT EDUCATION

BANGLADESH

Book

768.   Foundation for Research on Educational Planning and
        Development (FREPD). A Survey on Adult Education in
        Bangladesh. Dhaka: FREPD, 1979.

        Aim of this survey is to examine and evaluate the factors
        which motivate the participants, the teachers, and organizers
        of adult literacy programs, and to identify the factors which
        stand in the way of adult learners being literate.

INDIA

Books

769.   Adult Education Components in the Development Schemes of
        Government of India, a Compendium. New Delhi: Ministry of
        Education and Social Welfare. Directorate of Adult
        Education, 1979.

        This book tries to identify the non-formal education
        components in the schemes and programs of different
        ministries and departments of the Government of India, and to
        trace those programs in which adult education components can
        be introduced. The focus, however, has been mainly on the
        activities having educational elements directly addressed to
        specific groups and which have a bearing on their socio-
        economic and cultural development. For collecting pertinent
        information for this compendium, officers of the Directorate
        of Adult Education were assigned responsibilities for

different ministries, departments, and organizations.
Certain general guidelines and a format for preparing
writeups were provided to the individual officers concerned.

770. Ansari, N. A. Adult Education in India. New Delhi: S.
      Chand, 1984.

771. Bhatia, S. C., ed. Environmental Consciousness and Adult
      Education. New Delhi: Delhi University Adult Education
      and Continuing Education Cell, 1980.

      Seven essays in English and two in Hindi on environmental
      education. Part of the on-going attempt at integrating
      environmental education into the National Adult Education
      Programme. Covers areas such as environmental consciousness,
      education and training, the physical environment, energy,
      nutrition, noise, natural history museums, and the rural
      environment.

772. Bordia, Anil, ed. Adult Education in India: A Book of
      Readings. Bombay: Nachiketa, 1973.

773. Central Institute of Research and Training in Public Co-
      operation. People's Participation in Adult Education:
      Report of the National Seminar January 4-8, 1971. New
      Delhi: Central Institute of Research and Training in
      Public Co-operation, 1973.

      A compilation of the addresses and discussion papers
      presented at the seminar. Covers the changing concept of
      adult education, programs, people's participation, the use of
      mass communication, government and community resources,
      experiments in people's participation in adult education, and
      the recommendations of the seminar.

774. Gode, M. A., ed. Handbook for Functionaries of N.A.E.P. in
      Universities and Colleges. Bombay: University of Bombay,
      NSS Unit, 1979.

      A guide to the setting up and running of adult education
      centres, as part of the involvement of higher education
      institutions in the National Adult Education Programme
      (NAEP). Provides a perspective on the NAEP, covering issues
      related to curriculum, teaching methods, aims and evaluation,
      training and roles of functionaries, organization of courses,
      and on dealing with the bureaucracy. Includes the NAEP
      policy statement and guidelines on project formulation.

775. Kundu, C. L. Adult Education. New Delhi: Sterling, 1984.

A survey of the principles and practice of adult education.
Deals with conceptual clarification, the content of programs,
the process of adult education, relevant theories of
learning, training and methods, research undertaken, and
needs.

776. Kundu, P. D. Adult Education: Principles, Practice and
Prospects. New York: Apt, 1985.

This book surveys the principles and practice of adult
education and is a valuable source of information for
students and those embarking upon a career in adult
education.

777. Mali, M. G. Adult Education in India. New Delhi: Deep and
Deep, 1984.

778. Mathur, R. S. and Prem Chand. Adult Education Programme:
Appraisal Studies in Bihar, Gujarat, Maharashtra, Rajasthan
and Tamil Nadu; Summaries. New Delhi: Ministry of
Education & Culture. Directorate of Adult Education, 1981.

779. Ministry of Education and Social Welfare. Directorate of
Adult Education. Adult Education in India A Select
Bibliography. New Delhi: Ministry of Education, 1979.

780. Rao, T. V. and others. Adult Education for Social Change: A
Study of the National Adult Education Programme in
Rajasthan. New Delhi: Manohar, 1980.

Evaluates the National Adult Education Programme (NAEP) in
Rajasthan State on the basis of extensive field work in seven
agencies and in 125 of the 3,615 centres sanctioned during
1977-79. Surveys the position of adult literacy in the state
and studies the impact of voluntary and government agencies.
Concludes that NAEP has had a positive impact that belies the
fears of cynics. Suggests measures to bring out its full
potential.

     Articles

781. Adalene, M. "From Theory to Practice: Grihini Schools, and
Experiment in Adult Education." Social Action 18, no. 1
(1968): 56-64.

Argues for the education of tribal women and girls as an important aspect of preparing tribal people for life in modern India. Offers suggestions regarding the priorities and structure of such an education based on the experience of missionary workers in Grihini schools for home and family life education.

782.   Adisehiah, Malcolm. "Education of the Elderly in India." Convergence 18, nos. 1-2 (1985):   82-87.

783.   Aikara, Jacob. "Adult Education and Schooling of Slum Children." Indian Journal of Adult Education 418 (August 1980): 7-12.

784.   Bhandari, R. K. "National Adult Education Programme: An Appraisal." New Frontiers in Education 13 (April-June 1983): 1-16.

785.   Bordia, Anil. "India's New Challenge: The National Adult Education Programmes." Convergence 11, nos. 3-4 (1978): 27-35.

The National Adult Education Programme (NAEP) in India represents an unprecedented, massive effort of adult education linked to development needs and objectives. The program, which got underway in April 1979 after a preparation year, was implemented through a network of projects to be undertaken by all sectors, official and non-official development agencies, as well as voluntary organizations. This article presents a general overview of the aims, scope, and administrative and implementation structure of NAEP.

786.   Kidd, Ross and Krishna Kumar. "Co-opting Freire: A Critical Analysis of Pseudo-Freirean Adult Education." Economic and Political Weekly 16 (January 3-10, 1981): 27-36.

Examines the application of Freirean pedagogy in some recent adult education work. The first part presents a theoretical model of socio-political and economic aspects of Freire's work, contrasting it with its distorted absorption in a historical context. A case study of an international program in non-formal education, implemented by a non-government agency in India and Thailand, is presented in part two.

NEPAL

Article

787.   Hely, Arnold. "Adult Education in Nepal." Indian Journal of
          Adult Education 28 (May 1967):   3-4.

PAKISTAN

Article

788.   Khan, Ansar Ali. "Pakistan: Planning Literacy for 50
          Million." Literacy Work 4, no. 2 (October/December 1974):
          65-77.

          Each year, a million new illiterates are being added to the
          pool of fifty million illiterates in Pakistan. An adult and
          continuing education program is reviewed. Objectives and
          needs, program implementation, curriculum requirements, and
          the role of international cooperation are topics considered.

SRI LANKA

Book

789.   Roth, Klaus. Adult Education and Social Policy. Colombo:
          Sri Lanka Foundation Institute, 1977.

CHAPTER 19

STUDENTS AND STUDENT POLITICS

BANGLADESH

Books

790.   Islam, Rizwanul and Taherul Islam. Background, Attitude, and
        Expectations of Students in the Higher Education System of
        Bangladesh. Dhaka: National Foundation for Research on
        Human Resource Development, 1980.

        This monograph is part of a larger study on Higher
        Education and Employment and deals with the issue of the
        imbalance between the economy being unable to absorb all the
        educated job-seekers and the failure of the educational
        system to insure an adequate supply of skills demanded by the
        economy. The study is divided into four parts: methods of
        admissions in various institutions and socioeconomic
        backgrounds of students, evaluation of secondary education,
        examination of preference patterns of students for various
        specializations, and a look at expectations of students about
        the labor market and its correspondence with the actual
        situation.

791.   Rahman, N. Mizanur, et al. What University Students Think:
        A Profile of Chittagong University Students. Chittagong:
        Department of Sociology, University of Chittagong, 1975.

792.   Sattar, Ellen. Socio-Economic Survey of Dhaka University
        Students. Dhaka: University Grant Commission, Government
        of Bangladesh, 1975.

        In Bangladesh, very few students reach university level
        education (a mere 3 percent of all the students in the
        educational system). University education is therefore, a
        scarce commodity enjoyed by a fraction of the people of
        Bangladesh. Yet 10.86 percent of the total investment in the
        education sector goes to university education and another

7.66 percent to intermediate and Degree Colleges in the First
Five year plan.

This study presents facts about the students, the
educational levels of their parents, their guardians' monthly
income, their place of residence, family size, guardians
occupation, and many other facts which help to draw a more
realistic portrait of the students of Dhaka and in this way
help to facilitate the making of wise decisions concerning
the expansion and funding of university level education.

INDIA

Books

793.   Aikara, Jacob. Ideological Orientation of Student Activism.
        Poona: Dastane Ramchandra, 1977.

        An empirical study that attempts to test theoretical
        formulations. Views activism as normal behavior that is
        desirable and functional to the social system. Student
        unrest might lead to social movements for change, as well as
        to counter ideologies. Linkages between student unions and
        political parties are discussed. The study is based on a
        sample of college students from Trivandrum district in
        Kerala, a state that has had a marked number of political and
        student movements.

794.   Altbach, Philip G. Student Politics in Bombay. Bombay:
        Asia, 1968.

        A historical overview of the nature of student political
        activism in Bombay, including a discussion of the role of
        students in the struggle for Independence as well as post-
        independence student politics. The changing patterns of
        organization, ideology, and interaction with educational
        institutions and society are discussed.

795.   Altbach, Philip G., ed. Turmoil and Transition: Higher
        Education and Student Politics in India. New York: Basic,
        1968.

        A multidisciplinary analysis of student political activism.
        Authors from a variety of fields discuss aspects of student
        activism from historical, sociological, psychological, and
        political perspectives. Case studies of several regions as
        well as overall discussions are included.

796.   Bhattacharjee, Arun. Misconduct of Students: A Legal and
       Disciplinary Study. New Delhi: Deep and Deep, 1981.

       Discusses misconduct of students with respect to
       administrative control of educational institutions and its
       legal implications. Analyzes the Indian case law covering
       various aspects of student relationships with educational
       institutions. For comparative purposes, the legal context of
       student behavior in some commonwealth countries is cited.
       Covers forms of misconduct and punishment, quasi-judicial
       functions of educational institutions, procedures for
       inquiry, norms of natural justice and reasonable
       opportunities, and jurisdiction and functions of civil courts
       with respect to education.

797.   Coelho, George V. Changing Images of America: A Study of
       Indian Students' Perceptions. Glencoe: The Free Press,
       1958.

       A study of changes in the perception of America and India
       by sixty Indian students whose residence in the United States
       ranged from less than a week to seven years; based on essays
       written by the students and on interviews seeking to elicit
       attitudes toward the two countries.

798.   Cormack, Margaret L. She Who Rides a Peacock: Indian
       Students and Social Change. Bombay: Asia, 1961.

       The book deals with the state of higher education in India
       and, also provides the basis for the understanding the
       cultural transformation in India. The problem of student
       indiscipline seems to be the major concern of the period.
       The author tries to provide a scientific basis for this
       phenomenon. She also deals with topics such as the growth of
       India's nascent democracy, the progress and pitfalls of In
       dia's internal social revolution, and the critical problems
       Indian youth are facing, as elsewhere in the world, in this
       modern environment of rapid cosmic change. She concludes,
       India's real problem is not "student indiscipline",
       "corruption" or "party-politics" but the deep phenomenon of
       social change, the pace and direction of which can, in a
       community like India's, be influenced significantly by
       culture consciously molded by democracy and education, so
       that organized discontent can be directed into social
       dynamism.

799.   Damle, Y. B. College Youth in Poona: A Study of Elite in
       the Making. Poona: Deccan College, 1966.

800.   Desai, B. G. The Emerging Youth. Bombay: Popular
        Prakashan, 1967.

801.   Dowsett, N. C. and S. R. Jayaswal. Education of the Child.
        Pondicherry: Sri Aurobindo Society, 1974.

802.   Eakin, T. C. Students and Politics: A Comparative Study.
        Bombay: Popular Prakashan, 1972.

803.   Ganguli, H. C. Foreign Students: The Indian Experience.
        New Delhi: Sterling, 1974.

804.   Garg, Pulin K. and Indira J. Parikh. Profiles in Identity:
        A Study of Indian Youth at Crossroads of Culture. New
        Delhi: Vision, 1976.

        A systematic record of the feelings and experiential
        reality of growth of a sample students from the Indian
        Institute of Management, Ahmedabad, class of 1972. The data
        is classified into two streams, that of the intra-psychic
        phenomenology of the youth, presented in this volume, and the
        experience-based analysis of the Indian social systems
        impinging on the youth, presented in another volume. The
        data in this volume is presented in the form of twenty case
        studies, representative of seven types of growth patterns.

805.   Kakar, Sudhir and Kamla Chowdhry. Conflict and Choice.
        Bombay: Somaiya, 1970.

806.   Mansukhani, C. J., ed. Student Power in India. New Delhi:
        Oxford and IBH, 1975.

        States the causes and consequences of campus unrest in
        India and suggests some measures to resolve it. Comments on
        the role of students in changing existing politico-economic
        and social institutions. Surveys the student movements of
        Gujarat and Bihar. Contains five essays.

807.   Mehta, P., ed. Indian Youth. Bombay: Somaiya, 1971.

808.   Neelsen, John Peter. Student Unrest in India, A Topology and
        Socio-Structural Analysis. Munich, W. Germany: Welt Forum
        Verlag, 1973.

809.   Oommen, T. K. Student Unions in India. New Delhi: Vishwa
        Yuvak Kendra, 1970.

810.   Pandey, Ram Shakal. Our Adolescents: Their Interests and
        Education. Agra: Lakshmi Narain Agarwal, 1966.

A study on adolescent interests based on data collected
from over 4000 ninth and tenth standard students and 238
teachers in thirty-six schools in Uttar Pradesh state. The
interests are categorized as personal, social, recreational,
sexual, academic, and vocational. Concludes with suggestions
for the education of adolescents.

811.   Parker, Clyde A., ed. Selected Readings in Student Services
       for Indian Universities and Colleges. New Delhi: U. S.
       Educational Foundation in India, 1973.

A selection of readings drawn out of the Foundation
publications. Covers a variety of topics such as the need
for student services, student needs, service programs related
to admission, orientation, student activities, housing,
counseling job placement, health and the administration of
such services. The attempt is to apply concepts to the
Indian situation.

812.   Pattnaik, Surendra Kumar. Student Politics and Voting
       Behaviour: A Case Study of Jawaharlal Nehru University.
       New Delhi: Concept, 1982.

A study of student political behavior, that analyzes: the
character and orientations of student organizations, whether
agitational or electoral, in their relation to the larger
political system; student union elections and voting
behavior; political profiles of students, their ideological
orientations, forms of political participation, in relation
to their social background. Based on newspaper reports,
discussions with office bearers, and questionnaires to
students.

813.   Raghuvanshi, M. S. Modernising Rural Youth: On the Role of
       Formal Education. Delhi: Ajanata, 1984.

Studies 'modernity' as an individual psycho-cultural
syndrome on the lines of Alex Inkeles, Daniel Lerner and
others. Is based on interviews with the help of a structured
schedule, of 326 male Rajput youth between the ages of
eighteen and twenty in one ethnic region. Identifies the
character and extent of modernization among the youth, using
an inter-correlational of variables and explains variations
in modernity in relation to formal education and other
situational factors in the rural context. Concludes that
modern, formal education plays a primary role in changing the
attitudes, values, and behavior of rural youth in traditional
communities. However, the orientation and access to formal
education are found largely to be a function of the socio-

economic context of the youth, in which family income and level of family education play a crucial part. Both micro and macro-structural factors in their determination of individual modernity are considered.

814.   Ray, Anil B. Student and Politics in India. Columbia, Missouri: South Asia Books, 1978.

This book documents the inter-relationship between student politics, faculty politics, and party politics in India in the context of a national university--the Benaras Hindu University. It shows that student politics at BHU are often indistinguishable from, and largely a dependent variable of, faculty and party politics.
        It traces the history of the BHU from its inception and discusses the politicization of its students and their participation in the freedom struggle as also the growth of the parochial sentiment there in terms of vice-chancellors, caste, language, and sub-region. It deals specifically with three student agitations in 1958, 1965 and 1968.

815.   Ross, Aileen. Student Unrest in India. Montreal: Queens McGill University Press, 1970.

816.   Roy, A. B. Students and Politics in India. New Delhi: Manohar, 1977.

817.   Sarkar, S. N. Student Unrest: A Socio-Psychological Study. Calcutta: India Book Exchange, 1974.

818.   Sharma, Dev Datta. Bhil Students Between Tradition and Change: A Study in the role of Education. Udaipur: University of Udaipur, 1968.

819.   Sharma, Savitri. Women Students in India: Status and Personality. New Delhi: Concept, 1979.

Investigates the intelligence, values, and temperaments of college female students of different socioeconomic status. It also investigates their hobbies, interests, and extra-curricular activities. Part one of the study includes a brief review of previous studies, and forms the basis of the investigation. Part two is concerned with the various aspects of the present study. It also served the purpose of devising a new socioeconomic scale, as no other available Indian socioeconomic scale can be assumed to be suitable for the urban population.

820. Shinde, A. B. Political Consciousness Among College
      Students. Bombay: Thacker, 1972.

821. Singh, Amar Kumar. Indian Students in Britain. London:
      Asia, 1963.

      A study of the social and economic background of Indian
      students attending British institutions of higher learning in
      recent years and of the problems and adjustments stemming
      from this experience.

822. Singhal, Sushila. Academic Leadership and Student Unrest.
      New Delhi: Newman Group, 1977.

      The book focuses attention on one of the major problems of
      educational organizations in India, from a social-
      psychological and organizational theory perspectives. It
      traces the links of student unrest to the pre-independence
      era, evaluates its hypotheses over the last two decades, and
      operationalizes the problem for the present research.
      Academic leaders are identified, their impact on student
      unrest assessed and their roles discussed. The author
      concludes from the findings that student agitations
      represented complex, multidimensional and dynamic social
      behavior of students groups. The various forces in the
      human, organizational, and social domain interacted in a
      multiple order and produced congruent as well as incongruent
      reactions.

823. Sinha, D. Academic Achievers and Non-Achievers. Allahabad:
      United, 1970.

824. Sinha, D. The Mughal Syndrome: A Psychological Study of
      Intergenerational Differences. Bombay: Tata McGraw Hill,
      1972.

825. Srivastava, H. C. The Genesis of Campus Violence in Banares
      Hindu University, Varanasi. Allahabad: Indian
      International, 1974.

826. Vreede-De Stuers, Cora. Girl Students in Jaipur: A Study
      Towards Family Life, Marriage, and Career. Assen,
      Netherlands: Van Gorcum, 1970.

      Attempts to ascertain social factors which determine the
      attitudes and aspirations of female students at Rajasthan
      University. Based on interviews with 128 undergraduates and
      seventy-five graduate students. Examines attitudes toward

various facets of traditional Indian family life and female
employment.

Articles

827.   Altbach, Philip G. "Student Politics in the Third World."
        Higher Education 13 (1984): 635-56.

828.   Altbach, Philip G. "Student Politics and Higher Education in
        India." Daedalus 97 (Winter 1968): 254-73.

829.   Altbach, Philip G., ed. "Student Politics and Higher
        Education in India." Turmoil and Transition, pp. 917-73.
        New York: Basic Books, 1968.

830.   Anderson, Walter and Alok Pant. "Student Politics at
        Allahabad University-I." Economic and Political Weekly
        (June 1970): 941-43, 945-48.

831.   Chaudhari, D. P. and P. Rao. "Private and Social Returns to
        Higher Education -- A Case Study of Delhi Graduates."
        Economic and Political Weekly 5 (April 4, 1970): 605-608.

832.   Di Bona, Joseph. "Indiscipline and Student Leadership in an
        Indian University." Comparative Education Review 10 (June
        1966): 306-19.

        Deals with the problem of student indiscipline in India
        through analyzing student action and leadership on a single,
        north-Indian campus. The University of Allahabad, the locale
        of a number of student disturbances was chosen to conduct the
        field research during 1963 and 1964. Varieties of
        indiscipline are discussed and the political and economic
        explanations for the indiscipline are provided. The author
        concludes that the issue of indiscipline is not simple.
        Theories of economic deprivation, or of psychological
        alienation lack applicability. Since data in this study are
        presented from a single university, it is worth studying
        other institutions for a preliminary understanding of this
        problem.

833.   Haq, Ehsanul. "Education and the Emerging Patterns of
        Political Orientations: A Sociological Analysis."
        Sociological Bulletin 32 (March 1983): 35-59.

834.   Heredero, J. M. "Motivation Courses and College Students."
        Indian Educational Review 6 (July 1971): 165-81.

The author reports and discusses results of short
motivation courses given to Gujarat college students at camps
organized during 1968 and 1969. He compares the results
achieved with those achieved in similar courses organized
elsewhere separately by NCERT and the SIET Institute of
Hyderabad, and stresses the need for more such courses for a
wider range of participants.

835.   Ilchman, Warren F. and Trilok N. Dhar. "Student Discontent
        and Educated Unemployment." Economic and Political Weekly
        5 (July 1970): 1259-66.

Acts of what is commonly termed student indiscipline are
becoming more frequent. Indeed it is a fair guess that among
all the sources of violent agitation in recent years, student
dissatisfaction has been the most important.

However, none of the policy conclusions that flow from the
usual explanations of student unrest show any promise of
successfully tackling the problem. The participants in
student agitations are so varied--disproving, for instance,
the assumption that the vast increase in the number of first
generation students is a major cause of student violence--
and the proximate causes of unrest are so many that social
scientists' theories have proved to be of little predictive
or prescriptive value.

This article, therefore, argues for a more modest level of
explanation. It suggests that the explicit purposes of the
agitations be taken at face value as the more relevant
explanations of why students act the way they do. Starting
thus, there is considerable empirical evidence that a major
reason for indiscipline is the impact of certain academic or
political factors on the 'life chances' of students,
especially in fields where unemployment is greatest. It may
well be, insofar as educated unemployment is a cause of
student unrest, that reducing the educational inflation will
reduce the importance of or even eliminate one reason for
agitation.

It is too much to expect in a permissive society that all
agitation can be ended. But what needs to be recognized is
that there are many possibilities in coping with problems
such as student indiscipline and educational inflation. The
major need is not to explain the problem at too abstract and
encompassing a level as that eliminates or reduces the
possibilities of action.

836.   Jesudason, Victor. "Indian Students in the United States:
        Socio-economic Background, Academic Performance and Plans
        to Return Home." Indian Educational Review 14 (January
        1979): 1-21.

For a large sample of male Indian students who were enrolled in colleges and universities in the USA in 1966, the present study shows that compared to the general population in India, the students came from higher socioeconomic status. Among the students, those who were self-supporting were more affluent. Some subgroups were represented among the students in larger proportions than that can be expected from their size in the population. This simply reflects the socio-economic achievement of these subgroups in India. Some subgroups like the Moslems and scheduled castes were under-represented among the students. Compared to the number of Indian students from upper castes and upper classes in prestigious universities (as reported in other studies) the proportion of upper caṣte/upper class students in this sample is less. This suggests that more students from the lower classes attended less prestigious colleges and universities. A model of the process of plans to return to India was proposed and it was shown that the affluent families were able to ensure that their sons get better grades not only in India but also in the USA, more adequate financial support in the USA, lower degree of homesickness, more years of education in the USA and through these factors ensure that they were less certain to return to India.

837. Jones, Dawn E. and Rodney W. Jones. "The Scholars' Rebellion: Educational Interests and Agitational Politics in Gujarat." Journal of Asian Studies 36 (May 1977): 457-76.

This article explains how educational issues could be so explosive in state politics as to result in the overthrow of government of Gujarat, India. The first two sections of the article show how Chimanbhai, as an entrepreneur, was able to capitalize on the expansion of the collegiate base of Gujarat University so as to establish virtual control over its affairs. In the third and fourth sections, it explains the origins and development of the major teachers' association of Gujarat University in terms of conflicts between teachers and private managements over service conditions, institutional administration and other issues that surfaced in public policy competition outside the university. The final section describes the battle for control over the university under a new set of rules--the product of reform registration won by the teachers' association.

838. Katz, Alan N. "Changing Indian Student Perceptions of the Indian Government." Asian Survey 17 (March 1977): 264-74.

This study analyzes the reactions of a sample of Indian
students studying in the United States to the Indian
political crisis of the winter of 1971. The analysis tries
to indicate that those events engendered very different
perceptions of the Indian government than those articulated
during the months following the 1975 crisis. The students
indicated overwhelming support for the government as a result
of the events of 1971. They noted satisfaction with the
perceived "general progress" in India as well as with the
result of the struggle in Bangladesh. More importantly, the
students tended to evaluate the health and efficiency of the
Indian system according to the job Indira Gandhi was doing
and concomitantly expected solutions to political problems to
come from the Prime Minister's office. It is the thesis of
this study that those very positive attitudes and aspirations
of the system in general, and of Mrs. Gandhi in particular,
in some ways helped to explain, and to some degree helped to
create, the disillusionment and political conflict found in
India in recent months.

839.   Kazi, Khalid Ahmed and Rehena Ghadially. "Perception of
        Female Role by Indian College Students." Sociological
        Bulletin 28 (March-September 1979): 59-70.

840.   Khan, M. Z. and D. R. Singh. "College Youth, their Courses
        of Study and their View of Society." Journal of Higher
        Education 4 (Monsoon 1978): 57-66.

841.   Lakshminarayana, H. D. "Caste, Class, Sex and Social
        Distance among College Students in South India."
        Sociological Bulletin 24 (September 1975): 181-92.

842.   Mahadeva, Bani. "Values and Aspirations of College Students
        in India." Sociological Bulletin 26 (March 1977): 116-29.

843.   Malik, Yogendra K. and Jesse F. Marquette. "Changing Social
        Values of College Students in the Punjab." Asian Survey 14
        (September 1974): 795-806.

The study is done in a liberal and modernizing state of
India--Punjab. An attempt is made in this study to catalog
and analyze the direction and consistency of orientations
toward several aspects of social change among Punjab college
students. The focal concern of this research is the
students' view of the propriety and necessity of basic
changes in several traditional social institutions and their
general level of shared agreement on desirable social change.
The first important finding of this study is that
irrespective of class or caste, social status or religion,

rural and urban background, an overwhelming majority of Punjabi youth favors the abolition of such traditional institutions as caste and untouchability and strongly approves of a general social revolution in India. Social background, thus, has little impact on their attitude towards social change.

Another important finding is the fact that there is no relationship between a student's pro- or anti-democratic orientation and his attitude toward social change. This high degree of commitment to social change on the part of the young elites does conform to the general role of the intellectuals in underdeveloped societies.

844.   Nagla, Bhupendra K. "Youth Unrest in Contemporary Indian University." Journal of Higher Education 8 (Spring 1983): 289-98.

845.   Oommen, T. K. "Student Politics in India: The Case of Delhi University." Asian Survey 19, no. 9 (1974): 777-94.

846.   Oommen, T. K. "Student Power in India: A Political Analysis." Political Science Review 14, no. 1-2 (1975): 10-38.

847.   Parker, Clyde A., Sally Jo Power and Robert W. Ross. "Student Protest in the United States and India." Indian Educational Review 12 (April 1977): 1-18.

Student protest in varying forms and intensities has been a characteristic of institutions of higher learning. While all student protests have many features in common, there are also many features which vary with time and/or place. Comparative studies are useful tools in delineating these common and differentiating factors. Such knowledge provides insight not only into the phenomenon of student protest, but also into the cultures in which the protest occurs.

In this paper, quantitative data concerning the general trends manifested in student protest occurring in India in 1971-72, are compared to those manifested in data collected in the United States in 1968-69. Although some difference in the time period exists, we feel that student protest in America in 1968-69 was characteristic of that four to six-year period of intense social concern by American students in which it falls, and that student protest in India in 1971-72 was equally representative of that same time span in India.

848.   Ray, Anil Baran. "Reflections on Socio-Political Expectations of Students in India." Journal of Higher Education 4 (Spring 1980): 301-12.

849.   Reddy, P. H. "Indian Student Rebellion - Some Neglected
        Factors." Economic and Political Weekly 4 (February 15,
        1969): 357-60.

850.   Rudolph, Lloyd I., Susanne H. Rudolph, and Karuna Ahmed.
        "Student Politics and National Politics in India."
        Economic and Political Weekly 6 (July 1971): 1655-68.

        The emergence of youth as a new political class is a
        consequence of the creation and prolongation of youth as a
        distinctive life-stage with its attendant cultures and social
        arrangements. This has been made possible by the relatively
        rapid build-up of the educational system. And it has all
        been supported mainly by the requirements and rewards of
        industrial economies for literate, knowledgeable, and skilled
        labor forces working away from home and family, and also the
        aspiration that democratic citizens should be informed and
        responsible.
        One result, in India, of political capacity (in the sense
        of ability to make demands effectively within the political
        system) outstripping economic capacity (in the sense of the
        economy's ability to supply resources) has been the creation
        of a relatively large educational sector. In India, and in
        some other new and industrializing nations, modern
        educational institutions have created the new political class
        of youth prior to, or parallel with, the emergence of other
        modern political classes such as the middle and working
        classes. In consequence, this political class and
        particularly its vanguard, the students, has a significance
        in the politics of these countries uncharacteristic of the
        political change process in Europe and America during
        comparable periods of their democratization and industriali-
        zation.
        Given the special significance of students in the politics
        of many new nations, certain questions assume importance and
        interest. These are: whether or not their politics are like
        national politics and integrated with them; whether student
        politics are separate from, opposed to, or ahead of, national
        politics; and what conditions promote one or another of these
        tendencies. The relationship of student politics to national
        politics can range between the poles of congruence and
        incongruence, and student politics can be assessed within
        this range by reference to goals and methods in the
        categories: Ideological, Regime, Programmatic/Party,
        Interest, and Issue.
        Such an analysis of student politics in India is carried
        out in this article. While the findings do not tell us at
        what point, historically, students may become a political
        class, they do illuminate those factors in the college

environment that are likely to incline students toward
adhering or not adhering to their role as students, and throw
light on those conditions that, in India, have been
associated with student unrest and a readiness for activity
as a political class.

851.   Shekhawat, V. "Science Education and Scientific Attitudes of
        Indian Students." Indian Educational Review 7 (July 1972):
        1-10.

        The author postulates that the philosophy of science
        essentially conflicts with the native Indian philosophy and
        that therefore in spite of concerted efforts the majority of
        Indian youth remain alien to science. Another barrier to
        learning science is the foreign language employed. The
        author examines these issues and goes into the implications
        for the methods and materials of science teaching arising
        from this conflict.

852.   Singhal, Sushila. "Genesis of Student Unrest: Results of a
        Multimethod Analysis." Journal of Higher Education 3
        (Monsoon 1977): 27-53.

        Reports the results of a multi-method analysis based on
        events of unrest in University of Delhi in the year 1972-73,
        and seeks to identify where control towards containment could
        be exercised by using a tentative model. Also discusses, the
        egoistic attitude of teachers, the pragmatic attitude of
        authorities, perception of academic leadership and programs,
        organizational climate, faith in violence on the campus,
        police and governmental interference, belief in agitational
        tactics, absence of a code of conduct, economic factors, and
        political interests, in this context.

853.   Sivakumar, C. "Social Behaviour of Students: A Women's
        College in Mysore City." Economic and Political Weekly 10
        (May 31, 1975): 859-66.

854.   Uberoi, J. S. "Student Question." Economic and Political
        Weekly (May 29, 1981): 1098-1100.

855.   Unnithan, P. and others. "The Use of Psychotropic Drugs
        among College Youth in India." Sociological Bulletin 29
        (September 1980): 171-86.

NEPAL

Article

856.   Hayes, Louis. "Educational Reform and Student Political
        Behavior in Nepal." Asian Survey 16 (August 1976): 752-
        69.

        Assesses the impact of the New Education System (NES) upon
        the role of students as a political force in Nepal. The
        three parts of the paper review the political activities of
        students and their impact upon the development of Nepal's
        institutions and policies, describes the basic components of
        the NES and the changes anticipated as a result of its
        implementation, and analyzes these developments in the
        context of current knowledge of modernization and attempts to
        evaluate their importance for the future.

PAKISTAN

Books

857.   Abbas, S. Zia. Students and the Nation. Karachi: 1970.

858.   Khan, Shafique Al. The Age of Rage: An Academic Study of
        the Universal Youth Unrest, With Particular Reference to
        Pakistan. Hyderabad, Sind: Markez-i-Shaoorb-Adab, 1974.

859.   Pakistan. Commission on Student Problems and Welfare.
        Report. Karachi: Manager of Publications, 1966.

860.   Sweeney, Leo J. Islamic Republic of Pakistan: A Study of
        the Educational System of Pakistan and a Guide to the
        Academic Placement of Students from Pakistan in Educational
        Institutions of the United States. Washington: American
        Association of Collegiate Registrars and Admissions
        Officers, 1977.

861.   Zaki, Wali Muhammad and R. M. Akhtar. Study in Pakistan: A
        Handbook For Foreign Students. Islamabad: Ministry of
        Education, 1973.

Article

862.   Shah, Khalida.   "Attitudes of Pakistani Students Toward
        Family Life." Marriage and Family Living 22, no. 2 (1960):
        156-61.

        Assesses differences in attitudes toward family life of
        male and female college students in Lahore. Female students
        favored larger families, were more orthodox regarding
        religious practices, dower and dowry, parental authority, sex
        education for children and female employment, and were more
        liberal about female education and the husband's role in the
        home. Men considered themselves more intelligent while women
        stressed equality in intelligence. Based on questionnaires.

SRI LANKA

    Articles

863.   Babapulle, C. J. and A. L. S. Mendis. "General Intellectual
        Ability of University Entrants in Sri Lanka." Medical
        Education 18, no. 3 (1984): 142-46.

864.   Kearney, Robert N.   "Educational Expansion and Volatility in
        Sri Lanka: The 1971 Insurrection." Asian Survey 15
        (September 1975):   727-44.

        The 1971 insurrection in Sri Lanka was a product of many
        complex influences and a number of coincidences and chance
        happenings. This article concerned with some aspects of the
        socio-political environment that allowed an organization such
        as the Janathe Vimukthi Peramuna (JVP) to transform itself
        from a small clique of disaffected young Marxists into a
        significant movement of youths capable of launching an armed
        rebellion that left at least 1,200 persons dead and 14,000 in
        custody. It discusses the pace of educational expansion
        coupled with sluggish economic growth that led to staggering
        levels of unemployment for educated youths and an abrupt
        shattering of the new expectations contributed to a growth of
        disillusionment, alienation, and sense of deprivation among
        youths, which in turn heightened the potential violence.

CHAPTER 20

TEACHERS AND TEACHER ORGANIZATIONS

BANGLADESH

Books

865.   Rafique, A. A Study on Some Aspects of Staff Development
        Strategies for the Technical Education Programme of
        Bangladesh. Dhaka: the Author, 1980.

        This study examines the present situation of teachers and
        the different categories of teachers who need development.
        Based on the information gathered from teachers through a
        questionnaire, the findings point to the need for formulating
        a clear staff development policy considering constraints of
        resources and time of teachers, revising and updating the
        curriculum, and conducting more studies in the area of staff
        development.

866.   University of Dhaka. Institute of Education and Research.
        Teachers in East Pakistan. National Commission on Manpower
        and Education Research Study No. 13. Karachi: Manager of
        Publications, 1972.

867.   Zulfaqar Ali, S. N. Q. The Modern Teacher. Dhaka: Book
        Villa, 1968.

        Article

868.   Dove, Linda. "The Teacher and the Rural Community in
        Developing Countries." Compare 10 (1980): 17-29.

        Discusses position and role of the teachers of the
        developing countries, particularly of Bangladesh in rural
        community development.

INDIA

Books

869.   Ahuja, B. C. The Problems of Teachers in India. Ambala:
       Associated, 1981.

870.   Arora, K. Differences Between Effective and Ineffective
       Teachers. New Delhi: S. Chand, 1978.

871.   Chaurasia, G. New Era in Teacher Education. Delhi:
       Sterling, 1967.

       In nine chapters the book deals with all major developments
       in teacher education and brings together in one place the
       major forces shaping teacher education in India today.

872.   Chitnis, S. and P. G. Altbach, eds. The Indian Academic
       Profession: Crisis and Change in the Teaching Community.
       Bombay: Macmillan, 1979.

       A collection of essays concerning the academic profession
       from a range of viewpoints. Included are studies of the
       working habits of academics, structural problems of the
       profession, socialization patterns of academics, and related
       issues. Special attention is paid to the problems of college
       teachers.

873.   Kale, Pratima. The Career of the Secondary School Teacher in
       Poona. Bombay: Nachiketa, 1972.

       This study is an analysis of career of the secondary school
       teachers in Poona in a broad social context. It provides
       information on the social world of the school "as it really
       is". The various relationships which the teacher has with
       other participants in the school system--students, col-
       leagues, principals, parents, etc.--are studied from the
       point of view of the teacher.

874.   Kulshrestha, S. P. Emerging Value Patterns of Teachers and
       New Trends of Education in India. New Delhi: Light and
       Life, 1979.

       Attempts to identify the emerging value-patterns of
       teachers and, in the process, presents a scale of teachers'

values, a review of over fifty studies on teacher and student values, a survey of eighteen measures of values, a description of the sociocultural environment of Indian schools in their contribution to the values embodied in the educational system, and an evaluation of recent trends in education in terms of the values that they represent. Definitions of and distinctions between terms are presented in their theoretical context.

875.   Mangal, S. K. Dimensions of Teacher Adjustment. Kurukshetra: Vishal, 1985.

876.   Pethe, Vasant P. Living and Working Conditions of Primary School Teachers. Bombay: Popular Book Depot, 1962.

This book assesses the economic and social conditions of the teachers, with emphasis on the levels of living, ascertains the educational and other attainments which mainly form the professional equipment of the teacher, and examines the nature and volume of work and the conditions of service in the school in India. It also elicits the views of the teachers on some of the important problems prevailing at the present time in the field of primary education.

877.   Ramanamma, A. and Usha Bambawale. Academicians' Role Performance and Modernization. Poona: Continental Prakashan, 1983.

Analyzes the role and performance of teachers in Poona University so as to evaluate their impact on modernization. Based on questionnaires answered by a sample of postgraduate teachers. Presents a socioeconomic profile of the respondents, their self-image and attitudes toward teaching, research, updating of knowledge, and social issues.

878.   Ruhela, S. P., ed. Sociology of the Teaching Profession in India. New Delhi: NCERT, 1970.

879.   Shah, B. V. The Role of the Secondary School Teacher: A Sociological Investigation. New Delhi: NCERT, 1969.

880.   Sharpe, Brian. Bombay Teachers and the Cultural Role of Cities. Washington, D.C.: University Press of America, 1983.

This monograph illuminates some of the social and cultural processes at work in the complex environment of Bombay, India through a study of "education and the educated" at the primary and secondary levels. He focuses on teachers drawn

from a variety of schools which educate Bombay's youth:
schools employing different languages as media of instruction, those sponsored by municipal, private, religious, or
secular agencies, and those committed to a variety of social
and political philosophies. He examines systematically how
these factors, together with the diverse social and cultural
backgrounds of the teachers, affect the attitudes, beliefs,
aspirations, and life-styles of the students--students who
are destined to become India's educated urban elite and hence
influential far beyond their numbers.

881.   Singh, R. P. The Indian Teacher. Delhi: National, 1969.

A few case studies are discussed such as the strike of
Delhi teachers and status of secondary school teachers. It
also furnishes a glimpse into the working of various teacher
organizations and suggests a code of ethics for the teachers.

882.   Sinha, B. N. University Teachers and Their Problems. New
        Delhi: Puja, 1982.

Studies the professional and social problems of university
teachers in Bihar state, in the perspective of a history of
university education in the state and presents academic and
familial relations. A widespread dissatisfaction among university teachers at different levels, is found with respect
to their familial, professional, and social life.

883.   Swamy, S. Sreedhara. Teacher Organisations in India. New
        Delhi: All India Federation of Educational Associations,
        1980.

This book contains a detailed study on the working of
teacher organizations, their direction and purposes, their
strengths and weaknesses, the battles they have waged, and
their achievements and failures. It covers the period between the closing years of the nineteenth century till the
year of 1974.

        Articles

884.   Altbach, Philip G. "In Search of Saraswati: The Ambivalence
        of the Indian Academic." Higher Education 6 (May 1977):
        255-75.

College teachers in India are the focus of this article.
Working conditions, attitudes, and their organizational

milieu are surveyed. Data for this article are provided by a case study of the University of Bombay. The ambivalent role of the college teacher as an individual with an inadequate income, declining social status, and yet the pretensions of professionalism is a theme of this article. The Indian teaching community has been called on to function in a rapidly expanding higher education system but with inadequate resources. This situation has led to declining standards of education in general, and in a demoralization of the academic community in particular. A tradition of bureaucratic involvement in academic affairs and only a limited amount of academic freedom have further retarded the growth of a profession and effective teaching community.

885.   Basu, Asoke. "Politics of Academics: A Comparative Review." Journal of Higher Education 7 (Monsoon 1981): 59-72.

886.   Chitnis, S. "The Indian Academic Profession." Annals of the American Academy of Social and Political Sciences 448 (March 1980): 139-50.

887.   Desai, H. G. "Psychological Needs of College Teachers." Journal of Higher Education 1 (Autumn 1975): 250-54.

888.   Filella, S. J. "College Teaching in India: An Academic Function, A Personal Relationship, or Coaching for Examinations?" Journal of Higher Education 3, no. 3 (1978): 321-31.

889.   Gilbert, I. "The Indian Academic Profession: The Origins of a Tradition of Subordination." Minerva 10 (July 1972): 384-411.

890.   Gilbert, I. A. "The Organization of the Academic Profession in India, The Indian Education Services, 1864-1924." Pp. 319-41 in Education and Politics in India, eds. L. and S. Rudolph. Cambridge, Mass.: Harvard, 1972.

891.   Haragopal, G. and K. Jagannadha Rao. "Problems and Perceptions of Social Science Teachers in Higher Education." Journal of Higher Education 4 (Monsoon 1978): 67-74.

892.   Kale, Pratima. "The Guru and the Professional: The Dilemma of the Secondary School Teacher in Poona, India." Comparative Education Review 24 (October 1970): 371-6.

        This article analyzes the contradictions and dilemma of status and role as projected by the secondary school teacher

in Poona, India. The contradictions and adaptations can be
seen in a variety of occupational identities and self-images
of the teacher such as the traditional Indian Guru, the
modern western pedagogue, the professional, the academic
salesman, and the bureaucratic functionary. In part, the
image is formulated from an internalized set of positive and
negative values, attitudes, and ideology that the individual
teacher associates with his role. On the other hand, the
image is the result of historical developments and cultural
traditions to a large extent determine the status and the
role of the teacher in relation to the larger society.

893.   Malaviya, A. "Commitment and Rural Bias of Teachers for
        Rural Orientation of Home Science Education." Journal of
        Higher Education 10 (Monsoon-Autumn 1984):   77-83.

        An analysis of the origin of Home Science and its organiza-
        tion at the university level. Comments on the boost given to
        Home Science in agricultural universities and on the concern
        for rural orientation. Studies the rural background of Home
        Science teachers and measures the degree of commitment of
        Home Science teachers for giving a rural orientation to Home
        Science education.

894.   Passi, B. K. and S. P. Malhotra. "Effects of Authoritarian-
        Democratic Teachers Behaviour Upon the Likings of the
        Students Towards Their Teachers." Indian Educational
        Review 10 (January 1975):   43-51.

        This study aims at exploring the effect of teacher behavior
        upon likings of the students towards their own teachers.
        Besides this major objective, it was also thought to study
        the authoritarian and democratic behavior of the teacher in
        the light of the variables of age, sex, and training of the
        teachers. Through the correlational and t-test approaches it
        was found that democratic behavior of the teacher is more
        liked by the students. Aged teachers are more authoritarian
        in their behavior. Further, it is found that sex and train-
        ing do not have significant effect on the behavior of the
        teacher at higher secondary stage.

895.   Saraswathi, L. S. "Teacher Evaluation by the Taught."
        Journal of Higher Education 1 (Spring 1976):   315-24.

896.   Shils, Edward. "The Academic Profession in India." Minerva
        7 (Spring 1969):   345-72.

        The academic professions Shils talks about belong to
        traditions, which have grown up not in India but outside

India. The profession is itself new and its members are criticized for not being the same as their traditional analogue, the guru. The author describes the differences between academic tradition and Indian tradition, impediments which prevented the Indian academic profession from performing with distinction in its work of research and teaching and which has led it into becoming a "pariah class" rather than a self-confident and equal sector of the center of Indian society. He also explores some of the ways which the segmented structure of the center of the India of the Raj blocked the performance of other elite functions by the Indian academic.

897.   Singh, R. P. "Teachers in Higher Education: A Review of Their Problems and Status." Education Quarterly 37 (Spring 1985): 4-12.

898.   Singh, Satvir and Harjit Kaur. "The Relationship of Motives, Aspiration, and Anxiety Among Women Teachers at Different Professional Levels." Asian Journal of Psychology and Education 1 (July 1976): 1-11.

899.   Verma, M. R. and M. H. Ansari. "Classroom Behavior of Student Teachers." Indian Educational Review 10 (January 1975): 19-42.

The study analyzes the classroom behavior of student-teachers to find out if content differences are associated with differences in teacher behavior. The sample was drawn from a mixed group of thirty-seven male and female student-teachers of the Aligarh Muslim University, sixteen from social studies area, fifteen from languages area, and six from sciences area. Flanders' Interaction Analysis Category system (FIAC) was used to collect the data for this study.

Since behavioral data are valid to the extent of reliability of observations, an intensive training was given to the two observers who collected data for this study. Scott's formula was used for computing the inter-observer agreement which was as high as .86, indicating a sufficiently high degree of reliability.

The findings of the study show that on an average, student-teachers talked for about one-half of the total interaction time, pupils for about one-fourth of the time, and none talked for about one-fifth of the time.

Students' talk chiefly comprised giving specific information to narrow questions with very few ideas initiated by pupils themselves. There was strong evidence to demonstrate subject group difference on sixteen out of twenty behavior ratio variables. Teachers' talk was highest in social stud-

ies, pupils' talk in languages, and productive silence in
sciences group. Some other findings thought to be quite
provocative include: teachers' excessive concern for react-
ing only to the cognitive aspects of pupil behavior (least
use of Cat. 1) and their lack of concern for promotion of
divergent thinking in the pupils (low size of the PIB).

PAKISTAN

Books

900. Boewe, Charles E. The Green Book, American Scholar in
Pakistan. Islamabad: United States Educational Foundation
in Pakistan, 1977.

901. Institute of Education and Research. Punjab University. A
Study on Teachers in West Pakistan. Karachi: Planning
Commission, Government of Pakistan, 1970.

902. Pakistan Planning Commission. A Study on Teachers in West
Pakistan. Karachi: Manager of Publications, 1972.

Article

903. Ekanayade, S. B. "Training Teachers for Changing Roles in
Sri Lanka." Prospects 10, no. 4 (1980): 504-11.

Describes and evaluates a project undertaken to reform
teacher training in Sri Lanka so that it would be more
focused toward community development. Major successes of the
program were that it helped educators understand the
potential resources available at the village level and
encouraged them to stress multi-disciplinary approaches
toward teaching and learning.

CHAPTER 21

TEACHER EDUCATION

BANGLADESH

Book

904.   Sharafuddin, Abdullah Al-Muti and Howard C. Allison, eds.
        Improvement of Teacher Education: Proceedings of the
        Seminar of Teacher Education, October 15 to 22, 1968.
        Dhaka: Education Extension Centre, 1969.

Article

905.   Dove, Linda. "Teacher Training for Universal Primary
        Education in Bangladesh, 1981-86." International Review of
        Education 29, no. 2 (1983): 215-27.

        Between 1981 and 1986, the government of Bangladesh aims to
        enroll up to seventy percent of its twelve million five- to
        nine-year-olds in school, a program which involves the
        training or retraining of 156,000 teachers. To achieve this
        ambitious target demands great quantitative expansion but
        also requires a rethinking of what schools teach and the
        relations between schools and the communities they serve. An
        IDA-UPE project in forty thanas (ten percent of the country)
        aims to pilot the way towards achieving these linked
        qualitative and quantitative targets.
        Central to the project is the improvement of teacher
        quality both through regenerating the Primary Training
        Institutes and, in schools, through the appointment of a new
        category of supervisory officer, the Assistant Thana
        Education Officer. These ATEO's will each supervise a small
        number of schools and will be key figures in the organization
        of school-based in-service training and supervision, without
        which the quality of teaching and learning in the schools may
        not improve.

INDIA

Books

906.   Gupta, A. K. Teacher Education: Current and Prospects. New
        Delhi: Sterling, 1984.

        Collection of seminar papers on the subject. Reviews the
        current situation of education and teacher training.
        Presents recent innovations in teacher education and the
        prospects for the future.

907.   Jangira, N. K. Teacher Training and Teacher Effectiveness:
        An Experiment in Teacher Behaviour. New Delhi: National,
        1979.

        This book provides a model for validating Indian teacher
        education programs in terms of the real impact on the
        pupils--the ultimate goal of teacher education.   The
        experiment blazes a trail in research on teacher education
        and teacher effectiveness. The book has an implied message
        for teaching children from the weaker sections who remain
        deprived of the teacher responsiveness and are ultimately
        "pushed out" of the mainstream of education. The increased
        teacher responsiveness to these pupils, as suggested in the
        training program envisaged as a part of the Classroom
        Behavior Training, will go a long way in arresting the
        incidence of high level of wastage and stagnation plaguing
        Indian educational institutions which is so necessary for the
        universalization of elementary education.

908.   Khamborkar, K. R. Training Teaching Techniques. Akola: L.
        W. Deshmukh, 1980.

        A catalogue of methods of teaching and their variations,
        including lectures, group discussions, self-study, and the
        use of audio-visual aids. Contains a discussion on trends in
        the teaching-learning process with reference to educational
        thinkers like Gandhi and Piaget.

909.   Khan, M. S. Teacher Education in India and Abroad. New
        Delhi: Ashish, 1983.

910.   Kochar, S. K. Methods and Techniques of Teaching. New York:
        Apt, 1984.

The book has as its corner-stone the unique needs of the inexperienced teacher, his untested frame of reference for teaching, and his limited approach to resources that facilitate learning. An attempt is also made to update the knowledge of the experienced teacher.

911.   Lipkin, J. P. <u>Secondary School Teacher Education in Transition</u>. Bombay: Asia, 1970.

Secondary teacher training in India was set by the British in an academic mold. Since Independence in 1947, there has been a steady trend towards a pattern of training more suited to the Indian socioeconomic and political context. In this study, the author examines the motive forces for and the extent of transition in Bombay. He starts with an examination of the adoption of the British educational tradition in Bombay and then goes on to examine the new trends in the field of secondary teacher training in India with particular reference to change in secondary training colleges affiliated to Bombay University from 1953 through 1964. The final chapter sums up the progress of the evolution of an Indian system of secondary teacher training.

912.   Mukerji, S. N. <u>Education of Teachers in India Volume II</u>. Delhi: S. Chand, 1968.

Teacher education in all states of India, including Union territories, is discussed in its present comprehensiveness and sweep against the backdrop furnished by history. Each of the chapters on states and union territories covers largely the bases of development of teacher-education programs over a long period of time identifying policies and the recent trends.

913.   National Council of Educational Research and Training. <u>Gandhian Values, Socially Useful Productive Work and Community Work Under Teacher Education Programme; Report</u>. New Delhi: National Council for Teacher Education, 1979.

914.   National Council of Educational Research and Training. <u>Teacher Education Curriculum; A Framework</u>. New Delhi: NCERT, 1978.

The foreword points out that the success of any educational reform depends upon the abilities of the teachers. These in turn depend to a large extent on the quality of the teacher education program. Reports of education commissions and various meetings observe that present teacher education **programs appear to be static and inflexible to cope with new**

national goals, and fail to impress upon student teachers
their usefulness and applicability to society. This
publication presents a framework for a teacher education
curriculum which incorporates recommendations of a Committee
on 'Working with the Community'.

915.   Paliwal, M. R. Teacher Education on the Move: A Global View
        Today and Tomorrow. New Delhi: Uppal, 1985.

916.   Shanker, Uday. Education of Indian Teachers. New York:
        Apt, 1984.

        The theme of the book is teacher education yesterday,
        today, and tomorrow. The emphasis is on preparing primary
        and secondary school teachers in a professional manner. The
        author pleads for training of Indian teachers on the same
        footing as training of doctors and engineers, through an
        integrated course of academic and professional preparation.

917.   Shukla, R. S. Emerging Trends in Teacher Education.
        Allahabad: Chugh, 1978.

918.   Singh, L. C. Microteaching--An Innovation in Teaching
        Education. Agra: National Psychological Corporation,
        1979.

919.   Singh, R. P. Studies in Teacher Education: An Overview.
        New Delhi: Bahri, 1980.

920.   Srivastava, R. C. and K. Bose. Theory and Practice of
        Teacher Education in India. Allahabad: Chugh, 1978.

921.   Teacher Education Curriculum: A Framework Prepared for
        National Council for Teacher Education. New Delhi: NCERT,
        1978.

922.   Vasishtha, K. K. Teacher Education in India: A Study in New
        Dimensions. New Delhi: Concept, 1979.

        This study is an attempt to study the effect of training in
        the Flanders' Interaction Analysis System (FIAS) on some
        characteristics and verbal behavior of secondary science and
        mathematics student-teachers. The inferences are quite
        natural and have been presented in a generalized form. They
        have been substantiated with the flow of interaction analysis
        of the composite matrices of experimental and control groups.

Articles

923.   Ahmad, Karuna. "For Sociology in Teacher Education." *Sociological Bulletin* 27 (March 1978):   83-97.

924.   Joyce, Bruce and Beverly Showers. "Teacher Education in India: Observations on American Innovations Abroad." *Educational Researcher* 14 (October 1985):   3-9.

        Examines the structure of Indian teacher education, current criticisms of it, and the themes of research and innovation. Identifies many parallels between North American and Indian practices and asserts that, like the American system, the structure of Indian teacher education lacks mechanisms to promote experimentation and research.

NEPAL

Books

925.   *Alternative Structures and Methods in Teacher Education: Report of a Technical Working Group, Kathmandu, Nepal, 21-30 October 1975*. Kathmandu: Institute of Education, Tribhuvan University and Bangkok: UNESCO Regional Office for Education in Asia, 1975.

926.   Karmacharya, Uttam Krishna. *Teacher Training Through Distance Learning in Nepal*. Kathmandu: Institute of Education.

        The Institute of Education, Tribhuvan University, adopted an alternative scheme of teacher training through distance learning to train the backlog of untrained and unqualified teachers in the remote rural areas of Nepal. Self-learning materials were prepared, including a handbook of student teaching.

927.   Nepal.   Institute of Education. *Courses of Study for Certificate of Education, Phase I (primary school teacher)*. Bhaktapur: Division of Instruction and Curriculum, 1979.

        Presents the objectives and contents of the courses.

Article

928.   Pilain, Mary Ann Calkins. "Nepal: Training Women Primary
        School Teachers." Women, Education, Equality: A Decade of
        Experiment. Paris: UNESCO, 1965, 33-50.

PAKISTAN

Book

929.   Sulemani, I. H., ed. A Survey of Outcomes of In-Service
        Training Programmes. Lahore: Education Extension Center
        in Cooperation with UNICEF, 1977.

        A survey of an in-service training program to determine an
        instrument of evaluation of the outcome of the program. The
        program, begun in the Punjab in 1975, undertakes to equip the
        primary school teachers with knowledge for new course content
        and the required pedagogical skills.

Article

930.   Hughes, W. J. "Postgraduate Teacher Training in Pakistan."
        Teacher Education New Countries 11 (May 1970): 17-21.

CHAPTER 22

ADMINISTRATION OF EDUCATION

BANGLADESH

Book

931. Bangladesh. University Grants Commission. Role, Functions, and Procedure. Dhaka: UGC, 1977.

INDIA

Books

932. Aggarwal, J. C. Educational Administration, Inspection, Planning, and Financing in India. New Delhi: Arya Book Depot, 1972.

933. Bhat, K. S. and Ravishankar, eds. Administration of Education: New Perspectives and Viewpoints. Delhi: Seema, 1985.

934. Bhatnagar, R. P. and I. B. Verma. Educational Supervision. Meerut: Loyal Book Depot, 1978.

A democratic approach to aspects of supervision in education. Presents theoretical issues in supervision; methods of planning, organizing, and operating the supervisory program; evaluation of such programs; steps to improve the teacher-pupil relation, the curriculum, and the school environment; and finally, a vision of supervision in the future.

935. Desai, Daulatbhai and Others, eds. School of Management and Change. Baroda: Faculty of Education and Psychology, M.S. University of Baroda, 1979.

Discusses concepts involved in school management and
innovations, as related to the school system, backed by a
presentation of results from a number of research studies.
Includes deliberations of a national seminar on research
needs in the subject, held in December 1978.

936.   Gadgil, A. V. Supervision in Education. Pune: Shubhada-
        Saraswat, 1982.

A historical survey of school inspection in Maharashtra
over the last 120 years, based on secondary data,
questionnaires, and panel inspections.

937.   Gopal, M. V. Raja. Education in Andhra Pradesh.
        Machilipatnam: Telugu Vidyarthi Publications, n.d.

Discusses the practical problems faced by the educational
authorities in Andhra Pradesh, and presents omnibus
suggestions for several problems. The weaknesses of the
educational system in Andhra Pradesh are given. The problems
in primary and secondary education are discussed elaborately.
There is a lengthy presentation of the administrative network
of schools and colleges. Several suggestions are made for
the improvement of the quality of higher education and
equalization of educational opportunities.

938.   Goswami, D. H. University Administration in North-East
        India. Calcutta: Naya Prakash, 1982.

A history of the administration, functioning, and growth of
four universities that were, after 1947, set up in the East,
an area of poor educational facilities. Discusses the
establishment, administrative bodies, officers and councils,
finance, the expansion of affiliated colleges, and problem
areas such as student indiscipline, poor female education,
and educational standards.

939.   Gupta, L. D. Educational Administration at College Level.
        New Delhi: Oxford and I.B.H., 1983.

An administrator's view of the problems of higher education
and their solutions. Discusses at length aspects of college
administration, educational reforms such as the 10+2+3
system, innovations such as the open university and
educational policy in the context of the five-year plans.
Favors autonomy of educational institutions, open
universities, non-formal education, as steps towards a more
functional, educational system.

940. Guruge, Ananda, W. P. Towards Better Educational Management.
      New Delhi: Asian Institute, 1970.

941. Inamdar, N. R. Educational Administration in the Zilla
      Parishads in Maharashtra. Bombay: Popular Prakashan,
      1974.

      An evaluation of the change in the administration of the
      primary education, from the District School Boards to the
      Zilla Parishads, after the inception of Panchayat Raj in
      Maharashtra State in 1961-62. The role of the rural
      leadership in primary education through the administrative
      hierarchy of the village schools, Taluka Panchayat Samiti and
      the Poona Zilla Parishad is evaluated while discussing
      aspects such as relations between officials and non-
      officials, compulsory education, the functioning of village
      schools, finances, secondary education, and adult literacy.
      Concludes that while primary education has expanded, there
      has been a decline in its quality, negative interference by
      elected non-officials in the educational administration,
      slackening in inspection, and financial inadequacy.

942. Khan, M. S. School Administration. New Delhi: Jackson,
      1983.

      Analyses of basic policies and practices of secondary
      school administration and organization. Covers conceptual
      issues; the history and present setup of administration in
      Uttar Pradesh; issues related to the principal, staff, and
      students; curriculum, timetable; the physical structure and
      functioning of a school unit and evaluation.

943. Kochhar, S. K. Successful Supervision and Inspection. New
      Delhi: Sterling, 1981.

      An analysis of supervision and inspection in terms of both
      practice and research. Discusses the need for supervision
      and inspection, its objectives, types and trends, roles of
      officials, and innovations in the subject in different
      countries.

944. Kumar, Binod and Others, eds. Management of Education in
      India: Problems and Prospects. Calcutta: Indian
      Institute of Management, 1976.

945. Mathur, S. S. Educational Administration: Principles and
      Practices with Special Reference to India. Jullender:
      Krishna Bros., 1969.

946.   Matthai, Ravi and Others, eds. Institution Building in
        Education and Research. New Delhi: All India Management
        Association, 1977.

        Describes how institutions develop and grow. Develops a
        typology of decision-making from the feudal to the
        institution-building framework. Argues that institutions are
        built around men. Comments on the growing demand of students
        for participation in decision making and makes a few
        theoretical and practical observations on how the matter is
        to be tackled.

947.   Mukherjee, L. Problems of Administration of Education in
        India. Lucknow: Lucknow, 1970.

        Discusses the problems of educational administration in
        India, presenting a historical perspective of the evolution
        of the system. In the present situation, discusses the role
        of central, state, and local governments; of private agencies
        and the financing and inspection of education. Specific
        problems confronting educational administration at different
        stages are analyzed and necessary administrative reforms
        suggested.

948.   Mukherji, S. N., ed. Administration of Education in India.
        Baroda: Acharya Book Depot, 1962.

949.   Pinto, Marina. Federalism and Higher Education: The Indian
        Experience. Bombay: Orient Longman, 1984.

        A study of the role of the University Grants Commission and
        related administrative agencies in promoting national goals
        in higher education, analyzed in the context of the federal
        state structure. Based mainly on primary data gathered from
        individuals in government and academia, in Bombay and Delhi.
        Examines the constitutional and non-constitutional aspects of
        federalism in action in higher education. Stresses the need
        for state level institutions which would coordinate between
        the center and the states.

950.   Rao, T. P. R., T. V. Rao, and M. K. Singhvi. A Computer
        Model for Administration of Teachers Transfer. Ahmedabad:
        Indian Institute of Management, 1978.

951.   Sharma, M., ed. Systems Approach: Its Applications in
        Education. Bombay: Himalaya, 1985.

952.   Shukla, D. Administration of Education in India. New
        Delhi: Vikas, 1983.

Provides basic material and insights for the modernization of educational administration in India, taking into consideration modern management techniques. Covers legal and organizational aspects of education, administration at the district level and for higher education, administration of finance, and planning and inspection of institutions. The literature is directed at the academic community engaged in degree and postgraduate courses in educational administration, at planners and administrators. Underlines the need for efficient administration in a situation of limited resources and vast needs.

953.   Sidhu, K. S. School Organization and Administration. New York: Apt, 1984.

In view of the complex nature of school organization and administration there is a constant need to provide new guidelines to our administrators, would-be administrators, teachers, and students. The present book is an attempt to meet this need. It provides latest material on educational administration, organization, and supervision.

954.   Srivastava, Ramesh Chandra. College Administration: The Study of Faculty and Student Participation in College Administration. New Delhi: Metropolitan, 1980.

A report of a study of practices of faculty and student participation in administration. Analyzes university statutes, ordinances, and responses of a sample of teachers and students from Delhi University colleges. Discusses conceptual issues, perceptions of teachers and students, reasons for inadequate participation, and the relationship between participation and satisfaction.

955.   Srivastava, R. C. Educational Decision Making. New Delhi: Metropolitan, 1983.

A study of models of decision making in educational institutions to determine the extent and type of shift from traditional practices in which teachers had a negligible part, and its effects on the attitudes and perceptions of teachers and administrators. Based on a sample of teachers and administrators from thirty-two institutions of higher education throughout the country. Uses a Transactional Analysis of Personality and Environment questionnaire (TAPE), a Participation Scale, and a Participation Survey questionnaire.

956.   University Grants Commission. Report of the Committee on Governance of Universities and Colleges, Part-I, Governance of Universities. New Delhi: UGC, 1971.

       Articles

957.   Bhattacharya, Swapan K. and Manabendra Nath Pal. "Management Information Systems in University Administration." Journal of Higher Education 2 (Autumn 1976): 213-22.

958.   Chakravarty, Kumaresh. "Administration of Higher Education: An Overview." Journal of Higher Education 2 (Autumn 1976): 223-32.

       Analyzes the existing rules governing the structure of administration and management of education. Comments on the deficiencies of the system and expresses the need for an ideal one and finally suggests certain remedies. Reviews the Education Committee's report and the recommendations of the Gajendragadkar Committee.

959.   Desai, Uday. "University of Vice-Chancellors: Profile of the Educational Elites." Journal of Higher Education 8 (Spring 1983): 265-88.

960.   Desai, Uday. "Vice Chancellor: A Man for All Seasons." New Frontiers in Education 13 (July-September, 1983): 1-20.

961.   Dube, S. C. "Environment and the Challenge of Educational Management." Journal of Higher Education 6 (1980-81): 9-14.

962.   Garrett, C. Joanne and Larry N. Garrett. "Policy Analysis as an Adjunct Tool in the Prevention or Resolution of Managerial Crises in Higher Education." Journal of Higher Education 5 (Monsoon 1979): 13-20.

963.   Joshi, K. L. "Twenty-five Years of UGC: Dilemmas and Difficulties." Journal of Higher Education 6 (1980-81): 63-70.

964.   Kurien, C. T. "An Open and Participatory College Administration." Journal of Higher Education 2 (Autumn 1976): 203-12.

965.   Mathai, Samuel. "UGC--A Personal View." Journal of Higher Education 6 (1980-81): 55-62.

966.   Mathur, Kuldeep. "Leadership and Organizational Structure in
        a University." Journal of Higher Education 2 (Autumn
        1976): 233-42.

967.   Mukhopadhyay, M. "Management of Educational Technology: New
        Challenge in Education." Education Quarterly 37 (Summer
        1985): 10-19.

968.   Narain, Iqbal. "Rural Local Politics and Primary School
        Management." Pp. 148-64 in Education and Politics in
        India, eds. S. H. Rudolph and L. I. Rudolph. Delhi:
        Oxford, 1972.

969.   Raghaviah, Y. "The Midget Bureaucratic Phenomenon--
        Reflections on System Transformations in Universities."
        Journal of Higher Education 9 (Autumn 1983): 157-76.

970.   Sharma, Mahindra. "A Study of Conflict in a University."
        Journal of Higher Education 4 (Monsoon 1978): 1-10.

971.   Srivastava, R. C. "Faculty and Student Status in
        Administration." Journal of Higher Education 4 (Autumn
        1978): 225-44.

NEPAL

    Book

972.   Shrestha, Kedar Nath. Educational Management in Nepal.
        Kathmandu: Tribhuvan University, Institute of Education,
        1980.

    Article

973.   Graham, Jack W. and Belbase, Lekh Nath. "Status of Guidance
        in Nepal--Land of High Mountains and High Hopes."
        International Education 13, no. 1 (1983): 7-15.

PAKISTAN

Book

974.   West Pakistan. Education Department. Revised Handbook of
        Circulars and General Orders for Lahore and Rawalpindi
        Regions. Peshawar: Manager of West Pakistan Government
        Press, 1965.

SRI LANKA

Books

975.   Ariyadasa, K. D. Management of Educational Reforms in Sri
        Lanka.   Paris: UNESCO, 1976.

976.   Wijegunasekera, D. P., D. Gunaratne, and W. S. Perera.   The
        School and the Community: A Case Study of an Open-Plan
        School in Sri Lanka.   Bangkok: UNESCO Regional Office for
        Education in Asia and Oceania, 1979.

Articles

977.   Perera, Sterling W.   "The Sri Lanka Pilot School Cluster
        Project."   Education in Asia and the Pacific: Reviews,
        Reports, and Notes 20 (September 1983):   12-20.

        Discusses the project of clustering (grouping schools
        within a defined geographical area) in order to organize and
        manage the schools more effectively.   This project is
        intended to reduce inequalities of educational facilities.   A
        pilot plan would be implemented first on a small-scale order
        to be used as an example and also give opportunity to train
        administrators and cluster principals to develop the project
        on a nation-wide scale.

978.   Wanasinghe, Jauampati.   "The Concept of Cluster Schools and
        Its Relevance to Educational Development in Sri Lanka."
        International Journal of Education Development 3, no. 3
        (1983):   247-52.

CHAPTER 23

EDUCATION OF WOMEN

BANGLADESH

Books

979.   Chaudhury, Rafiqul Huda and Nilufer Raihan Ahmed. Female
       Status in Bangladesh. Dhaka: Bangladesh Institute of
       Development Studies, 1980.

       Chapter Four of this study covers education of women in
       Bangladesh in relation to the country's constitution,
       literacy and adult education, school attendance and achieve-
       ment, higher education, and the proportion of expenditure
       allocated to female education.

980.   Gerard, Renee, Meherunnessa Islam and Mehraj Jahan. Training
       for Women in Bangladesh: An Inventory and Sample Survey of
       Training Programmes. Dhaka: Women's Development
       Programme, UNICEF, 1977.

       Study of 196 governmental and nongovernmental, formal and
       informal training programs for poor women in Bangladesh.
       Reviews goals and operations of the various programs,
       evaluates them and attempts to determine which women are
       being reached and identify areas in which training programs
       are needed.

981.   Hoque, Naseem. Informal Education for Women in Bangladesh:
       With Emphasis on Agency and Organizational Programs Serving
       Economically Disadvantaged Women. East Lansing: Agency
       for International Development and Institute for
       International Studies in Education, Michigan State
       University, n.d.

       Report of study of voluntary and nongovernmental
       organizations assisting semiliterate and illiterate, poor,
       young and old, unskilled women. Assesses such programs as a

239

group and examines four in detail. The study conducted in
1974-75 examines the programs in the context of the history
of Bangladesh.

982.   Hossain, Monowar, Raihan Sharif, and Jahanara Huq, eds. Role
        of Women in Socio-Economic Development in Bangladesh:
        Proceedings of a Seminar Held in Dhaka, May 9-10, 1976.
        Dhaka: Bangladesh Economic Association, 1977.

        Reproduces various addresses, fifteen English and seven
        Bengali papers and reports of the various panels. Main
        topics are productive activities, rural women and
        development, education, and population planning. Jahanara Huq
        says in her introduction, "For the first time in the history
        of Bangladesh, women from diverse walks of life (about 300)
        submitted the fruits of their wide experience, deep insight
        and painstaking research, and ... were able to articulate
        their views on various social and economic issues confronting
        members of their sex."

983.   Islam, Shamima. Women's Education in Bangladesh: Needs and
        Issues.   Dhaka: The Foundation for Research on Educational
        Planning and Development, 1982.

        This study is an attempt to see how much opportunity has
        been provided to women in the educational system of
        Bangladesh in order to make them self-reliant, improve their
        self-concept and expose them to the idea of change.   The
        state of women in literacy, primary, and secondary education,
        has been dealt with a major emphasis since very few pupils go
        beyond that.   An effort has been made to focus understanding
        at the district level.   The overview of female education
        reveals that extreme imbalances exist in educational
        opportunities for females in Bangladesh.   The total effort of
        the Government to provide for educational needs for females
        indicate some achievement.   But the advance is evident
        quantitatively rather than qualitatively.   Educational
        opportunity has not been given to all, and the system has not
        been reconstructed to meet the needs of the nation.

984.   Krippendorf, Sultana.   Women's Education in Bangladesh:
        Needs and Issues. Content Analysis. Dhaka: Foundation
        for Research in Educational Planning and Development, 1977.

        This report is based on a quantitative content analysis of
        school textbooks to ascertain what ideas and attitudes about
        women are currently being taught children.   The study
        indicates that the textbooks are clearly biased against women
        both in terms of: (a) the representation of women; and (b)

the attitudes expressed about the social value, and capabilities of women to cope with their environment.

985. Women and Education: Bangladesh, 1978. Dhaka: Women for Women, Research and Study Group, 1978.

Collected papers from the Women for Women collective, Dhaka. Contents: "Women's Education and Emancipation in a Purdah Society: The coeds of the 50s" by Roushan Jahan, "Data on Attitudes Towards Urban Girls' Education" by Noorunnahar Fyzunnessa, "Mother's Attitudes Toward Freedom of Children and Academic Achievement of the Child" by Hamida Akhtar, "Female Primary Education in Bangladesh" by Mahmuda Islam, "The Position of Women in Secondary School Education in Bangladesh: A Case Study of Dhaka Division" by Ellen Sattar, "Married Female Students in Higher Education" by Khurshid Jalal and Ishrat Shamim, "Women in Education Administration" by Jahanara Huq, "Non-formal Education in Bangladesh: Some Selected Lessons and Choices of Strategy" by Shamima Islam and "Rural Women's Education: A Case for Realistic Policy Making" by Perveen Ahmad and Nazmunnessa Mahtab.

986. Omitted.

Articles

987. Islam, Mahmuda. "Women at Work in Bangladesh: A Sample Survey of Working Women." Pp. 93-120, Women for Women: Bangladesh 1975. Dhaka: University Press, 1975.

This is a study of 200 women working in remunerative occupations outside the home in metropolitan Dhaka. It reports occupational distribution, marital status, age distribution, education, socioeconomic background, husbands' occupation, parents' education and occupation, motivation to work, attitudes toward work, and effects on home life.

988. Islam, Shamima. "Strengthening Non-Formal Education for Women in Bangladesh." Pp. 379-401 in Women and Development: Perspectives from South and Southeast Asia, eds. R. Jahan and H. Papanek. Dhaka: Bangladesh Institute of Law and International Affairs, 1979.

The paper discusses the importance of non-formal education for women in Bangladesh. Deficiencies in the existing non-formal education efforts are criticized. The few non-formal

educational opportunities for women that exist at the present
time are concentrated in urban or semi-urban areas. They do
not reach the target clientele most in need of the programs.
Although women's participation forms a major role in
production activities, rural women are seriously neglected by
the major extension services of the country. Existing non-
formal education programs are trying to initiate new roles
for women instead of trying to improve their present level of
knowledge and competence in the roles they already fill. The
new skill training programs for women clearly demonstrate an
urban-bias and preconceived notions.

On the basis of the criticisms of the present state of non-
formal education, a number of suggestions are made for the
planners to improve the situation for women. It is argued
that to realize the national goals of development,
participation of the previously bypassed half of the human
resources of Bangladesh is essential. Therefore, the top
priority will need to be given to devising and implementing
educational programs, which will reach the vast majority of
rural women with new knowledge and skills which, in turn,
foster attitudes and behavior patterns more conducive to
change.

989.   Islam, Shamima. "Women Drop-Outs in Non-Formal Education: A
        Case Study." Pp. 154-79 in Women for Women: Bangladesh
        1975. Dhaka: University Press, 1975.

        This study provides a descriptive profile of participant
        dropouts in the Bangladesh Women's Rehabilitation Program,
        uncovering some thematic problems and some relevant
        socioeconomic information. Covers trainees and production
        workers who dropped out in 1973-74 after one month or more
        participation.

990.   Khatun, Sharifa. "Women's Education in a Rural Community in
        Bangladesh." Pp. 253-74 in Women and Development:
        Perspectives From South and Southeast Asia, eds. R. Jahan
        and Hanna Papanek. Dhaka: Bangladesh Institute of Law and
        International Affairs, 1979.

        Historically, education in Bangladesh, especially for the
        masses, has been neglected. Within this mass of population,
        the most educationally disadvantaged group is the rural
        women. It is increasingly viewed that without the use of a
        country's full human resource potential, development cannot
        be materialized. Education is regarded as an important
        instrument to achieve the goal of reconstruction and
        transformation of the society.

This study assesses the educational requirements of the community in a village in Bangladesh through observation of its socioeconomic and educational characteristics. It categorically discusses the inadequacy of the present school system to meet the needs of the rural community, especially women. The author provides a more relevant guideline for reconstructing the educational system for girls, especially for the age group five to fifteen in the rural areas. The necessity of decentralization of educational strategies and planning, in order to achieve the developmental goals of the country, is felt essential. It is believed that without community participation and use of local resources it will not be possible for the government to cope with the task of such magnitude as that of making education meaningful to its recipients.

991.   Smock, Audrey Chapman. "Bangladesh: A Struggle with Tradition and Poverty." Pp. 81-126 in Women: Roles and Status in Eight Countries, eds. Janet Zollinger Giele and Audrey Smock. New York: John Wiley, 1977.

The article summarized the historical background of Bangladesh and recent research on women with respect to family, education, economy and employment, fertility and family planning, and politics. Bibliography lists numerous published and unpublished sources. Author's conclusion to the volume (pp. 383-421) puts some of this material in comparative perspective.

992.   Teel, J. H. and R. K. Ragade. "Simulation Modeling Perspectives of the Bangladesh Family Planning and Female Education System." Behavioral Science 29, no. 3 (1984): 145-61.

INDIA

Books

993.   Aggarwal, J. C. Indian Women: Education and Status. New Delhi: Arya Book Depot, 1976.

A presentation of extracts from documents on the education and status of Indian women, with a brief commentary. Covers views of Indian educational philosophers, recommendations of the National Committee on the Status of Women in India (1971-74) and of the Committee on Differentiation of Curricula for

Boys and Girls (1961), and the positions taken by various other committees, the Indian Constitution, and the United Nations on the education of women. The author presents a historical review and statistics on the question.

994. Ahmad, Karuna. The Social Context of Women's Education in India, 1921-81: Tentative Formulations. New Delhi: Nehru Memorial Museum and Library, 1983.

995. Bhandari, Arvind. Ethnicity, Women, and Education. Meerut: Anu Prakashan, 1978.

996. Bhandari, R. K. Educational Development of Women in India. New Delhi: Ministry of Education and Culture, 1983.

997. Blumberg, Rhoda Lois and Leela Dwaraki. India's Educated Women: Options and Constraints. Delhi: Hindustan, 1980.

Focuses on the options open to higher educated women and the constraints caused by role expectations relating to marriage, education, and work. Findings of a 1966-67 study in Bangalore are combined with data collected a decade later, while analyzing the problems that arise from the intermeshing of marriage, education, and employment. Employment is found to be generally restricted to teaching, medicine, and clerical work. The working wife is beginning to question the traditional division of household labor.

998. Brockway, K. Nora and Getsie T. Samuel. A New Day for Indian Women: The Story of St. Christopher's Training College, Madras, 1923-1963. Madras: Christian Literature Society, 1963.

Brockway, who wrote the larger section of the book, was closely connected with the college from its founding in 1923 until her retirement. Considers establishment of school and growth of curriculum, facilities, and personnel.

999. Deble, I. School Education of Girls: An International Comparative Study on School Wastage Among Girls and Boys at the First and Second Levels of Education. Paris: UNESCO, 1980.

1000. Desai, Chitra. Girls' School Education and Social Change. Bombay: A. R. Sheth, 1976.

Relates changing social circumstances in nineteenth and twentieth century Gujarat to changing patterns.

1001. Desai, Saroj. A Critical Study of the Development of
       Secondary Education for Girls in Gujarat: Its History and
       Present-Day Problems. Baroda: Faculty of Psychology and
       Education, Maharaja Shivajirao University, 1972.

1002. Deshmukh, Durgabai. The Stone that Speaketh, Vol. 1: The
       Story of Fifty-seven Years. Hyderabad: Andhra Mahila
       Sabha, 1979.

       A history of the Andhra Mahila Sabha, an institution
       devoted to adult women's education and employment, from 1922
       to 1979. Covers its activities in education and vocational
       training and the growth of projects such as the nursing home.

1003. Deshmukh, Laj. Women and Continuing Education Programme of
       S.N.D.T. Women's University. Bombay: SNDT Women's
       University, 1983.

1004. Doraiswami, S. Educational Advancement and Socioeconomic
       Participation of Women in India: Perspectives, Problems,
       Impediments, Concerns. New Delhi: Directorate of Non-
       formal (Adult) Education, Ministry of Education and Social
       Welfare, Government of India, 1975(?).

1005. Goldstein, Rhoda L. Indian Women in Transition: A Bangalore
       Case Study. Metuchen, New Jersey: Scarecrow, 1972.

       Report of questionnaire survey of graduates from Bangalore
       University to learn about their place in a changing society.
       Chapters discuss the study itself, socioeconomic background
       of the sample, significance of education, attitudes toward
       marriage, attitudes toward employment, and conclusions.

1006. Gorwaney, Naintara. Self-Image and Social Change: A Study
       of Female Students. New Delhi: Sterling, 1977.

       This is a study of female students at the University of
       Rajasthan, Jaipur, India, that explores educated women as
       agents of modernization. Focuses on the relationship of
       one's family background to level of self-esteem and level of
       self-esteem to attitudes toward and performance of other
       roles. Includes extensive theoretical and methodological
       considerations.

1007. Gupta, Sen. Women's Education of India. Bombay: Asia,
       1962.

1008. India. Committee on Adult Education Programmes for Women.
       Adult Education Programmes for Women: Report of the

Committee Appointed by the Ministry of Education and Social
Welfare. New Delhi: Ministry of Education and Social
Welfare, Government of India, 1978.

Argues that traditional social patterns and traditional
policy of planners and administrators have limited the
progress of adult education programs for women. Proposes
revised goals and the operational means to reach them.

1009. India. Directorate of Non-formal Education. Misconceptions
Influencing Non-formal Education for Women. New Delhi:
Directorate of Non-formal (Adult) Education, Ministry of
Education and Social Welfare, 1975.

Discusses misconceptions about development, illusions about
education, and prejudices about women. "The problem of
women's education ... is, therefore, an inseparable component
of fundamental, general, and deep-rooted socioeconomic,
sociopolitical, and sociocultural aspirations, needs, and
trends."

1010. India. Education Commission. Recommendations on Women's
Education: A Compilation Prepared by the Education
Commission. New Delhi: Education Commission, Government
of India, 1965.

Digest of the recommendations made by various Indian
councils and committees from 1949 to 1965, grouped by topic.

1011. Kalia, N. N. Sexism in Indian Education: The Lies We Tell
Our Children. New Delhi: Vikas, 1979.

Documents the collision between optimism and the ingrained
predilection of sexism. The content analysis of Indian
textbook indicates that 93 percent of all male occupations
are high prestige, while 87 percent of all female occupations
fall in the low-prestige category. To perpetuate sex-
segregated differential motivation through negative
socialization, only 13 percent of all occupations presented
in the lessons are shared by both the sexes. Women are
excluded from three-fourths of all occupations held by
characters in the plots. Of fifty-four biographies, only
seven feature women as exceptional achievers.

1012. Kundu, C. L. Women's Education in India, Retrospect and
Prospect: Silver Jubilee Issue. Agra: Women's Training
College, 1971.

1013. Maskiell, Michelle. Women Between Cultures: The Lives of
       Kinnaird College Alumnae in British India. Syracuse:
       Maxwell School of Citizenship and Public Affairs, Syracuse
       University, 1984.

1014. Mathur, Y. B. Women's Education in India, 1813-1966.
       Bombay: Asia, 1973.

       This is a well-documented survey with a basic bibliography.
       Key documents reproduced in appendixes.

1015. Mazumdar, Vina, ed. The Challenge of Education: Studies on
       Issues in Women's Education. Bombay: Allied, 1985.

       Papers sponsored jointly by the Indian Council of Social
       Science Research and Shreemathi Nathibai Damodar Thackersey
       Women's University.

1016. Mehta, Rama. The Western Educated Hindu Woman. Bombay:
       Asia, 1970.

       Study of fifty women from various areas of India who were
       educated in convent schools and Indian universities.
       Documents their attitudes toward a variety of topics.
       Concludes that these women generally do not maintain a
       commitment to or transmit Hindu traditions.

1017. Misra, Lakshmi. Education of Women in India, 1921-1966.
       Bombay: Macmillan, 1966.

       The author extensively documented study of formal
       education, organized chronologically: the background (1700-
       1921), 1921-1937, 1937-1947, independence through First Five-
       Year Plan, and Second, and Third Five-Year Plan of India.
       Focused on legislation and missionary, governmental, and
       women's organizational activities.

1018. Mitra, Ashok. The Status of Women: Literacy and Employment.
       Bombay: Allied, 1979.

       Separate sections discuss trends in female literacy and
       employment. Numerous tables. The book is a part of a joint
       project of the Indian Council of Social Sciences Research and
       Jawaharlal Nehru University to analyze trends of 1872 to 1971
       censuses and related data.

1019. Nayak-Tellis, Jessie B. Education and Income Generation for
       Women: Non-Formal Approaches. New Delhi: Indian Social
       Institute, 1982.

1020.   Panandikar, Sulabha, Neera Desai, and Kamalini Bhansali, eds.
        Future Trends in Women's Higher Education and the Role of
        the S.N.D.T. Women's University: Report of the Round Table
        Discussion. Bombay: Shreemati Nathibai Damodar Thackersey
        Women's University, 1975.

        This report includes history of SNDT, description of its
        recent programs, results of survey of students (primarily
        with respect to socioeconomic background), paper on "The Role
        and Relevance of the University in Changing Times," a working
        paper highlighting women's higher educational issues,
        discussions, highlights, and recommendations of the editorial
        committee.

1021.   Patel, Tara. Development of Education Among Tribal Women.
        Delhi: Mittal, 1984.

        Reviews several available studies and surveys on different
        aspects of education among tribal women in Gujarat and places
        it in context through an account of the socioeconomic
        conditions of the tribals, a history of education among
        tribals, and an analysis of secondary data on literacy,
        enrollment, and level of education. Some of the aspects
        examined are norms of female education in tribal society;
        reasons for wastage, stagnation, and low development of
        education among tribal women and a comparison with
        educational attainment in other communities.

1022.   Popal, B. F., ed. Women's Education in India (1957-76).
        Bombay: SNDT University, 1972.

1023.   Ramanamma, A. Graduate Employed Women in an Urban Setting.
        Poona: Dastane Ramachandra, 1979.

1024.   Saran, Raksha. Education of Girls and Women in Rural Areas,
        India. New Delhi: Ministry of Education, Government of
        India, 1962.

1025.   Sen, N. B., ed. Development of Women's Education in New
        India. New Delhi: New Book Society of India, 1969.

        Numerous brief articles concerning general and specific
        aspects of female education in India.

1026.   Sengupta, Padmini. Women's Education in India. New Delhi:
        Ministry of Education, Government of India, 1960.

1027. Thackersey, Premlila V. Education of Women: A Key to
       Progress. New Delhi: Ministry of Education and Youth
       Services, Government of India, 1970.

       Reviews history of women's education in India from 1813
       through the post-Independence period. Also considers access
       to higher education and presents problems and future aims.
       Appendixes compare female education trends in India with
       those of other major nations of the world, reproduce
       recommendations of the 1964-66 Education Commission, provide
       recommended readings, and present major educational trends in
       graphic form.

1028. Towards Equality: A Report on the Committee on the Status of
       Women. New Delhi: Ministry of Education, 1975.

1029. Trivedi, Sheela. Non-Formal Education for Women Officers,
       Education Department, U.P.: Report of the State-Level
       Orientation Seminars on Non-Formal Education. Lucknow:
       Literacy House, 1977.

       Report of 1976 seminars organized by the Family Life Centre
       of Literacy House for selected administrators of girls'
       schools and teacher training institutions. Main objective
       was to assess concept and programs of non-formal education
       for girls and women. Includes reports, statistics,
       discussion sheets, list of participants, and so forth. In
       English and Hindi.

1030. Wasi, Muriel. The Educated Woman in Indian Society Today.
       Bombay and New Delhi: McGraw-Hill, 1971.

1031. Y.W.C.A. of India. Educated Women in Indian Society Today:
       A Study. New Delhi: Tata-McGraw Hill, 1971.

       Regarding the Indian woman with higher education and "how
       to use her education most profitably." Many articles are
       relevant to work and employment topics.

       Articles

1032. Agarwal, Bina. "Exploitative Utilisation of Educated
       Womanpower." Journal of Higher Education 2 (Autumn 1976):
       185-96.

       Quantifies the extent of ineffective utilization of women's
       potential among the higher educated, by considering three

aspects in which this gets manifested, viz. women not seeking employment; women seeking employment, but having to wait much longer than men for jobs; women finding employment, but in jobs which do not give the same credit to their qualifications as a man would get. Suggests some methods for improvement.

1033. Ahmad, Karuna. "Equity and Women's Higher Education." Journal of Higher Education 5 (Monsoon 1979): 33-50.

Analyzes the trends in women's higher education with a view to estimate the position and prospects of women. Examines the historical background of the educational development of women and provides a general picture using statistics regarding enrollment, outturn, and women teachers. Draws conclusions from the same.

1034. Ahmad, Karuna. "From Secondary to Higher Education: Focus on Women." Journal of Higher Education 9 (Spring 1984): 349-62.

1035. Ahmad, Karuna. "Studies of Educated Working Women in India; Trends and Issues." Economic and Political Weekly 14 (August 1979): 1435-40.

Studies on Indian women generally assume that better educational and employment opportunities are fundamental to any improvement in the status of women. There is, however, little objective basis to warrant such an assumption; for one thing, women in rural areas as well as urban women from economically weaker sections have always labored hard, and yet their status has always been low.

This paper briefly surveys the dominant trends in the employment of working women in India and argues that what is called for is a new orientation of the research into the question of working women. Since sex-related attributes are rooted in social structure, the contention of the paper is that studies of women in India have to be more contextual than has been traditionally the case, if they are to be relevant.

1036. Ahmad, Shabans. "Education and Purdah Nuances: A Note on Muslim Women in Aligarh." Social Action 27, no. 1 (1977): 45-52.

Studies the relationship between education and observances of purdah among middle-class Muslim women in Aligarh City. Despite completing a secondary education, over one-fourth continued to observe purdah to some extent. Suggests that while the community values secular education for women, it is valued for the most traditional of reasons--enhancement on the marriage market.

1037. Amba Rao, U. "Higher Education and Occupational Values of College Girls." Journal of the Karnataka University (Humanities) 20 (1976): 180-89.

1038. Amba Rao, U. "A Sociological Study of Occupational Choice of Undergraduate Girl Students." Indian Journal of Social Work 37 (April 1978): 1-11.

1039. Bhandari, R. K. "Development of Women's Education." New Frontiers in Education 12 (October-December 1982): 32-7.

1040. Bhasin, Kamala. "Role of Educated Young Women in Changing India." Pp. 214-23 in The Crisis of Changing India, ed. V. D. Sudhir. Delhi: National, 1974.

The article criticizes the small proportion of Indian women receiving vocational, college, or university educations; the quality of the education they are receiving; and the extent to which their educations are wasted. Argues that the potential role of educated Indian women in the future of their country is great.

1041. Bhasin, Kamala. "The Why and How of Literacy for Women: Some Thoughts in the Indian Context." Convergence 17, no. 4 (1984): 37-43.

1042. Bose, Koylaschunder. "On the Education of Hindu Females." Nineteenth Century Studies 10 (April 1975): 193-216.

Impassioned plea for the cause of women's education. Discusses its power to transform Hindu society and the reasons why it has not become widespread. With special reference to conditions in Bengal.

1043. De, S. K. "Women's Education in Bengal from the Battle of Plassy to Sepoy Mutiny." Calcutta Review 161, no. 3 (1961): 255-65.

Describes efforts of Christian missionaries and Bengali merchants and zamindars to foster education since government assumed no responsibility, 1757-1857.

1044. Desai, Neera. "The Pattern of Higher Education of Women and Role of a Women's University." Journal of Higher Education 3 (Monsoon 1977): 5-19.

Examines the existing pattern of women in higher education, and the relevance of a women's university in this context. Conducts an introspective analysis of the SNDT Women's University regarding its evolution, women in higher education, goals and objectives, utilization of education, social composition of women students, and the place of women's universities and institutions in society.

1045. Doraiswami, S. "Educational Advancement and Socioeconomic Participation of Women in India." Design of Educational Programmes for the Promotion of Rural Women. Tehran: International Institute for Adult Literacy Methods, 1975.

Evaluates various efforts to educate rural Indian women and describes literacy and non-formal programs in operation at the time of writing.

1046. Goldstein, Rhoda L. "Students in Saris: College Education in the Lives of Young Indian Women." Journal of Asian and African Studies 5, no. 3 (1970): 193-201.

This is a study of Bangalore college graduates for whom a college degree is a mark of status, an economic asset and an asset or a liability in college education upon marital choice.

1047. Goldstein, Rhoda L. "Tradition and Change in the Roles of Educated Indian Women." Pp. 268-87 in Explorations in the Family and Other Essays: Professor K. M. Kapadia Commemoration Volume, ed. Dhirendra Narain. Bombay: Thacker, 1975.

Attitude survey of ninety-seven female graduates of Bangalore University concerning the importance of marriage; the effects of education and employment on marriage choices, · marital roles and adjustments, and preferred marriage age.

1048. Gould, Ketayun. "Sex Inequalities in the Dual System of Education: The Parsis of Gujarat." Economic and Political Weekly 18 (September 24, 1983): 1668-76.

1049. Jhabvala, Renana and Pratima Shinha. "Girl Students: Between School and Marriage--A Delhi Sample." Pp. 281-87 in Indian Women, ed. Devaki Jain. New Delhi: Publications Division, Ministry of Information and Broadcasting, Government of India, 1975.

Case study material from questionnaires and interviews with female students at Delhi University, India. Concludes that for most, college is a means of spending the time till they get married. Those girls to whom college means more than a period of waiting are definitely the exceptions.

1050. Kale, B. D. "Contours of Female Education and Age at Marriage in Urban India: A District Level Study." Journal of the Institute of Economic Research 4, no. 2 (1969): 34-49.

This article presents average female literacy and age at marriage rates by districts of India in tabular and map forms. Based on 1961 census data.

1051. Kamat, A. R. "Women's Education and Social Change in India." Social Scientists 5, no. 1 (1976): 3-27.

This article is concerned about various aspects of formal education since independence. Major sections describe trends, assess achievements and shortcomings, and consider effects upon employment in other areas.

1052. Kaur, Amrit. "Women Education in India Today." Teacher Today 21 (April-June 1979): 9-24.

1053. Krishnaraj, Maithreyi. "Employment Pattern of University Educated Women and Its Implications." Journal of Higher Education 2 (Spring 1977): 317-28.

1054. Krishnaraj, Maithreyi. "The Status of Women in Science in India." Journal of Higher Education 5 (Spring 1980): 381-93.

1055. Kumar, Kamala and Sadhara Khitha. "Women in Science and Technology." Education Quarterly 34 (October 1982): 8-11.

1056. Mazumdar, Vina. "Higher Education of Women in India." Journal of Higher Education 1, no. 2 (1975): 155-65.

Reviews the progress of women's education in India. Mentions enrollment statistics of women in university education (1951-71), of degree holders and technical personnel in each subject, and of number of women teachers in colleges and universities. Comments on the inter-state variations and examines issues such as differentiation of roles, coeducation, and the social factors governing women's education.

1057. Mazumdar, Vina and Kumud Sharma. "Women's Studies: New
       Perceptions and the Challenges." Economic and Political
       Weekly 14 (January 1979): 113-20.

       Why has the process of understanding women's contribution--
       social, economic, and political--been shrouded in mystery?
       Why were women's concerns generally seen by planners and
       social scientists as welfare rather than development, or as
       peripheral rather than central to the development process?
       What were the historical and ideological dimensions of
       women's roles and status in Indian society?
       Do the empirical dimensions selected by social scientists
       to analyze women's roles and status actually represent
       operational indicators of women's status and are they
       applicable to all groups of women?
       The conceptualization of these problems raises some
       substantial issues and is a challenge to researchers in the
       area of women's studies.

1058. Mehta, Sushila. "Women in Indian Universities." Pp. 162-80
       in Crisis in Indian Universities, ed. G. S. Mansukhani.
       New Delhi: Oxford and IBH, 1972.

       Stresses the rapidly increasing numbers and proportion of
       women in Indian universities and its impact upon these women
       in terms of age at marriage, individualistic values, and
       career opportunities.

1059. Pandey, Rajendra. "Youth's Aspirations for Women's Education
       and Some Correlates." Journal of Social and Economic
       Studies 2, no. 1 (1974): 57-77.

       Attitude survey of rural and urban Male College Students in
       Varanasi District. Correlates results with socioeconomic
       factors.

1060. Phadke, Sindhu. "Special Problems of the Education of
       Women." Pp. 173-200 in Papers in the Sociology of
       Education in India: Papers Prepared as Part of a Project
       in the Sociology of Education in India, Sponsored by the
       Education Commission and the National Council of
       Educational Research and Training, New Delhi, eds. M. S.
       Gore, I. P. Desai, and Suma Chitnis. New Delhi: National
       Council of Educational Research and Training, 1967.

       Reviews nineteenth and twentieth century changes in formal
       education that affected female education, problems associated
       with contemporary female education, and the relationship of
       female education to other socioeconomic factors.

1061. Richey, J. A., ed. "The Beginning of Female Education."
       Selections From Educational Records, Part 2 (1840-1859).
       Delhi: Manager of Publications, Government of India, 1965,
       32-63.

       Extracts from minutes, reports, addresses, and so forth
       regarding female education in mid-nineteenth century India.
       Much information on the founding of particular institutions.

1062. Sen, Keshab Chundra. "The Improvement of Indian Women." Pp.
       205-20 in Sociology in India: An Enquiry into Sociological
       Thinking and Empirical Social Research in the Nineteenth
       Century with Special Reference to Bengal, ed. Bela Dutt
       Gupta. Calcutta: Centre for Sociological Research, 1972.

       Paper read before the Bengal Social Science Association in
       1871. Argues for blending of Oriental and Occidental
       civilizations. Reviews progress of female education and
       women's literary activities in Bengal. Urges establishment
       of Normal Schools, establishment of position of "Inspectress"
       to oversee public and private educational efforts, adult
       classes, secular zenana teachers, "visits to interesting
       places", periodical examinations, and prize distributions.
       Urges conservative fellow countrymen to consider the general
       merits in and benefits of the education of women.

1063. Shah, Madhuri R. "Status and Education of Women in India."
       Journal of Gujarat Research Society 38-39 (1976-77): 15-
       24.

       Briefly reviews formal educational trends in India since
       independence, by sex. Considers goals and objectives of
       women's education and argues that higher education is not
       wasted when married women do not work outside the home.
       Education for women must, however, become more oriented
       toward employment skills.

1064. Sharma, Radha Rani. "Education of Women in India: Inequal-
       ities and Bottlenecks." Education Quarterly 34 (October
       1982): 20-8.

1065. Singhal, Sushila. "The Development of Educated Women in
       India: Reflections of a Social Psychologist." Comparative
       Education 20, no. 3 (1984): 355-70.

       This article is concerned with three broad topics: (1) the
       position of women in educational development in India during
       post-independence period; (2) the existent employment pattern
       of educated women in India; (3) the emergent socio-

psychological perspectives within which research may be
undertaken, and data support can be generated to provide an
understanding of the problems specific to their development
and change.

The percentage of women at different levels of education,
the participation of women in different courses or curricula,
proportion of males and females at various stages of
education as well as a comparison between educational levels
and the rates of participation by women in the labor force
are discussed elaborately. The author then concludes how
social system, and education in particular, promote practices
which maintain exploitative, economic, political, and social
arrangements which reinforce feelings of despair,
resignation, and helplessness among half of the population in
India.

1066.   Srivastava, Vinita. "Professional Education and Attitudes to
        Female Employment: A Study of Married Working Women in
        Chandigarh." Social Action 27, no. 1 (1977): 19-32.

        Survey found that length of education, particularly
        exposure to a college education, and work experience have a
        greater effect upon job satisfaction than does type of
        education in Chandigarh, India.

1067.   Swaminathan, M. S. "Women and Rural Development." New
        Frontiers in Education 12 (July-September 1982): 56-63.

1068.   Vreede-De Stuers, Cora. "Attitude of Jaipur Girl Students
        Towards Family Life." Pp. 151-62 in Explorations in the
        Family and Other Essays: Professor K. M. Kapadia
        Commemoration Volume, ed. Dhirendra Narain. Bombay:
        Thacker, 1975.

        Results of interviews and participant observation with 203
        university students concerning their attitudes toward the
        joint family in Jaipur, India. Although overall attitudes
        varied considerably, low-income students were more likely to
        favor and high-income students to dislike joint family life.
        Notes a degree of ambivalence in students' responses.

1069.   Wasi, Muriel. "Educating Women in India: Ends and Means."
        Education Quarterly 34 (October 1982): 1-5.

NEPAL

Books

1070. Ghimire, Durga, ed. Women and Development. Kathmandu:
       Centre for Economic Development Administration, Tribhuvan
       University, 1977.

       Papers and proceedings from a 1975 seminar on women and
       development in Nepal sponsored by CEDA. Includes
       introduction, program schedule, list of participants,
       photographs and the following papers, with commentary:
       "Social Status of Nepali Women" by Durga Ghimire, "Role of
       Women in Economic Development" by Meena Acharya, "A
       Daughter's Right to Inherit Family Norm and the Role of
       Women" by Chapala Pandy, "Women and Education" by Lila Devi,
       and "Role of Women (sic) Organization for the Development of
       Women" by Punya Prabha Devi Dhungana.

1071. Junge, Barbara and Shashi M. Shrestha. "Another Barrier
       Broken: Teaching Village Girls to Read in Nepal." Reading
       Teacher 37 (May 1984): 846-52.

       Points out that overcoming illiteracy among females in
       Nepal requires overcoming cultural bias as well. Describes a
       program designed especially for young girls with no
       schooling.

1072. Shrestha, Bihari K. Equality of Access of Women to Education
       in Pokhara: A Sociological Survey. Kathmandu: Centre for
       Economic Development and Administration, 1973.

       Results of a sociological survey that focused on
       socioeconomic factors relating to local education for girls,
       teacher training for women, and the extent of migration from
       surrounding villages and its effect on recruitment of female
       teachers. Relates female education to local hierarchy,
       economic condition of family, and education of household
       head. Points to various limitations on female recruitment to
       teaching profession.

PAKISTAN

Books

1073.   Ahmad, Anis. Muslim Women and Higher Education: A Case for
        Separate Institutions for Women. Islamabad: Institute of
        Policy Studies, 1984.

1074.   Education and the Veil. Karachi: Peer Mahomed Ebrahim
        Trust, 1975.

1075.   Harley, Barry. Mohalla Schools, Old Traditions Lead to New
        Hopes for Educating Girls; A Case for UNICEF Support.
        Islamabad: UNICEF, 1979.

1076.   Hashmi, Salima. Education of Rural Women in West Pakistan.
        Lyallpur: West Pakistan Agricultural University Press,
        1968.

        Argues for widespread rural female education. Chapters on
        primary, secondary, and higher education briefly review
        nineteenth and twentieth century history in India and
        Pakistan, discuss contemporary circumstances, describe
        programs in other countries, and present recommendations
        regarding the levels. Also considers education for the
        gifted, vocational and technical education, religious
        education, adult education, role of youth organizations, and
        views of various Pakistani educationists.

1077.   Hassan, Iftikhar. Future Educational Aspirations of Rural
        Females. Islamabad: National Institute of Psychology,
        1970.

1078.   Hussain, Asaf. The Educated Pakistani Girl: A Sociological
        Study. Karachi: Ima Printers, 1963.

        Presents a generalized picture of various types of educated
        females and their attitudes. Discusses conservative and
        modern women, love, marriage, career women versus homemakers,
        sex consciousness, and leisure activities. Author states
        that he undertook the study out of concern for the clash
        between modern educated women and the inability of most men
        to accept them. Based on questionnaires, diaries, personal
        observations, etc., which are liberally quoted. Probably
        conducted in Karachi.

1079. Qurashi, Salma Mustafa. Female Education in the Peshawar
       District, West Pakistan. Peshawar: Board of Economic
       Enquiry, N.W.F., Peshawar University, 1960.

       Reviews types of institutions, financial support,
       curricula, family influences, and details education.
       Includes numerous statistics, recommendations, and
       photographs. Considers all levels of formal education.
       Based upon interviews with heads of institutions, teachers,
       parents, and students.

1080. Qureshi, Nuzat K. Role of Female Education in Development
       Planning of N.W.F.P. Peshawar: Board of Economic Enquiry,
       North West Frontier Province, University of Peshawar, 1972.

       Interviews with educated and uneducated women of Peshawar
       District document the substantial positive effects of
       education on what are generally considered their primary
       duties to family and household and on their secondary duties
       to community. Briefly reviews the history of Muslim
       education in the subcontinent and surveys contemporary female
       education and professional employment patterns in N.W.F.P.
       With recommendations and numerous tables.

       Article

1081. Korson, J. Henry. "Career Constraints Among Women Graduate
       Students in a Developing Society: West Pakistan." Journal
       of Comparative Family Studies 1, no. 1 (1970): 82-100.

       Data from interviews with female graduate students from
       Karachi and Lahore. Presents socioeconomic profile of this
       group, family attitudes toward daughter's employment, and a
       discussion of the developmental drain of educated but
       nonemployed women. With comparison between the two cities.

SRI LANKA

       Book

1082. Sri Lanka Foundation Institute. Education of Women for
       Involvement in National Development: Report of Regional
       Seminar, S.E. Asia Held at the Sri Lanka Foundation
       Institute, Colombo, November 6-11, 1975. Colombo: Sri
       Lanka Foundation Institute, 1975.

CHAPTER 24

EDUCATION OF MINORITIES: GENERAL

INDIA

Books

1083. Beg, Nasirullah. Educational Rights of Minorities. Lucknow:
National Herald Press, 1978.

1084. Patel, Surabhi P. Equality of Educational Opportunity in
India: A Myth or Reality? New Delhi: National, 1983.

1085. Yagin, A. Constitutional Protection of Minority Educational
Institutions in India. New Delhi: Deep and Deep, 1982.

Discusses the opposing claims of the state and of
minorities, in conducting educational institutions. Some of
the questions discussed, from a judicial and constitutional
perspective, are: minority status and rights, recognition
and affiliation of institutions, state aid, medium of
instruction, admission, reservations, and administrative
questions.

Articles

1086. Garg, V. P. "Equality in Education: An Indian Profile."
New Frontiers in Education 15 (April-June 1985): 67-88.

1087. Ramaswami, Uma. "Education and Inequality." Economic and
Political Weekly 20 (September 7, 1985): 1523-29.

CHAPTER 25

EDUCATION OF RELIGIOUS MINORITIES

INDIA

Book

1088. Sharma, Krishna Dev. Education of a National Minority: A
      Case of Indian Muslims. New Delhi: Kalamkar Prakashan,
      1978.

      Studies the question of equal educational opportunities and
      the factors within the educational system and the Muslim
      community that inhibit the education of a minority, in the
      context of a history of Muslim education. Based on different
      data collecting techniques and respondents such as students,
      teachers, parents, administrators and community leaders
      connected with schools in Delhi. Some of the conclusions are
      that Muslims are not proportionately represented in schools,
      generally go to schools with poorer facilities and factors in
      the community, such as favor of Urdu medium and religious
      education and discouragement of women's education, tend to
      inhibit educational development.

Articles

1089. Ahmad, Imtiaz. "Muslim Educational Backwardness: An
      Inferential Analysis." Economic and Political Weekly 16
      (September 1981): 1457-65.

      The central argument of this paper is that the explanations
      often advanced to account for the educational backwardness of
      Muslims in contemporary India rest upon certain questionable
      assumptions. These are, one, that Muslims are an aggregate
      community; and two, that the appeal of education is universal
      to all social strata. Following from this, if indeed Muslims
      are educationally backward, it is because of some innate

religious conservatism which discourages pursuit of secular
education, or because of an acute 'minority complex'.

This paper questions these assumptions and argues that
educational opportunities are likely to be exploited in any
community by those sections that are oriented to employment
in the professions and services. Amongst the Muslims, this
social strata has not only been historically quite small, but
was further reduced in size in the wake of the creation of
Pakistan.

The educational backwardness of Indian Muslims should
therefore be attributed not to any 'religious fanaticism' or
'minority complex' but to the small size of the social strata
whose members can be expected to seek educational
opportunities.

1090. Al-Nadui, Rashid and S. M. Wazeh. "Traditional Muslim
        Education in India: Origin, Curricular Revisions and the
        Present-Day Condition." Muslim Education Quarterly 2, no.
        4 (1985): 37-60.

1091. Kamat, A. R. "Literacy and Education among Muslims: A
        Note." Economic and Political Weekly 16 (June 6, 1981):
        1031-33.

        Examines the educational status of Muslims in post-
        Independence India and questions some of the assumptions
        regarding the causes of the backwardness of the community.
        Suggests that this is due to the lack of a continuing
        formation of a lower and middle class employed in the
        professions. The identity crisis following the partition of
        the country, neglect of and discrimination against Muslims by
        the larger Hindu community are seen to be factors
        discriminating against Muslims in the matter of education and
        jobs.

1092. Lalwani, K. C. "Equalizing Educational Opportunities."
        Indian Educational Review 11 (April 1976): 18-28.

        For this paper, education is taken as a whole overlooking
        its break-up into primary secondary and higher.
        Illustrations are drawn from the personal experience of the
        writer. Statistical data are avoided.

1093. Mohiuddin, Syed Ghulan. "Modern Education and the
        Educational Problems of the Indian Muslim." Muslim
        Education Quarterly 2, no. 4 (1985): 61-75.

1094.   Sharma, K. D.   "A Comparative Study of Educational
        Opportunities: Muslims vis-a-vis Other Communities."
        Indian Educational Review 11 (April 1976):   47-55.

        The approach to education is always conditioned by the
        system of government that a country chooses for itself.
        Democracy puts more premium on the individual, and provides
        him greater freedom.   But a socialistic form of government,
        with its emphasis on social good, comparatively affords
        lesser freedom for the individual.   India after attaining in-
        dependence struck the golden mean between 'pure' democracy
        and 'pure' socialism.   In December 1954, the Indian
        Parliament ratified the broad objectives of the government
        policy as the attainment of 'Socialistic Pattern' of society
        through democratic means.

1095.   Wright, Theodore P.   "Muslim Education in India at the
        Crossroads: The Case of Aligarh."   Pacific Affairs 39
        (Spring-Summer, 1966):   50-63.

        Discusses the problems facing by the Muslim University-
        Aligarh--in India in socio-political context.   The main focus
        of the article is on the attitude and interests of four types
        of Muslims: traditional, fundamentalists, modern and
        secular, in events in Aligarh.   It seems that most
        individuals and organization in the first three categories
        regard the preservation of some degree of Muslim
        distinctiveness in the University as symbolic of a condition
        vital to the survival of community in India.   The
        secularists, who have isolated themselves by arousing fears
        that Aligarh will be "de-Muslimised," could probably reassure
        the modernists if only they could demonstrate that Muslim
        youth and culture will not be discriminated against elsewhere
        in India and this they cannot do in short run with the best
        good will.   For the modernist is basically more concerned
        with the fate of Muslims than with Islam.   It was for them
        that Aligarh was founded.   The traditionalists and
        fundamentalists who opposed Sir Syed Ahmad Khan's ideas and
        efforts cannot expect by championing the university now
        belatedly to transform it into their own image.

CHAPTER 26

EDUCATION OF SCHEDULED CASTES AND TRIBES

INDIA

Books

1096. Adiseshiah, M. S. and S. Ramanathan. Educational Problems of
       Scheduled Castes and Scheduled Tribes in Tamil Nadu.
       Madras: Institute of Developmental Studies, 1974.

1097. Aikara, Jacob. Scheduled Castes and Higher Education: A
       Study of College Students in Bombay. Poona: Dastane
       Ramchandra, 1980.

       Evaluates the impact of the provisions made by the Central
       and State Governments for scheduled caste students and the
       academic performance of the beneficiaries in colleges in
       Bombay city. The scale of dropout and stagnation is
       estimated and factors responsible are analyzed. Scheduled
       caste students who persist in education are found to be
       inferior in socioeconomic and academic background and in
       performance in studies as compared to non-scheduled caste
       students. There is a high incidence of stagnation and
       dropout. However, enrollment shows increase. Selective
       enrollment from the scheduled castes accompanied by greater
       academic assistance and facilities in the college environment
       are suggested as remedial measures.

1098. Ambasht, N. K. A Critical Study of Tribal Education: With
       Special Reference to Ranchi District. Delhi: S. Chand,
       1970.

1099. Chauhan, B. R. Scheduled Castes and Education. Meerut:
       Anu, 1975.

1100. Chitnis, Suma. Literacy and Educational Development among
       the Scheduled Castes of Maharashtra. Bombay: Tata
       Institute of Social Sciences, 1974.

1101. Chitnis, Suma. A Long Way to Go: Report on a Survey of
       Scheduled Caste High School and College Students in 15
       States of India. New Delhi: Allied, 1981.

       A descriptive and analytical study that offers insights
       into several problems of education of this disadvantaged
       community. Covers issues such as investment and returns on
       the education of the scheduled castes, prejudices
       encountered, changes in the outlook of the community and
       prospects of occupational mobility. Offers suggestions for
       further action and research. This all-India report is based
       on a survey of the educational problems of scheduled castes
       sponsored by the Indian Council of Social Science Research.

1102. D'Souza, Victor S. Educational Inequalities among Scheduled
       Castes: A Case Study in the Punjab. Chandigarh:
       Department of Sociology, Punjab University, 1980.

       An attempt to explain the gap in educational attainment
       that exists between the scheduled castes and the rest of
       society and the growing gap that exists among the scheduled
       castes themselves. The arguments are based on census and
       other data. Concludes that the structured division of
       scheduled castes into mutually exclusive occupations and
       their distribution over educationally and socioeconomically
       differentiated regions, is responsible for their growing
       disparity. Points out that state educational aid assumes a
       certain supplementation from the family, which certain groups
       are unable to provide by virtue of their economic position,
       which in turn is determined by their caste occupation and
       residence in poor areas. State initiated institutional
       structures that would, apart from financial aid, look after
       supplementary needs and ensure that education reaches the
       socio-economically lowest, is suggested.

1103. Gangrade, K. D. Educational Problems of Scheduled Castes in
       Haryana. Delhi: Delhi Schools of Social Work, 1974.

1104. Goyal, Bhagat Ram. Educating Harijans. Gurgaon: Academic,
       1981.

       Presents a history of the Harijans within the context of
       efforts for their upliftment, educational and otherwise. The
       data on the conditions of Harijans is primarily based on
       government records, reports, and other primary data.
       Evaluates the approaches and efforts of government, social
       reformers and the impact of socio-religious reform movements.
       A perspective for the future is drawn out this analysis of
       past and contemporary situations.

1105. Lal, Sheo Kumar and Umed Raj Nahar. Higher Education:
       Scheduled Castes and Scheduled Tribes. Jodhpur: Jainsons,
       1978.

       A survey of the social background, academic life and
       progress of scheduled caste and tribe, school and college
       students in five districts of Rajasthan. Also covers their
       social life and outlook, their perceptions of status and
       facilities provided. The opinions of concerned teachers are
       presented. Draws out the implications for policy,
       administration, and research.

1106. Lokshmanna, C. and N. Inniah. Depressed Group Students:
       Between Yesterday and Tomorrow. Trivandrum: College Book
       House, 1977.

       A survey of high school level, scheduled caste/tribe
       students in Andhra Pradesh, based on a sample of students and
       teachers from nine districts. Examines the use of
       educational facilities and the socio-cultural climate in
       which educational schemes are being implemented. Presents an
       educational profile of the scheduled castes/tribes in the
       state and of the students, in particular.

1107. Malik, S. Social Integration of Scheduled Castes. New
       Delhi: Abhinav, 1979.

1108. Ministry of Education and Culture. Development of Scheduled
       Castes and Scheduled Tribes in India 1967-68 to 1977-78.
       New Delhi, 1983.

       This volume describes the development of education for
       scheduled castes and scheduled tribes in the states over a
       ten-year span. This report covers mainly the enrollment of
       children belonging to S.C. and S.T. at different levels of
       education with all possible bifurcations into a different
       standard of education. Sex-wise and state-wise comparison
       has also been given. A brief description of the general
       steps taken by government for the rapid expansion and
       qualitative improvement of education is also given.

1109. Naik, T. B. Impact of Education on the Bhils: Cultural
       Change in the Tribal Life of Madhya Pradesh. New Delhi:
       Research Programme Committee, Planning Commission, 1969.

       An intensive, social anthropological study of the impact of
       education on different social institutions among the Bhil
       tribals, based on a selection of fifteen villages in all,
       from two different regions in Madhya Pradesh state, taking

into consideration proportions of schools and tribal population. Data drawn from a multi-technique approach are presented as a history of education among the Bhils, a description of their present state, an analysis of change brought about by education in different institutions such as marriage, family and kinship, political and social structures. Also attempts to discover the social base of those who get educated.

1110. National Institute of Educational Planning and Administration, New Delhi. Scheduled Castes and Scheduled Tribes in IITs: A Study of Five States. New Delhi: NIEPA, 1983.

This monograph investigates the exposure of scheduled castes and scheduled tribes, the two deprived groups, to industrial training facilities in the country. The five states selected for intensive study are Andhra Pradesh, Bihar, Gujarat, Madhya Pradesh, and Maharashtra. Besides analyzing the utilization of facilities and reasons for under-utilization and dropout, an attempt is also made to assess the impact of training in terms of employment, emoluments, and sector and place of work of the ex-trainees. Finally the availability, adequacy, and implementation aspect of various incentives and facilities for the deprived in these institutions has been studied. The monograph raises some important questions regarding the industrial training institutes, viz., relationships with the +2 vocational stream; the scope for vertical linkages between industrial training institutions and polytechnics, and the scope for collaboration between the industrial training institutions and industries.

1111. Nautiyal, K. C. and Y. D. Sharma. Equalisation of Educational Opportunities for Scheduled Castes and Scheduled Tribes. New Delhi: National Council of Educational Research and Training, 1979.

A macro-level analysis of the educational achievements of scheduled castes and scheduled tribes through data on enrollment at different stages of school education. Presents a state and community-wise, comparative, statistical profile of the progress of education in order to find out the extent of regional disparaties at different levels of education. A sharp decline in the co-efficient of educational equality in several states during the period 1960-61 and 1970-71, is one of the findings. Strategies for realizing the goal of equalization of educational opportunities are suggested. Calls for planning, based on a fuller understanding of educational needs and the cultural milieu of this section of the population.

1112.   Pimpley, Prakash N.   Profile of Scheduled Caste Students: The Case of Punjab. Chandigarh: Department of Sociology, Punjab University, 1980.

Examines the status of scheduled caste school and college students in Punjab State. Data collected through the multi-stage random sampling method were earlier presented in two reports sanctioned by the Indian Council of Social Science Research, as part of a national survey of scheduled caste students. Covers demographic characteristics, academic progress, study habits, comprehension abilities, educational and occupational aspirations, politicization, social life, and views on various social issues. Stresses the need to educate the parental generation in the causes of backwardness and in the ways towards structural transformation.

1113.   Rangari, Ashok D.   Indian Caste System and Education. New Delhi: Deep and Deep, 1984.

A comparative study of scheduled caste and non-scheduled caste college students in Aurangabad district, with respect to their self-images, social relationships, intelligence, and academic achievement. Among the conclusions is that the differences between scheduled caste and non-scheduled caste students are minimized in cases where they are of the same socioeconomic class.

1114.   Rathnaiah, E. V.   Structured Constraints in Tribal Education: A Regional Study. New Delhi: Sterling, 1977.

Analyzes the ecological, socioeconomic, and educational constraints on the educability of the tribal community of Adilabad district, Andhra Pradesh state. Views structural variables as playing a predominant role in either facilitating or constraining the diffusion of education and modernization. Assesses the pattern of educational facilities available to and the educational attainments of the scheduled tribes, as compared to that of the general population.

1115.   Shah, Vimal P.   The Educational Problems of Scheduled Castes and Scheduled Tribe School and College Students in India: A Statistical Profile. New Delhi: Allied, 1982.

Contains tables presenting state-wise distribution, by sex and hostellers/non-hostellers of almost all the variables on

which data were collected for an Indian Council of Social
Science Research sponsored, nation-wide study covering
fourteen states for the scheduled castes and twelve states
for the scheduled tribes.   Data are provided to enable
further examination.

1116.   Shah, Vimal P. and Tara Patel.   Who Goes to College?:
        Scheduled Caste/Tribe Post-Matric Scholars in Gujarat.
        Ahmedabad: Rachana Prakashan, 1977.

        An empirical study with secondary data analysis on the
        utilization of government assistance for higher education by
        the scheduled castes/tribes residing in different districts
        of Gujarat.   The data is based on fresh/renewal application
        forms filled in by awardees in 1967-68 and 1971-72.   Examines
        characteristics such as academic background and courses
        taken, socioeconomic status, and place of residence of the
        beneficiaries.   Concludes that although the scheduled
        castes/tribes have been able to modestly improve their
        educational achievement, and policy of financial assistance
        and facilities in admission to educational institutions has
        not put them on par with other sections of society.   Only a
        few scheduled caste and tribal groups are able to benefit
        from the scholarships and males predominate among them.
        Residential nearness to the institutional concentrations
        facilitates achievement of higher education.

1117.   Siddiqui, M. K. A.   Educating a Backward Minority.   Calcutta:
        Abadi, 1984.

1118.   Yadav, S. K.   Harijan Awareness of Educational Schemes:
        Antecedents and Consequences.   Gurgaon: Academic, 1983.

        The specific focus of the study is on the Harijans'
        awareness of the schemes set up for their educational
        progress.   The Harijans have been considered the lowest rung
        of the caste system.   This study involves identification of
        specific schemes for promoting the education of the Harijans
        in a selected location, and a study of the awareness by heads
        of family and students of the schemes for their educational
        progress.   The book outlines the operational plan and
        strategy for conducting the investigation.   The study focuses
        on the problem faced by the heads of family at the time of
        availing themselves of educational schemes and the solutions
        suggested by them to tackle the same.   The problems have been
        discussed with particular reference to the conditions of
        eligibility, value of scholarship, selection of candidates,
        duration and renewal of stipends/scholarships, mode of
        payment, mode of publicity, and submission of applications.

The last chapter is divided into two major sections. The
first section deals with the summary of findings. The second
section outlines implications of the study.

Articles

1119.   Amba, Rao U. "Higher Education and Occupational Mobility
        among the Scheduled Caste Youth." Journal of Higher
        Education 1, no. 3 (1976): 305-14.

1120.   Chaudhuri, Saroj Kanti. "Educational Progress in Rural
        Bengal: A Study of Four Villages." Economic and Political
        Weekly 5 (February 1970): 301-306.

        An attempt is made in this article to assess educational
        progress among backward castes in rural West Bengal. Four
        villages of south Bengal in which Scheduled Castes and Tribes
        predominate numerically, have been studied. The period
        covered is roughly that of the Second and Third Plans.
        The conclusion that emerges is that the educational
        condition of the backward castes did not improve during this
        period. At the end of the period, from 65 to 90 percent of
        the backward caste population was still illiterate. Among
        females, illiteracy levels ranged between 90 and 100 percent.
        School registration of children of school-going age, a
        crucial indicator of future trends in literacy, went up in
        two of the four villages studied and down in the other two.
        It is significant that the deterioration had taken place in
        those villages where the backward castes were mainly
        agricultural laborers or share-croppers.

1121.   Chauhan, B. L. and G. Narayana. "Problems of Education among
        Scheduled Caste Students in Uttar Pradesh." Social Change
        6 (March-June 1976): 13-17.

1122.   Chitnis, Suma. "Education for Equality: Case of Scheduled
        Caste in Higher Education." Economic and Political Weekly
        7 (August 1972): 1675-81.

        The effort to educate the Scheduled Castes may be viewed as
        part of a two-pronged attempt to improve their status. Laws
        against untouchability and against discrimination by caste
        and the reservation of seats in educational institutions and
        jobs are, between them, expected to clear the ground for the
        equality of the Scheduled Castes. Education is expected to
        clear the ground for the quality of the Scheduled Castes.

Education is expected to equip them to occupy the ground thus cleared.

While the purpose behind the generous provision of educational facilities for the Scheduled Castes is clear and well-reasoned, the approach is naive in its assumptions, viz, (a) that the facilities provided would be optimally and equitably used; (b) that given the opportunity for school and college education, members of the Scheduled Castes would measure up on par with those who are backed by a tradition of formal education; and (c) that the policy of reservations would best serve the attainment of equality for the Scheduled Castes. Experience indicates that these assumptions are unrealistic and educational programs based on them have led to the perpetuation of old inequalities and the creation of some new ones.

This paper presents some data regarding the situation of Scheduled Caste students in higher education in the country in general and in Maharashtra in particular to indicate the nature of the anomalies that exist.

1123. Chitnis, Suma. "Education of the Scheduled Castes." Journal of Higher Education 1 (Autumn 1975): 167-78.

Reviews the policy of protective discrimination for the scheduled castes, its effects on enrollment and literacy. Data is given out from a study on the educational problems of the scheduled caste and a scheduled tribe school and college students, sponsored by the ICSSR and a series of studies on education of the scheduled castes conducted by the Tata Institute of Social Sciences. Highlights issues such as poor enrollment in professional and technical courses, enrollment in inferior institutions, poor performance, interstate and interdistrict differences, disparity between sexes and intercaste inequality, and suggests the need for continuing assistance.

1124. Kamat, A. R. "Education and Social Change Amongst the Scheduled Caste and Scheduled Tribes." Economic and Political Weekly (August 1981): 1279-84.

This paper discusses some features of social change associated with the advance of education among the scheduled castes and scheduled tribes during the post-independence period.

It considers these changes in their three constituents: changes within the segment of SC/ST, changes in the wider caste Hindu society, and changes in the inter-relations between caste Hindu society and the SC/ST segment. The discussion of the inter-relation between the SC and caste

Hindu society touches mainly upon the problem of
untouchability and caste discrimination while in the case of
scheduled tribes, the problem of transition from tribal
isolation and backwardness to assimilation into and greater
interaction with the rest of Indian society is touched upon.

1125. Omitted.

1126. Karlekar, Malavika. "Higher Education and the Scheduled
        Castes." Journal of Higher Education 1 (Autumn 1975):
        179-88.

1127. Kirpal, V. "Higher Education for the Scheduled Castes and
        Scheduled Tribes." Economic and Political Weekly 13
        (January-February 1978): 165-69.

        The Scheduled Castes and the Scheduled Tribes form a large
        community and the educational facilities and incentives
        offered to them are substantial. Yet the community remains
        educationally backward.
        This paper seeks to find out why education has not spread
        among the Scheduled Castes and Scheduled Tribes, and why
        seats reserved for them in institutes of higher education
        cannot be filled for absence of qualified applicants.
        It also offers some suggestions for the spread of education
        among Scheduled Castes and Tribes and concludes with a brief
        case study of the programme of reservation of seats for
        Scheduled Caste and Scheduled Tribe students in the Indian
        Institute of Technology, Bombay.

1128. Kirpal, V. and others. "Scheduled Caste and Tribe Students
        in Higher Education: A Study of an IIT." Economic and
        Political Weekly 20 (July 20, 1985): 1238-48.

1129. Lal, Shivkumar. "Scheduled Caste College Students in
        Rajasthan." Journal of Higher Education 1 (Autumn 1975):
        244-99.

1130. Minz, Nirmal. "Higher Education in the Tribal Context." New
        Frontiers in Education 12 (January-March 1982).

1131. Premi, Kusum K. "Educational Equality and Economic
        Opportunities: A Comparative Study of Scheduled Castes and
        Non-Scheduled Castes." Journal of Higher Education 9
        (Spring 1984): 363-73.

1132. Premi, Kusum K. "Educational Opportunities for the Scheduled
        Castes: Role of Protective Discrimination in

Equalisation." Economic and Political Weekly 9 (November 1974): 1902-10.

Marked progress has been made by the scheduled castes in education, as is manifest from the rise in their literacy rates, enrollment co-efficients, and the proportion of their numbers in Class I and II categories of jobs in Central and state services. Two questions still seem relevant from the point of view of equalisation of educational opportunities for the scheduled castes vis-a-vis others. (1) To what extent can this educational progress be attributed to the special concessions?; (2) Is the scheme of special facilities conceived in the spirit of ensuring equality to all the members of the scheduled castes or, in the process, do they suffer from deficiencies that tend to create certain subtle inequalities among them?

1133. Rath, R. "Problems of Equalization of Educational Opportunities for the Tribal Children." Indian Educational Review 11 (April 1976): 56-74.

1134. Shah, B. V. "Education and Social Change among Tribals in India." Sociological Bulletin 28 (March and September 1979): 25-45.

1135. Singh, T. P. and others. "Educational Aspirations of Scheduled Caste Students in Eastern Uttar Pradesh." Social Change 6 (March-June 1976): 18-25.

1136. Srivastava, L. R. N. "The Role of Education in Modernization of Two Tribes in Chotanagpur." Indian Educational Review 6 (January 1971): 162-82.

This study was undertaken to find out the role of education in the modernization of two tribes of Bihar--the Munda and the Oraon. The findings reveal that the educated tribesmen, as compared to the uneducated ones, are more mobile spatially, occupationally, and socially. Their emphatic capacity has increased and they are capable of choosing new individuals, roles, and situations, and participating in socioeconomic and political activities. Education has also made the tribesmen more competent to take interest in public matters and to express opinions thereon.

1137. Verghese, Alexander V. "Education, Earning and Occupation of Weaker Castes." Journal of Higher Education 9 (Spring 1984): 373-80.

1138. Zachariah, Matthew. "Positive Discrimination in Education
      for India's Scheduled Castes: A Review of the Problem,
      1950-1970." Comparative Education Review, 16 (February
      1972): 16-29.

      This paper discusses the legal and other steps taken in
      India from about 1950 to approximately 1970 for implementing
      educational discrimination in favor of certain "weaker
      sections of the people." Examines the various problems which
      have arisen in the wake of this government policy of positive
      discrimination, such as legal, administrative, and socio-
      political problems. Finally, it raises questions such as
      whether the disadvantages of the Scheduled Castes are
      primarily due to poverty or untouchability.

CHAPTER 27

EDUCATION OF THE URBAN/RURAL POOR

BANGLADESH

Book

1139. Mia, Ahmadullah, ed. Working with the Poor in Bangladesh:
Ten Case Studies and Lesson Plans for Social Work Education
and Allied Fields. Manila: United Nations Social Welfare
and Development Centre for Asia and the Pacific, 1980.

INDIA

Books

1140. Bag, Dulal Chandra. Impact of Education on Some Backward
Communities of West Bengal: Study Based on West Dinajpur.
Calcutta: OPS, 1984.

Studies the diffusion of education and its effects on
backward communities in West Dinajpur district of West Bengal
state, through an empirical study placed in historical
context and a multi-disciplinary approach. Probes the intra
and inter-community social relations in their linkages with
the peripheral society. Finds that instead of education
filtering down to the grass root level there is a rise of
multi-elitism and the stimulation of a process of
'bhadraization' in behavior and attitudes. Underlines the
weakness of educational policies in their politico-economic
context.

1141. Mathur, Anil K. Educational and Learning Needs of Slum
Dwellers: A Report of Survey (Psychosocio-Economic Survey
of Five Slums of Bikaner, India). Bikaner: Vikas Bal
Niketan, 1980.

279

1142. Patel, Surabhi. Education of Children From Urban Slums. New
       Delhi: Department of School Education, National Council of
       Educational Research and Training, 1980.

       Deals with major dimensions of the slum situation such as
       its growth, factors responsible for the slow spread of
       education in the slum areas, the current education process,
       teaching and evaluation strategies, organizational aspects,
       and community participation.

1143. Rath, R. and others. Cognitive Abilities and School
       Achievement of the Socially Disadvantaged Children in
       Primary Schools. Bombay: Allied, 1979.

       Studies the cognitive abilities of school children from
       different socioeconomic backgrounds, with a view to improving
       the academic achievement of children from disadvantaged
       groups. Data are based on testing 110, fifth standard
       children each from Brahmin, scheduled tribe and scheduled
       caste households, for cognitive abilities. These data are
       analyzed in their relation to examination marks, home
       background, and attitudes of students, teachers, and parents,
       to see how these latter contribute towards the development of
       cognitive abilities. The study underlines the retardation of
       the cognitive development of disadvantaged groups during the
       school years, as a result of an irrelevant pattern of
       education, and suggests alternatives.

SRI LANKA

       Books

1144. Gnanamuttu, G. A. Education and the Indian Plantation Worker
       in Sri Lanka. Colombo: Gnanamuttu, 1977.

1145. Workers Education in Asia. Colombo: Sri Lanka Foundation
       Institute, 1980.

       Article

1146. Kapferer, Judith. "Four Schools in Sri Lanka." Comparative
       Education 11 (March 1975): 31-41.

One of the most disturbing aspects of education in Sri Lanka is the tremendous gap in provision of educational facilities for rural and urban children. Although this problem slightly redressed by the establishment of government central schools, these are limited in number, and serve merely as recruiting agencies for the elite. The authors examines four schools, their memberships (staff and students), and facilities provided, and illustrates that rural children in Sri Lanka are, despite government efforts, disadvantaged in terms of social mobility through educational achievement.

CHAPTER 28

EDUCATIONAL POLICY AND PLANNING

BANGLADESH

Books

1147. Bangladesh. Planning Commission. Manpower Section. An Educational Geography of Bangladesh: Locational Availability Against Ideal Requirement. Dhaka: The Section, 1974.

1148. Development in Education in Bangladesh 1975-77: A Country Report, 1977.

The report on education in Bangladesh summarizes educational trends since 1971 and objectives of the first five-year plan (1973-78). Population growth and illiteracy are the two major national problems. During the liberation war, many students left schools to join the army, and most school buildings were either demolished or closed down. Thus, immediate tasks for education involve reopening schools to provide minimum physical facilities, and defining the function of education in the changed sociocultural context. Strategies for national educational development include integration of education with rural development, promotion of nonformal education, and introduction of population education. Efforts to eliminate illiteracy are aimed mainly at the adult population. Attitudes must be changed to accept technological developments; literacy programs must encourage self-reliance and introduce technological innovation. Nonformal and community education programs stress these needs. In the schools, Bangla has replaced English as the language of instruction, but textbooks are not readily available in Bangla. Reorganization of the overly centralized system of educational administration is needed.

283

1149. Ritzen, Jozef M. and Judith B. Balderston. Methodology for
      Planning Technical Education: With a Case Study of
      Polytechnics in Bangladesh. New York: Praeger, 1975.

Articles

1150. Dove, Linda A. "Educational Policy in Bangladesh, 1978-81:
      Promise and Performance in Political Perspective."
      Comparative Education 19, no. 1 (1983): 73-88.

      Examines the main thrust of educational policymaking in
      Bangladesh during 1971-81 and compares policy goals with
      achievements. Finds there have been failures, but suggests
      underlying explanations for the persistent gap between policy
      goals and implementation come from the wider socio-political
      context in which educational policy is formulated and carried
      out.

1151. Hossain, Serwar. "The Development of Libraries for Education
      in Bangladesh." International Review of Education 29, no.
      1 (1983): 77-82.

INDIA

Books

1152. Adiseshiah, Malcolm S., ed. Education Perspective for Tamil
      Nadu: Backdrop to the Learning Society. New Delhi:
      Indian Council of Social Science Research, 1978.

      Part of a research project that reviews the implementation
      of the recommendations of the Kothari Commission and
      formulates plans for the development of education during 1976
      to 1986. These background papers view the formal and non-
      formal educational system in Tamil Nadu state, in retrospect
      and prospect, and discusses questions of education,
      employment, and management of education.

1153. Adiseshiah, Malcolm S. Indian Education in 2001. New Delhi:
      National Council of Educational Research and Training,
      1975.

      Two lectures delivered in September, 1975. The first
      presents a profile of population, production, poverty, and

unemployment in 2001. The second predicts developments in education--quantitative aspects, innovations, vocationalization, and democratization of education. Concludes with suggestions for curriculum design, technologies, evaluation, planning and restructuration in education.

1154. Agarwal, J. C. Development and Planning of Modern Education, with special Reference to India. New Delhi: Vikas, 1982.

A presentation of the state of education in India, its policies and development since independence. Based on and presents data from various commissions, committees, surveys, reports, and the 1971 census. Draws out the recommendations made by these bodies and includes a discussion of education the six five year plans. This is a comprehensive account of policy level initiatives in the field at different stages and on various problem areas.

1155. Agarwal, J. C. Evaluation of the New Pattern and the Report of the Review Commission, 1977. New Delhi: Arya Book Depot, 1978.

1156. Biswas, A., et al. The New Educational Pattern in India. Delhi: Vikas, 1976.

The National Policy Resolution on Education laid down the new educational pattern to transform the school system in India. This work analyzes in detail the concepts behind this directive and the hurdles to be overcome for its implementation. The authors stress the necessity for reform at all stages of school education highlighting the need for providing it a scientific and vocational bias. The book emphasizes the need for orientation in dynamic methods of teaching and learning and for a redefinition of the present pattern. Concepts such as work-experience, pupil growth and development, and the changes envisaged in curriculum and structural pattern have been discussed in both historical and comparative perspectives.

1157. Chaurasia, G. Challenges and Innovations in Education. New Delhi: Sterling, 1977.

1158. Chawla, S. P. Co-ordination between Education and Population Policies: A Case Study in India. New Delhi: National Council of Educational Research and Training, 1978.

Attempts to analyze the relation between the population and education policies in India, in particular, the relation between the degree of convergence or divergence between these policies and their achievements. Based primarily on census records, government documents and reports, the study discusses the different policies and programs, their target groups, the extent of co-ordination and contact, their performance in diverse situation in different parts of the country, and the role of private and public agencies.

1159. Desai, Dhanwant, M. Some Problems of Education in the Gujarat State. Baroda: Faculty of Education and Psychology, Maharaja Sayajirao University of Baroda, 1967.

A review of the educational situation in Gujarat and issues arising from government policy. Deals with elementary, secondary, and teacher education, and includes discussions on science education, educational experiments and government's finance policies, backed by statistical data.

1160. Heredia, Rudolf C., ed. Perspective on Education in India. Bombay: Somaiya, 1983.

Presents part of a lecture series that honours the memory of Joseph Duhr, an eminent educationist. The three lectures published cover a review of educational developments as a basis for projecting to the year 2000, the role of the university in the pursuit of equality and an analysis of the crisis of character in colleges and society.

1161. India. National Education Policy. New Delhi: Lok Sabha Secretariat, 1985.

1162. Kaur, Kuldip. Education in India, 1781-1985. Chandigarh: Center for Research in Rural and Industrial Development, 1985.

1163. Kochhar, S. K. Pivotal Issues in Indian Education. New Delhi: Sterling, 1981.

Analyzes, in a historical perspective, certain critical issues emerging as a result of the change in form, structure, content, and techniques in education and as part of policy changes in the post-independence period. Some of the areas covered are the Indian Constitution on education, stages of education, innovations, wastage and stagnation, educational research, the language problem, and equalizing of educational opportunities.

1164. Laska, J. A. Planning and Educational Development in India. New York: Teachers College Press, 1968.

1165. Mukerji, S. N. Education in India Today and Tomorrow. Baroda: Acharya Book Depot, 1964.

The book examines some of the major problem facing education in India today with schemes for reconstruction. It has chapters on the organization of education, basic education, primary education, secondary education, university education, education of girls, technical education, teacher education, miscellaneous branches, and some experiments in education. Adequate statistical data are provided to indicate the present state of educational system.

1166. Naik, Chitra. Educational Innovation in India. Paris: UNESCO Press, 1974.

1167. Naik, J. P. Education in the Fourth Plan. Bombay: Nachiketa, 1968.

Analyzes the first three educational plans of India since independence and provides some constructive suggestions for the Fourth Educational Plan. Major programs of educational reconstruction, which should be incorporated in the fourth and subsequent plans, how these programs are different from the past, and why a different planning is important for future are some of the concepts of this book.

1168. Naik, J. P. Educational Planning in India. Bombay: Allied, 1965.

1169. Naik, J. P. Equality, Quality and Quantity: The Elusive Triangle in Indian Education. Bombay: Allied, 1975.

Examines the way in which equality, quality and quantity have been evolved, interpreted and implemented in Indian education, and whether education has had an impact on social structure. The discussion is presented in the context of education from 1813 to the present. Advocates a transformation of the formal educational system with an emphasis on social goals. The appendix contains suggestions for structural changes in elementary education, suggestions of the Education Commission on quality improvement and statistical data on institutions, enrollment, expenditure, and literacy.

1170. Naik, J. P. Policy and Performance in Indian Education, 1947-1974. Bombay: Orient Longman, 1975.

Reviews briefly the main educational developments of the post-independence period to analyze the factors which have

created the crisis in India. The book then suggests
alternative courses of action for the future to rebuild
healthier educational system which would be more conducive to
national development.

1171.   National Institute of Educational Planning and
        Administration. Education for International Understanding:
        the Indian Experience; Report of a Unesco Sponsored
        Project. New Delhi: National Institute of Educational
        Planning and Administration, 1980.

1172.   Patil, V. T. and B. C. Patil. Problems in Indian Education.
        New Delhi: Oxford and IBH, 1982.

        A discussion on major issues in Indian education, with
        suggestions for government policy. Among the questions
        discussed are the language issue, education and leadership,
        the Gandhian philosophy of education, education for social
        change and rural reconstruction, vocational education, adult
        education, the role of teachers, the open university, and
        student activism.

1173.   Prakash, Shri. Educational System of India: An Econometric
        Study. New Delhi: Concept, 1977.

        Discusses different models of educational planning and the
        problems of educational planning in a system of dynamic
        general equilibrium. Examines the working of the Indian
        educational systems in terms of two and inter-temporal and
        multi-sectoral input output models of education. Analyzes
        supply demand factors of education and their repercussions.

1174.   Prakasha, Veda. Extending Educational Opportunity in Sikkim.
        New Delhi: National Staff College for Educational Planners
        and Administrators, 1976.

        Studies the school system of Sikkim with special reference
        to educational administration. Contains a chronological
        study of the development of the educational system in Sikkim
        from monastic days to the introduction of the recent 10+2
        formula. Comments on the growing demand for education and
        recommends several measures to improve various facets of
        education, especially its administration.

1175.   Premi, M. K. Educational Planning in India: Implications of
        Population Trends. New Delhi: Sterling, 1972.

1176.   Raj, Samuel. India's Educational Policy. New Delhi:
        Select Books, 1984.

1177. Raza, Moonis, ed. Educational Planning: A Long Term
       Perspective. New Delhi: Concept, 1986.

1178. Roy, Binoy. U. S. Infiltration in Indian Education. New
       Delhi: Perspective, 1973.

1179. Rusia, P. N. A Study on Earn While You Learn Programme:
       Madhya Pradesh. Bhopal: Directorate of Public
       Institution, Madyha Pradesh, 1984.

       The document, which is an exemplar handbook for planning as
       much as it is a study of an action program, reviews the
       situation in the state of Madhya Pradesh where the dropout
       rates were 53 percent for the enrolled six-eleven year age
       group and 23 percent for the eleven-fourteen year age group.
       The document provides a vast array of critically analyzed
       details from the design to the implementation level, and
       impact of the Earn While You Learn Programme.

1180. Saxena, Sateshwari. Educational Planning in India: A Study
       in Approach and Methodology. New Delhi: Sterling, 1979.

1181. Sharma, G. S., ed. Educational Planning: Its Legal and
       Constitutional Implications in India. Bombay: N. M.
       Tripathi, 1967.

1182. Shukla, P. D. Towards New Pattern of Education in India.
       New York: Apt, 1984.

       This handbook is a useful guide for introducing,
       developing, and administering the new 10+2+3 pattern of
       education currently under implementation in the country. It
       is intended for those concerned with planning, imparting, and
       administration of education as well as for the general
       reader.

1183. Singhal, R. P. Revitalising School Complexes in India. New
       Delhi: Concept, 1983.

       This book gives a critical appraisal of the scheme School
       Complex over the last fifteen years. It also probes into the
       recent innovative experiment of Maharashtra's Rapport Based
       Program of School Complex. The Maharashtra experiment
       assumes considerable significance against the backdrop of
       halfhearted or unsuccessful attempts of some States in the
       past to introduce the idea of School Complex and the
       challenging task that lies before the schools to achieve the
       targets of universalization of elementary education
       increasing the retention rate and improving the quality of

education. The author not only gives suggestions for further
strengthening of Maharashtra's innovation but also examines
the feasibility of revitalizing school complexes all over the
country.

1184. Singhal, R. P. and V. A. Kalpande. The 10+2+3 Pattern of
       Education at National Level, A Research Study. Pune:
       Indian Institute of Education, 1984.

       The document is a research study report which surveys the
       progress in the implementation of the 10+2+3 pattern of
       education across India. The scheme has been adopted in
       principle by fifteen states and eight Union territories in
       India over the last five years. Concludes with suggestions
       for the future, with emphasis being placed upon the 10+2+3
       pattern being considered as a means to reorganize the entire
       education system rather than as a mere mechanical structural
       change in the system.

1185. Sinha, Jai B. P. The School Complex: An Unfinished
       Experiment. New Delhi: Concept, 1981.

       The School Complex aims to integrate the neighboring
       primary schools to a centrally located middle school, and the
       middle schools to a nuclear secondary school so that the
       schools of a geographical area may function as a whole--
       drawing on each other's resources and planning their
       development with minimum of external control and support.
       The scheme was formulated by the Kothari Commission (1966)
       and has been tried out in Bihar. This monograph examines the
       salient features of the scheme, its implementation,
       successes, and failures in the existing power structure of
       the educational administration and community. It also
       explores the feasibility of integrating the School Complex
       with the community so that the resources may flow bi-
       directionally and enrich both systems.

1186. Siqueira, T. N. Modern Indian Education. Calcutta: Oxford,
       1960.

       Discusses the problems of Indian education against a
       historical background. Issues covered include women's,
       adult, religious, and physical education; reports and
       recommendations of education commissions and the language
       question. Holds that education must be based on moral and
       philosophical principles and that the problem is poor
       quality, resulting from uncritical imitation of Western
       models.

1187. Tewari, R. P., ed. Critique of Education for Our People. New Delhi: South Asian, 1980.

Five essays that critically discuss J. P. Naik's 'Education for our People: A Policy Frame for the Development of Education (1978-87)', and that present alternate suggestions for educational reform, based on the principle of pragmatism. In his document, J. P. Naik had viewed the failure of the educational system as arising from the failure to link educational reforms with a popular struggle for socio-economic transformation, both within and without the educational system.

1188. Tiwari, D. D. Education at the Crossroads. Allahabad: Chugh, 1976.

1189. UNESCO/NCERT. Study of World Problems in Schools: Human Rights, Disarmament and New International Economic Order; India Report. New Delhi: NCERT/UNESCO, 1983.

Three world problems, namely human rights, disarmament, and new international economic order, were selected for the project to be implemented in four schools in New Delhi (at Class IX of two associated schools, one public school and one government-aided girls' school. In the Preparatory Phase (May-October 1982), NCERT undertook to develop appropriate materials, lesson plans and evaluation tools. In the Implementation Phase (November 1982-March 1983), it carried out field implementation, evaluation of impact on students and evaluation of the project, and prepared a final report. Recommendations for future work at national, regional, and international level are included in the report.

1190. Verma, R. Education, Planning and Poverty of India: A Comparative Study, 1944-77. New Delhi: Lancers, 1978.

Articles

1191. Adisesheah, M. S. "New Education Pattern: Opportunity to Face Basic Issues." Economic and Political Weekly 12 (December 3, 1977): 2021-22.

1192. Bhalawdekar, M. V. "Integration of Educational and Economic Plans." Economic and Political Weekly 6 (July 1971): 1641-48.

1193. Bhandari, R. K. "Crisis in Education in India." New Frontiers in Education 14 (July-September 1984): 74-81.

Criticizes the present pattern of growth of education and its failure to form linkages with national development. Lists the major causes of failure. States the recommendations of the Kothari Commission for reconstruction of the educational system and the ensuing national policy on education. Comments on elementary, adult, secondary, higher, and technical education.

1194. Bhandari, R. K. "Education in the Sixth Five Year Plan." New Frontiers in Education 12 (July-September 1982): 31-49.

Studies the financial outlays for education in the Sixth Plan and the progress of expenditure in the central and State sectors. States the targets set up by the Plan for elementary education, adult education, and enrollment. Discusses various programs set up for this purpose. Comments on education in the "new twenty-point programme."

1195. Bhandari, R. K. "Educational Development during Six Five Year Plans: An Evaluation." New Frontiers in Education 15 (April-June 1985): 52-66.

1196. Bhandari, R. K. "Educational Development in the Seventh Five Year Plan." New Frontiers in Education 13 (October-December 1983): 50-61.

Studies the causes for discontent in our educational system. Reviews the Sixth Plan and its role in the progress of education at different levels. Makes a list of the unfinished tasks and formulates an approach to educational development in the Seventh Plan.

1197. Bose, P. K. "Role of Universities in Pursuit of Quality Science." Journal of Higher Education 10 (Monsoon-Autumn 1984): 101-105.

Lists a few suggestions made by the Education Commission (1964-66), regarding essential programs for strengthening science education. Reviews these recommendations and considers their actual implementation. Comments on the growth of universities regarding enrollment, allocation of expenditure, faculty, and grants. Mentions possible reasons for the downward trend of the efforts to strengthen science education.

1198. Chandra, Satish. "The University Grants Commission and its Role: A Review." Journal of Higher Education, 10 (Monsoon-Autumn 1984): 3-8.

Reviews the policies of the UGC to upgrade the standards of education during the period 1973-1980. Mentions various measures taken by the Commission to improve teaching examinations and syllabi. Comments on the efforts made to expand non-formal, adult, and continuing education along with extension and community services. Brings out the defects in these efforts.

1199. Datt, Ruddar. "Higher Education and Future Educational Policy." Journal of Higher Education 3 (Autumn 1977): 189-97.

Notes the new avenue of obtaining university degrees through correspondence courses, the permission to students to appear as private candidates and the related difficulty in availability of data to assess the exact demand for higher education. Presents a broad picture of enrollment in higher education in India, subject to such limitations. Describes trends of outlays at different levels of education and gives certain directions for future educational policy.

1200. Deshpande, Kalidas. "Area Based Research-cum-Research Centre: A Role for Colleges to Play." Journal of Higher Education 3 (Monsoon 1971): 89-93.

Emphasizes the need for a relevant science education related to the time-honored developmental programs framed for the upliftment of the people. Suggests a stepwise transformation of colleges into recourse-cum-research centre especially in rural areas. Discusses changes in curricula and the role of teachers in the entire process.

1201. Deshpande, R. D. "Scientific and Technical Education steps to Improve Quality and Extend Scope." Economic and Political Weekly 7 (August 1972): 1661-66.

An attempt has been made here to identify some of the steps which could be taken by the Central and state governments and universities to more effectively utilize the existing facilities for scientific and technical education. The success of these efforts would depend on proper planning and identification of suitable institutions and personnel for their execution.

A number of these programs have to be implemented on a
'pilot project basis' and suitable changes could be made in
the light of the experience gained in their operation.

1202. Deva, Satya. "The New Education Policy." Economic and
Political Weekly 20 (September 28, 1985): 1647-49.

1203. Kamat, A. R. "Educational Policy in India: Critical
Issues." Sociological Bulletin 29 (September 1980): 187-
205.

1204. Kamat, A. R. "Educational Progress in Rural Maharashtra."
Economic and Political Weekly 3 (October 5, 1968): 1534-
36.

1205. Kamat, A. R. "The Educational Situation." Economic and
Political Weekly 7 (June 1972): 1229-37.

It may well be said that in contrast to most other sectors
of development, the country has indeed done better in the
educational sector and, in fact, has overfulfilled the
targets of enrollment and turnout in certain sub-sectors like
higher education, including engineering and technology. But
the whole educational structure betrays serious weaknesses of
a fundamental character which appear to be more or less
inherent in our economic-political system.

A number of surveys clearly show that the spread of
literacy and education is much more in evidence among the
affluent and socially advanced sections of society. Elite
formation during the post-Independence period is, therefore,
very important for assessing the educational situation. In
terms of social differentiation, the fall-out from our
educational system can be briefly described as follows: (i)
emergence and consolidation of a 'super' elite at the top--
consisting of the old urban intelligentsia and a sprinkling
of the more enterprising elements of rural stock--in
technology, industry, business and in the higher echelons of
the bureaucracy and the defense services (ii) formation of a
fairly large 'common' and 'regional' elite, consisting of the
urban middle and lower salaried groups, skilled and semi-
skilled technicians, professionals, and of the newly emerging
rural groups; and (iii) continuance of stark illiteracy in
the rest of society at the base of the pyramid, with a slow
and sluggish movement among small sections towards basic
literacy and rudimentary education. It becomes obvious that
this situation is full of strains, full of contradictions and
confrontations.

1206. Kattackal, Joseph A. "Education in India's Five Years Plans:
       A Historical Review (1951-76) and Critical Appraisal."
       Canadian and International Education 7 (June 1978): 5-26.

       Educational Planning in India began in 1951. The first and
       foremost achievement of planned development in education
       since then has been the tremendous expansion which has taken
       place in all sectors and levels of education. Planning has
       been responsible for the reform in the curricula, and as a
       result has produced a large cadre of high-level trained
       manpower and promotion of research. Expansion has also taken
       place in the neglected areas of girls' education and of the
       socially and economically weaker sections of the population.
       However, the disproportionate expansion of secondary and
       higher education has favored an economically and socially
       privileged minority at the expense of the vast majority of
       the masses. The comparative neglect of the education of the
       masses constitutes, perhaps, the greatest weakness of planned
       development.

1207. Khan, Q. U. "Applications of Manpower Requirement Approach
       to Educational Planning." Indian Educational Review 8
       (January 1973): 18-36.

       Four approaches, simple correlation, residual, returns to
       education, and manpower forecasting relate education to the
       economy. The basic methods applied in the manpower
       forecasting approach are detailed and the transformation of
       manpower targets into enrollment targets for education is
       described. Modifications necessitated by cultural
       requirements, wastage in the educational system, etc. are
       listed. It is also noted that the approach has inherent
       difficulties such as the change in manpower requirements on
       account of change in technology, changing equivalence between
       jobs, and education, etc.

1208. Mathew, A. "The Role of the University Grants Commission in
       Framing the Policy of Higher Education." Journal of Higher
       Education 9 (Autumn 1983): 177-92.

       Discusses the role and functions of the UGC after its
       establishment in 1956 as a statutory body for co-ordination
       and maintenance of standards of university and higher
       education. During the final decade of its existence, the
       Commission's major focus was on the implementation of the
       programs initiated and sponsored by the Ministry. An attempt
       is made to study the changing perceptions of the role of the
       UGC vis-a-vis the Ministry over the last two and a half
       decades. The primary concern is to discuss the dynamics of

organizational changes resulting from the changing
perceptions of the UGC. The role and functioning of the UGC
as an autonomous body is studied planwise till the fifth
plan. The UGC's vision for ten-fifteen years ahead of 1978
is also discussed.

1209. Mohan, Dinesh. "New Education Policy: Promises, Promises,
Promises." Economic and Political Weekly 20 (September 21,
1985): 1615-20.

1210. Mukhopadhyay, M. "Actors and Reactors in Educational
Change." Indian Educational Review 12 (January 1977): 18-
29.

Various attempts have been taken to reform Indian
education. The major research organization and change agent
in the country (NCERT) perceived the difficulties in
promoting new ideas. This paper reviews the research studies
undertaken after a first seminar in the area of educational
reform in 1966 at Osmania University. This review has been
done in terms of objectives, methodology, and results of the
study.

1211. Naik, J. P. "The Search for a National System of Education:
The Indian Experience." Prospects 6, no. 2 (1976): 196-
208.

This article examines the achievements and failures of
India's search for a national system of education for the
last seventy years in order to indicate some probable future
trends. It emphasizes the role of the government in
radicalization of educational system. It advocates the
reconstruction of Indian education in the line of teachings
of Mahatma Gandhi and Karl Marx and by an appropriate
amalgamation of science and technology with the traditional
cultural values recommended by Jawharlal Nehru.

1212. Panchmukhi, P. R. "Decision-Making in Education - Some
Issues." Economic and Political Weekly 5 (1970): 219-22.

1213. Panchmukhi, P. R. "Devaluation of Education: A Quantitative
Analysis." Journal of Higher Education 1 (Monsoon 1975):
15-30.

Examines the implication that over-expansion in education
had led to the devaluation of education. Quantifies the
degree and pattern of devaluation of education in general and
higher education in particular in the context of the Indian
economy. Suggestions are made to tackle the problem.

1214. Premi, M. K. "Planning Educational Programmes: Implications
      of Population Trends." Economic and Political Weekly 3
      (February 24, 1968):   363-66.

1215. Ramasubban, Radhika. "Economic Dualism and Educational
      Policy: Reflections of an Amateur." Journal of Higher
      Education 8 (Autumn 1982):   179-83.

1216. Rosenthal, Donald B. "Educational Politics and Public
      Policy-making in Maharashtra." Comparative Education
      Review 18 (February 1974):   79-95.

      Examines the political controversy which evoked in the
      state of Maharashtra, India when a plan for educational
      development was put forward for public consideration by the
      state cabinet in 1968. It provides broad background of the
      conflict and concludes that despite verbal commitments of
      socialist planning, a multitude of self-interested groups
      strive to manipulate the resources they already control or to
      gain additional resources in order to enhance their own
      particular interests in the policy realm. There is little
      relationship between paper plans and the effective capacities
      of existing governmental structures or to the nature of
      political and social realities.

1217. Sancheti, Neelu. "The Ford Foundation and Indian Education:
      Some Issues of Motives and Power." Journal of Higher
      Education 10 (Monsoon-Autumn 1984):   9-22.

1218. Sancheti, Neelu. "Institutional Transfer and Educational
      Dependency: An Indian Case Study." Pp. 108-18 in
      Dependence and Interdependence in Education: International
      Perspectives, ed. Keith Watson. London: Croom Helm, 1984.

      This article examines the concepts and beliefs in
      institutional transfer and dependency in education in the
      specific historical context of the Indian Institute of
      Management at Ahmedabad and Calcutta. These institutions
      were closely modeled on the Harvard Business School and the
      Sloan School of Management at the Massachusetts Institute of
      Technology. The author analyzes whether these institutions
      can be appropriately cited as concrete instances of
      educational dependency, created through the process of
      institutional transfer. She then questions the validity of
      two important sets of generalizations on educational
      dependency. She indicates firstly the institutional transfer
      in the Indian case was certainly not a one-sided imposition.
      Even recognizing the importance of the Ford Foundation as the
      major catalyst and broker for the idea as well as the major

donor agency, it is evident that major strategy decisions
remained in the hands of the concerned Indian elite group.
Secondly, statements concerning perpetual dependency do not
seem to be justified in the Indian case study. Despite the
strong initial dependency well acknowledged in the IIMC, the
absence of formal linkages as well as of reduced foreign
assistance and also a gradual growing consciousness within
the Institute of the importance of "indigenising" management
materials and techniques, seems to indicate a significant
shift toward independence.

1219.   Shukla, S. "Priorities in Educational Policy." Economic and
        Political Weekly 6 (July 1971): 1649-54.

        In the present circumstances, one can either insist on a
        fully democratic and modern program of educational
        reconstruction and await--or work for--the creation of the
        political prerequisites thereof, or alternatively, one may
        offer suggestions which look sensible in a more immediate and
        'practical' sense. The educational system, like most other
        systems, is essentially dependent on economic and political
        developments, but nevertheless, has a certain autonomy, or at
        least persistence, or structural and behavioral
        characteristics which, in their turn, tend to have important
        bearings on educational as well as other issues.
        Creativity and conceptualization of the problems of our
        society are more likely to emerge from an appropriate--
        rather than from a borrowed, inappropriate and, therefore,
        sterile--educational framework which is closely linked with
        socially relevant work. This is, again, a programmatic
        position which may result only from a changed balance of
        social power. For, as it is, the present arrangements give
        the currently emergent elite, a position of monopolistic
        advantage vis-a-vis the rest of society.
        In any case, conventional pedagogical assumptions and
        stereotypes prevalent even among some of our most creative
        and knowledgeable academics require to be controverted.

1220.   Singh, Amrik. "The Dynamics of Change." Journal of Higher
        Education 9 (Autumn 1983): 197-206.

1221.   Singh, Amrik. "Reconstituted UGC." Economic and Political
        Weekly 5 (August 15, 1970): 1377-82.

1222.   Singh, Amrik. "Restructuring Our Universities." Economic
        and Political Weekly 10 (November 1975): 1847-53.

        The real pressure in higher education is at the
        undergraduate level. To establish new universities to cope

with this pressure is to make the wrong kind of response to the problem.
The right response would be to establish new institutional structures to cope with the growing numbers at the undergraduate level. Among other things, this can be done by redefining the concept of the university. Even an association of colleges which does only undergraduate teaching may be legitimately accepted as a university.
It in this way, problems of postgraduate and undergraduate education can be dealt with separately, there would be enormous saving of resources.
The expansion of postgraduate education, which is really expensive, has to be more carefully planned. The experience of the last two decades has shown that planning at the Central level has not worked. Nor have the procedures adopted by the Centre or the UGC to deal with the universities and the state governments been effective. The emphasis, therefore, must now change from the Centre to the states.
If this shift of responsibility can be accomplished, the universities, the overwhelming majority of which are state universities, are likely to breathe more easily and give a better account of themselves. At the same time, this might release more funds for undergraduate education than are available today.

1223.   Staley, Eugene. "Towards a more Work-Oriented Schooling." Economic and Political Weekly 7 (August 1972): 1667-74.

It is argued here that the schools can help substantially in the fight against poverty if, and only if, they undergo a fairly drastic process of curriculum reform. This means changes in the content of instruction, in the methods of instruction, and in the evaluation of achievement (examination reform). Merely more of the same could be counter-productive by generating more alienated youth, unable to find ready-made jobs for which they are suited or which suit them, and unable to generate their own jobs by self-employment and entrepreneurship.
Educational leaders in India are agreed that instruction in the schools should be made more relevant to the world of work, to the future job needs of the youngsters, and to the country's need for efficient producers who can carry development forward. Strong recommendations to this effect were contained in the report of the Education Commission, 1966, and these have since been re-emphasized by many leaders.
There is more agreement on these general aims, however, than on any strategy for implementing them. And, even where

there is substantial agreement on strategy, experience
demonstrates that much thought and effort are required to
move from statements of objectives to actual implementation
in the schools. Implementation in this field is a difficult
and time-consuming process, and has not yet gone very far--
though there are some promising efforts under way in certain
states.
This article, therefore, focuses on implementation. It
offers for consideration a broad strategy by which the
general aims can be sought. It also puts forward some
specific suggestions on the designing of curriculum
development and on the preparation of new instructional
materials and methods.
While the discussion that follows will be in terms of what
can be done at the primary-secondary level in the formal
school system, it will be obvious that many of these ideas
are applicable (with appropriate adaptation) at other levels
and in non-formal, out-of-school education as well.
While this discussion concentrates on ways to prepare young
people for better performance as producers and organizers--
and thus as contributors to economic development--it is not
intended to suggest that this is the only purpose of
education. However, it is certainly one of the purposes. It
is particularly important in a country where there is need
for a radical increase in productivity as a foundation for
progress towards major goals being sought--viz., better
livelihood, social justice, and self-reliance.

1224.   Subramaniam, V.   "Rationalising Communication Strategy in
        College Classes."   Journal of Higher Education 5 (Spring
        1980):   335-42.

1225.   Tilak, Jandhyala B. G.   "Block Level Planning in Education."
        Indian Journal of Public Administration 30 (July-
        September):   673-87.

1226.   Udgaonkar, B. M.   "New Directions for International
        Scientific Co-operation II."   Journal of Higher Education 2
        (Autumn 1976):   167-84.

1227.   Udgaonkar, B. M.   "Scientific Co-operation."   Journal of
        Higher Education 2 (Monsoon 1976):   33-48.

1228.   Verma, M. C.   "Review of Skilled Manpower Forecasts and
        Changes in Occupational Structures of India."
        International Journal of Educational Development 4, no. 3
        (1984):   173-222.

1229. Wood, G. "National Planning and Public Demand in Indian
       Higher Education: The Case of Mysore." Minerva 10, no. 1
       (1972): 83-106.

       In India, the great expansion of educational facilities at
       all levels which has taken place since Independence in 1947
       is a product of the belief of government that the
       advantages-- pecuniary, deferential, cultural, etc.--of
       higher education should be available to greatly increased
       numbers. State governments in India have the major
       responsibility for education, although the national or
       central government exercises influence through its planning
       powers, through its direct control of certain higher
       institutions and through its program of subsidy by the
       University Grants Committee. Certain educational policies
       are consonant with the aims of both national and local
       politicians. In most instances, however, the result is less
       happy. Conflict between national and local interests,
       concerning the allocation of resources to education as a
       consumption good or education as a production good, make up a
       good part of the actual--not the theoretical--debate about
       higher education in India. This article studies this problem
       in the state of Mysore during the period of the first three
       five-year plans (1951-66).

1230. Wood, G. L. "University of Mysore - Case Study of
       Decentralization." Economic and Political Weekly 6 (June
       12, 1971): 1177-82.

1231. Yadav, R. K. "Tasks Ahead for Indian Education."
       Comparative Education 16 (October 1980): 311-22.

       This article discusses the various aspects of education
       system and planning of India in comparative perspective. It
       examines the problems of realizing various reform efforts and
       plans. And it concludes, in the absence of complementary
       economic and political policies, educational decisions will
       remain only tantalizing blueprint.

NEPAL

       Books

1232. Nepal. Ministry of Education. The National Educational
       System: Plan for 1971-76. Kathmandu: The Ministry, 1971.

1233. Shrestha, Kedar Nath. Educational Experiments in Nepal.
       Kathmandu: Institute of Education, Tribhuvan University,
       1981.

           The document contains six papers on different aspects of
       educational development, covering primary education,
       secondary education, school management, school financing,
       instructional supervision, and popular participation. It
       gives a historical review of development, the National
       Education System Plan (NESP) and its consequences, and the
       'seventh amendment to the educational code.'

1234. UNESCO. Long Term Projection for Education in Nepal.
       Bangkok: Unesco, 1966.

           This report outlines the country's background and its
       economy and planning. Provides present situation of
       educational system, the cost of education, past educational
       planning. Estimates the future resources for educational
       expenditure. Provides long-term projection for future
       educational development.

       Articles

1235. Bhatt, Dibya Deo and Mohammad Mohsin. "Restructuring the
       Educational System in Nepal." Prospects 5, no. 1 (1975):
       96-100.

           This is an explanation of the educational plan of Nepal--
       the National System of Education: 1971-76, which aimed at
       reconstructing the entire system. National integration and
       development of human resources are the two major emphases of
       the plan, which is quite comprehensive and touches upon all
       aspects of educational reform. Discusses revamping the
       formal structure, teachers role, the national development
       service, lifelong education in the plan. The experience of
       plan implementation, despite some impediments, is encouraging
       and the author concludes Nepal's educational plan has the
       potential to give the skill knowledge and attitude needed for
       the country to overcome the legacy of the past.

1236. Brubacher, John W. and Richard H. Pfau. "Skill Development
       for Nepal (or What Can An American University Provide a
       Himalayan Kingdom?)." University Council for Educational
       Administration Review 19 (February 1978): 7-11.

During the late 1960s and early 1970s, a national plan was developed to guide educational activities in Nepal. With assistance from the United States Agency for International Development, the Nepalese government delineated guidelines for a cooperative program with a U. S. university that would provide practically oriented formal academic training for planners and managers of Nepalese educational agencies. The University of Connecticut's proposal, which was accepted, incorporates three major features: 1) an initial analysis of the job responsibilities of each Nepalese participant, 2) design of an individual course of study for each participant that reflects his training objectives and job responsibilities, and 3) design and implementation of a special work-related project endorsed by the participant's superiors in Nepal and executed with the help of University of Connecticut professors. Participants in the "Education Skills Training Project-- Nepal" project completed their job analyses and the initial planning of their work-related projects while still in Nepal, prior to coming to the U.S. Another facet of the project is a series of workshops for administrative and technical personnel to be conducted each year in Nepal by university of Connecticut professors.

1237. Singh, Mrigendra Tal. "Educational Wastage in Nepal."
        Educational Quarterly 16 (1973): 47-55.

PAKISTAN

    Books

1238. Baloch, Nabi Bakhsh, (compiler). The Education Policy, 1972:
        Implications and Implementation. Hyderabad: Institute of
        Education, Sind University, 1972.

        Contains address to the nation by the President of
        Pakistan, statement of the policy by the Minister for
        Education and Provincial coordination, and the papers read at
        the Seminar organized by the Institute of Education,
        University of Sind, Hyderabad, March 29, 1972.

1239. Bokhari, Khalid H. and Jefferson N. Eastmond. A
        Participatory Planning Model for Village Education in
        Pakistan. Islamabad: Ministry of Education, 1977.

        Successfully field tested in four villages in the Federal
        Capital Area, Pakistan, the model is designed to: identify

and prioritize village concerns and educational needs;
validate and analyze the needs with respect to village values
and goals; and select, develop, implement, and evaluate a
best solution. Major steps in the model are: data
collection; induction of the local primary school teacher
into the research and planning effort; establishment of
village Needs Assessment Committees and scheduling of
meetings; training facilitators; and conducting Committee
meetings to define, prioritize, and plan solutions for
village needs. Enthusiastic response of facilitators,
teachers, and villagers call into question conventional
assumptions about rapid educational improvements and supports
the conclusions that: total village improvement is the most
productive strategy for improving primary school attendance;
uncoordinated services to village (such as current
governmental programs) are unproductive; and village specific
solutions are best. The model should be piloted in every
Pakistan province and used to generate solutions to primary
education problems. Research, experimentations, monitoring,
and evaluation should continue in the test villages.
Appendices list the four villages' educational needs,
alternative solution strategies, and outlines of each
village's adopted plans.

1240. Curle, Adam. Planning for Education in Pakistan: A Personal
       Case Study. Cambridge, Mass.: Harvard University Press,
       1966.

       Two themes are interwoven in this study. The first
       concerns the problems of educational planning in Pakistan;
       the second, the position and difficulties of the adviser
       grappling with those problems. Discusses the planning
       organization of Pakistan and its two wings: East and West
       Pakistan and problems they face. Argues how education could
       contribute to development and provide a strategy.

1241. Khan, Janbaz. Progress of General Education in N. W. F. P.,
       1965-66 to 1970-71. Peshawar: Board of Economic Enquiry,
       N. W. F. P., University of Peshawar, 1974.

1242. Pakistan Commission on National Education Report January-
       August 1959.

       Reports the needs and problems of the educational system of
       Pakistan. The present condition of all aspects of education
       from higher education to medium of instruction and Maktab and
       Madrasa (religious schools) education are pointed out and a
       series of recommendations are made to effect the desired
       reorientation and meet the national needs and aspirations in

accordance with available resources.

1243. Pakistan. Education Policy 1972-80. Islamabad: Ministry of Education, 1976.

1244. Pakistan. Ministry of Education. Action Plan for Educational Development (1983-88). Islamabad: 1983.

This policy document is important in its function as a practical action plan derived from, and coherent with the National (Sixth) Development Plan priorities and objectives, such as the emphasis on the expansion of literacy and primary enrollment with special attention to rural areas and to female education, curriculum improvement, improvement of teacher competencies, enlargement of technical/vocational education, emphasis on excellence in higher education.

1245. Pakistan. Ministry of Education. Second Five-Year Plan Development Projects and Their Evaluation. Karachi: Central Bureau of Education 1967.

1246. Pakistan. Ministry of Education and Scientific Research. Proposals for a New Educational Policy. Karachi: Manager of Publications, 1969.

1247. UNESCO. Longterm Projections for Education in Pakistan. Bangkok: Unesco, 1965.

This report sketches the picture of the educational system, covering all levels of education in Pakistan. It uses projections of school population and estimates of resources, under different assumptions to show some of the inter-relationships within which an education system evolves. This plan is supposed to be integrated into the framework of national plans of economic and social development.

1248. West Pakistan. Directorate of Education, Lahore Region. Decade of Progress in Education, 1958-68. Lahore: The Directorate, 1968.

SRI LANKA

Books

1249. Mendis, George. Resource Center for Learning and Development, Sri Lanka. Colombo: School Organization Branch, Ministry of Education, 1980.

A network initiated in January 1980, which will provide
support in education and allied fields, and will supplement
and compliment the efforts of the schools through specialized
human resources, learning materials and specially designed
learning/discussion sessions and field stations for out-of-
centre practical work.

1250. Narasimhan, V. The Illumination Climate and the Design of
       Openings for Daylighting of School Buildings in Southeast
       Asia and Ceylon. Colombo: Asian Regional Institute for
       School Building Research, 1970.

1251. Peiris, Kamala. Educational Change at Primary Level in Sri
       Lanka. Colombo: The Author, 1981.

       The paper deals with the educational reform program in Sri
       Lanka at the Primary school level. There is a need to create
       a classroom climate conducive to promoting love of learning
       through allowing freedom to learn and making learning
       meaningful. Specific objectives are enumerated; and
       teachers' role, methods, and materials are described.

1252. Sri Lanka. Development of Small Schools in Sri Lanka; Report
       of a Seminar Sponsored by the Ministry of Education in
       Collaboration with UNICEF and Colombo and the Sri Lanka
       Foundation Institute. Colombo: Small Schools Unit,
       Ministry of Education/UNICEF, 1978.

       Discussion of topics: Development of small schools, role
       of small school in community development, supply and
       distribution of equipment, emerging alternative strategies in
       development relating especially to rural development and
       vocational training, and relevant activities.

1253. Swedish International Development Authority (SIDA).
       Education and Training in Sri Lanka: A Sector Analysis.
       Stockholm: SIDA, Education Division, 1981.

       Description of current situations in education sector.
       Discussion of on-going changes and proposed reforms. The
       discussion continues with a look at the salient problem areas
       within education and gives an analysis of problem areas,
       concluding with a number of recommendations on possible areas
       of future co-operation between Sri Lanka and Sweden in field
       of education.

1254. UNESCO. Long Term Projections for Education in Ceylon.
       Bangkok: Unesco, 1965.

Describes the present state of the educational system at all stages, trends and problems in general education, and future problems. Estimates the financial resources of both internal and external assistance to meet the educational cost. Projects the future educational needs.

Articles

1255. Jayaweera, S. "Recent Trends in Educational Expansion in Ceylon." International Review of Education 15 (1969): 277-94.

1256. Sirisena, U. D. I. "Education Legislation and Educational Development: Compulsory Education in Ceylon." History of Education Quarterly 7 (1967): 329-48.

CHAPTER 29

EDUCATIONAL REFORM

INDIA

Books

1257. Airan, J. W., A. Barnabas and A. B. Shah, eds. Climbing a
Wall of Glass: Aspects of Educational Reform in India.
Bombay: Manaktalas, 1965.

1258. Bhatnagar, S. Kothari Commission; Recommendations and
Evaluation. Meerut: International, 1967.

1259. Griffin, Willis H. and Udai Pareek. The Process of Planned
Change in Education. Bombay: Somaiya, 1970.

1260. Gupta, A. K., ed. Examination Reforms Directions Research
and Implications. New Delhi: Sterling, 1975.

1261. Gupta, M. P. Education Systems: Analysis and Reforms. New
Delhi: Agricole, 1984.

1262. Naik, J. P. The Education Commission and After. New Delhi:
Allied, 1982.

Surveys the Indian educational scene during the twelve
years since the Education Commission (1964-66). Discusses
the events preceding the Commission, modifications of the
report as a result of the intervention of politicians and
government, and the continuing crisis in education. Suggests
lessons for the future in the light of past recommendations.
The functioning of the political economy of education in the
implementation of educational programmes is discussed, taking
the Report of the Commission as a focus.

1263. Naik, J. P. Educational Reform in India: A Historical
Review. New Delhi: Orient Longman, 1978.

1264. Thomas, T. M. Indian Educational Reforms in Cultural
       Perspective. Delhi: S. Chand, 1970.

Articles

1265. Altbach, Philip G. "Problems of University Reform in India."
       Comparative Education Review 16 (June 1972): 251-66.

       Analyzes the process and problems of university reform in
       India by studying the University of Bombay as an example. It
       does not denigrate the achievements of Indian higher
       education nor claim that it has no useful role in Indian
       society. Rather it focuses on some of the problems and
       solutions which the universities have themselves identified
       and proposed.

1266. Srivastava, H. S. "Some Conceptual Variations in Examination
       Reform." Indian Educational Reform 12 (January 1977): 1-10.

       Discusses how examination reform has suffered from the
       infiltration of some conceptual confusions. Some of these
       originated from uncritical use of some concepts of foreign
       origin, other are an outcome of following the way of least
       resistance, in selecting for implementation projects which
       are administratively the easiest. Still other have
       germinated from ignorance. The article seeks greater clarity
       about the merits and demerits of different issues, with a
       view of adopting approaches that are academically sound and
       practicable in Indian situation.

1267. Udangama, Premadara. "Reforms in Secondary and Technical
       Education." New Era 55 (January/February 1974): 12-15.

       Changing secondary education curriculum to meet the needs
       of Sri Lanka entails the replacement of British, colonial
       education with a less elitist, more vocationally oriented
       institutions.

1268. Wood, G. "Planning University Reform: An Indian Case
       Study." Comparative Education Review 16, no. 2 (1972):
       267-80.

PAKISTAN

Books

1269. Koraishy, Taj Ali. How to Reform Education System to
       Pakistan and Other Muslim Countries. Lahore: Mirza Book
       Agency, 1972.

1270. Pakistan. Ministry of Education. Educational Innovation in
       Pakistan. Islamabad: Ministry of Education, 1978.

       The educational innovations described in this report are
       working towards: 1) providing access to basic education, 2)
       relating education to the development of the individual and
       the nation, 3) increasing resources by drawing on the hidden
       resources of the community for the purpose of expanding and
       improving educational programmes.

SRI LANKA

Book

1271. Sri Lanka. Education Proposals for Reform: General,
       University and Tertiary. Colombo: Ministry of Education,
       Ministry of Higher Education and Ministry of Youth Affairs
       and Employment, 1981.

       This White Paper was prepared by several Committees which
       have examined the role of education from a perspective of
       broad national development needs, and have presented their
       proposals for reform in the White Paper.

Article

1272. Lewin, Keith and Angela Little. "Examination Reform and
       Educational Change in Sri Lanka, 1972-1982: Modernisation
       or Dependent Underdevelopment?" Pp. 47-94 in Dependence and
       Interdependence in Education: International Perspectives,
       edited by Keith Watson. London: Croom Helm, 1984.

       Examines in detail the historical context of the 1972
       educational reforms, particularly focused on the school

examination reform in Sri Lanka. The article traces through
the aftermath of these reforms in order to indicate the
conditions that led to the abandonment of many of them after
1977. Finally it relates these processes to development
theory in ways which highlighted its adequacy to explain
events within a framework that extends beyond variables of
internal educational policy.

CHAPTER 30

EDUCATION-EMPLOYMENT RELATIONSHIPS

BANGLADESH

Books

1273. Bangladesh. Planning Commission. Employment Market for the
Educated in Bangladesh. Dhaka: Government of Bangladesh,
Planning Commission, 1974.

1274. Combining Education and Work; Experiences in Asia and
Oceania: Bangladesh. Bangkok: UNESCO Regional Office for
Education in Asia, 1978.

Bangladesh stresses the importance of education responsive
to the country's development needs and capable of producing,
through formal or non-formal methods, skilled, employable
manpower. Although no pre-vocational training exists, new
curricula have introduced practical work experience in the
primary schools and have integrated agriculture, industry,
social welfare, and home economics with general education at
the secondary level in order to help reduce school dropout
and youth unemployment problems. Post-secondary education
remains remote and theoretical despite the push to combine
work experience and education. Only highly specialized professional degree or vocational/technical programs utilize
productive work experience during training. While Bangladesh
plans more polytechnics and vocational/technical institutes,
current emphasis appears to be centered on improving the
quality of life and lowering the seventy-five percent illiteracy rate in the poverty ridden country through practical
adult education programs of rural development, functional
literacy, health, family planning, home economics, agriculture, and fisheries. The Bangladesh Rural Advancement Committee attempted to provide non-formal education in these
areas in a self-sustaining program of rural development in
the Sylhet district. The program continued for four years

but had little funding, an ill-trained staff, and met with
limited success.

1275. Dhaka, University of. Institute of Education and Research.
       A Study on the Relevance of Education to Work in
       Bangladesh. Paris: UNESCO, 1982.

       Education plays a vital role in building up the most
       appropriate human resources to sustain rural development.
       Education should be considered in the context of: (a) rural
       development conceived in the framework of national
       development and as an integral part of it; (b) education for
       rural development conceived within the national system of
       education; (c) education conceived in a broader sense
       including formal, non-formal and informal types for all age
       groups.

1276. Dhaka, University of. Institute of Education and Research.
       Supply of Educated Manpower in East Pakistan (Students).
       National Commission on Manpower and Education Research
       Study No. 11. Islamabad: Planning Commission, Government
       of Pakistan, 1971.

1277. Huq, M. Shamsul, Bikas C. Sanyal and Others. Higher
       Education and Employment in Bangladesh. Dhaka: University
       Press, 1983.

       The study explores the relationship between the employment
       of graduates and the development of higher education in both
       quantitative and qualitative terms. In Bangladesh, the num-
       ber of educated unemployed and inappropriately employed has
       been rising at an alarming rate. It was forty-four percent
       in 1973. In contrast to this, the country also suffers from
       a shortage of educated manpower in certain categories like
       engineering graduates, engineering technicians, doctors,
       medical technicians, agricultural professionals, teaching
       professionals, and so on. The following topics are included
       in the eight chapters of this book: socioeconomic framework
       of the country, development of educational systems, analysis
       of the employment situation, background, attitude and expec-
       tations of students in the higher education system in
       Bangladesh, employment of graduates and earnings, the higher
       education system and the labor market as perceived by
       employers and implication for policy.

Article

1278. Hossain, Najmul and Larry J. Crisler. "Perceived Earnings of
       Bangladeshi Students: The Effects of a Foreign Degree."
       Canadian and International Education 13, no. 2 (1984): 62-
       72.

INDIA

Books

1279. Bhattacharya, A. K. The Problem of Educated Unemployment in
       India. Meerut: Meenakshi Prakashan, 1982.

       Analyzes the views of leading economists on the question of
       employment, in the context of a historical review of the
       educational system in India. Suggests that unemployment,
       with its socioeconomic costs, cannot be solved only by great-
       er investment, but requires manpower planning at all levels.
       Educational output should be adjusted to societal needs
       through planning and work-orientation.

1280. Blaug, M., P. R. G. Layard, and M. Woodhall. The Causes of
       Graduate Unemployment in India. London: Oxford
       University, 1969.

       The book discusses the relation between supply and demand
       for educated manpower in a developing country--India. The
       authors have tried to explain how the paradox of educated
       unemployment arises and what can be done about it. They
       conclude that the persistence of educated unemployment in
       India can be explained by the resistance of educated people
       to the fall in their earnings which, according to economic
       theory, should accompany the increase in their relative
       supply. This resistance is strongly reinforced by the high
       correlation between starting salaries and life-time income
       resulting from the low mobility of labor in India. But how
       is it that the supply of educated people continues to grow
       faster than the demand for their services? The authors
       calculate private rates of return to primary, secondary, and
       higher education and show that even with unemployment, the
       pursuit of higher education is a financially profitable
       investment for the individual. But then using social rates
       of return they demonstrate that from society's point of view
       there has been serious under-investment in primary schooling

and relative over-investment at the higher levels of education. They end by suggesting a number of ways which the Indian authorities might consider in trying to control the explosion of higher education.

1281. Burgess, T., R. Layard, and P. Pant. Manpower and Educational Development in India, 1961-86. Toronto: University of Toronto Press, 1968.

1282. Committee on Education and Total Employment. Educated Unemployment in India: Challenge and Responses. Delhi: Hindustan, 1972.

This report makes a clear analysis of the problem of educated unemployment and puts due stress on the possible solutions which are open to the authorities in India. It discusses the general employment problem, extent of educational development during post-independence period, growth in educated manpower, evolving solutions--pedagogical diversification, economic framework, mobilization of resources--ways and means. Finally, it has a section on observations and recommendations.

1283. Dhar, T. N., and others. Education and Employment in India: The Policy Nexus. Calcutta: Minerva, 1976.

Discusses the perceptions and expectations of university students in India on educational patterns, job opportunities, etc. Investigates the socioeconomic background of the students and its impact on the educational and occupational expectation of the students. Is based on a survey on 'The Political Economy of Educated Unemployment in India", assisted by the University of California, covering 1151 college students from nine faculties belonging to five university campuses. Points out policy measures to check hyper-educational inflation.

1284. Dhar, T. N. The Politics of Manpower Planning--Graduate Unemployment and the Planning of Higher Education in India. Calcutta: Minerva, 1979.

A critical approach to manpower planning whose limitations are seen to arise not so much from conceptual limitations, but from the practical difficulties of operationalization. Discusses the implications of the social and political framework within which manpower and educational planning is taking place. Graduate unemployment is a major concern of this study.

1285. Institute of Applied Manpower Research. Wastage in Indian
       School Education: A Review and Further Analysis. New
       Delhi: IAMR, 1972.

1286. Kidder, E. Education and Manpower Planning in India.
       Bombay: Progressive, 1973.

1287. Parmaji, S. Education and Jobs. Delhi: Leeladevi, 1979.

       Investigates the relationship between general higher
       education and job aspirations, job satisfaction and job
       efficiency of non-professional job holders, in particular, of
       clerical workers. A secondary question discussed is the
       relation between clerical efficiency and job satisfaction on
       the one hand and length of education and service on the
       other. That general higher education raises the level of job
       aspiration towards salaried jobs and a positive correlation
       exists between education and clerical efficiency, are some of
       the conclusions.

1288. Parvathamma, C. Employment Problems of University Graduates.
       New Delhi: Ashish, 1984.

       This study suggests some long-term and short-term measures
       to tackle the problem of unemployment of university
       graduates. The study was based on a three percent sample of
       undergraduate and postgraduate students in the various
       faculties in Karnataka, Bangalore Mysore.

1289. Shah, K. R. and S. Srikantiah. Education, Earnings, and
       Income Distribution. New Delhi: Criterion, 1984.

1290. Rao, V. K. R. V. University Education and Employment: A
       Case Study of Delhi Graduates. Bombay: Asia, 1961.

1291. Tilak, Jandhyala B. G. Educational Planning and Unemployment
       in India. New Delhi: National Institute of Educational
       Planning and Administration, 1982.

1292. Wastage and Stagnation in Primary and Middle Schools in
       India. New Delhi: NCERT, 1973.

       Articles

1293. Bhattacharya, P. K. "Development of Need Based Curricula in
       Postgraduate Education in Organic Chemistry." Journal of
       Higher Education 3 (Autumn 1977): 181-88.

1294. Bhiday, M. R. "Integration of Higher Education for Effective Vocational Training." Journal of Higher Education 5 (Spring 1980): 371-80.

1295. Bose, P. K. and S. P. Mukherjee. "Graduate Employment and Higher Education in West Bengal." Journal of Higher Education 5 (Spring 1980): 281-300.

      Studies the particular characteristics of graduate unemployment in West Bengal. States reasons for the pursuit of higher education and compares the relevance of the degree and education to jobs. Talks about matching education with employment and suggests various measures against unemployment.

1296. Chandrakant, L. S. and Others. "New Perspectives for Technical Education--Industry Interaction." Journal of Higher Education 7 (Spring 1982): 201-10.

      Discusses the need for technical institutions and their role in economic development which needs industrialization. Describes these institutions as they exist in India, their shortcomings and problems. Comments on the technical education and industry interaction as it exists and suggests some measures to improve the system.

1297. Chaudhuri, D. P. "Rural Education and Agricultural Development--Some Empirical Results from Indian Agriculture." Pp. 372-86 in The World Yearbook of Education, 1974--Education and Rural Development, eds. Philip Foster and J. R. Sheffield. London: Evans, 1974.

      Examines the role of education in economic development. More specifically this article examines the relationship between education and productivity in the context of an underdeveloped country--India. The author concludes that the level of agricultural productivity is significantly related to the level of education.

1298. Choudhury, P. N. and R. K. Nandy. "Towards Better Utilization of Scientific Manpower." Economic and Political Weekly 6 (June 19, 1971): 1241-49.

1299. Choudhury, P. N. and R. K. Nandy. "Pattern of Employment of Agricultural Scientists." Economic and Political Weekly (June 20, 1970): 981-85.

1300. Dey, B. "Scientific and Technical Personnel: Inter-State
       Flow and Distribution." Economic and Political Weekly 4
       (August 23, 1969): 1373-81.

1301. Hommes, E. W. and N. Trivedi. "Market for Graduates--A Field
       Report." Economic and Political Weekly 6 (December 11,
       1971): 2486-91.

1302. Hone, K. "Unemployed Engineers." Economic and Political
       Weekly 3 (April 13, 1968): 616-17.

1303. Ilchman, Warren F. "People in Plenty': Educated
       Unemployment in India." Asian Survey 9 (October 1969):
       781-95.

       This essay discusses India's unemployment problem among the
       graduates of arts, science, and commerce fields. Major
       growth characteristics of supply of graduates and the major
       utilization facts of the demand for their services are used
       as empirical indicators. The author argues the problem is
       not merely irrelevant education, rather lack of job openings.
       The numbers of young people finishing degrees and seeking
       employment far exceed the potential of the economy to provide
       them with jobs.

1304. Indiresan, Jayalakshmi. "Profile and Index of the
       Polytechnic--Industry Collaboration--An Empirical Study."
       Journal of Higher Education 10 (Monsoon-Autumn 1984): 29-
       44.

       Comments on the need for a more decisive interaction
       between industry and technical education. Highlights the
       causes for its absence and points out possible areas for
       collaboration. Reviews the attempts made in this direction,
       with an example of industry--polytechnic collaboration.
       Suggests various measures for reform.

1305. Jetley, S. "Education and Occupational Mobility, a U.P.
       Village." Economic and Political Weekly 4 (April 1969).

1306. Khan, Q. V. "Higher Education in India--Some Issues."
       Journal of Higher Education 5 (Autumn 1979): 167-82.

       Attempts to answer the following questions: (a) whether
       India is over-educated with respect to higher education; (b)
       whether the mismatch between demand for and supply of higher
       education arrests the further expansion of higher education;
       (c) whether the absorptive capacity of the economy could be
       increased to improve the intake of higher educated persons,

and its demographic implications; (d) whether unemployment is
the result of lack of jobs or because graduates do not
possess the required skills and abilities? Also suggests
certain policy measures to control the situation.

1307. King, A. D. "IIT Graduate: 1970--Aspects, Expectations, and
Ambitions." Economic and Political Weekly 5 (September 5,
1970): 1497-1510.

1308. Mathur, P. N. "Medical Manpower Requirements and Supply up
to 2000 A.D." Manpower Journal 18 (October-December 1982):
39-58.

1309. Nair, K. Narayanan and Others. "Education, Employment, and
Landholding Pattern in a Tamil Village." Economic and
Political Weekly 19 (June 16-23, 1984): 948-56.

1310. Papanek, H. "Class and Gender in Education--Employment
Linkages." Comparative Education Review 29, no. 3 (1985):
317-46.   ·

1311. Patel, S. K. "Education, Employment, and Income Inequality:
A Marxian Perspective." Indian Educational Review 14
(October 1979): 13-23.

Explains the pattern of educational expenditure, the
distribution of benefits of educational expansion and labor
market slots among various socioeconomic groups, greater
educated unemployment and underemployment among weaker group
workers, relatively lower rate of return to human capital
formation accruing to the lower and lower-middle income
groups, repressive effect of educational expansion on the
income equality and the dynamic behavior of various
socioeconomic groups with respect to job search and
educational investment and the perpetual economic
subordination of the weaker group. The explanation is based
on Marxian theoretical perspective.

1312. Prasad, K. V. Eswara. "Education and Unemployment of
Professional Manpower in India." Economic and Political
Weekly 14 (May 1979): 881-88.

This paper examines the influence of several factors on the
unemployment of highly qualified manpower. It does so using
multiple regression with dummy variables.
Taking a sample from the 1971 Special Census on Degree
Holders and Technical Personnel, first an attempt is made to
study (a) the incidence and (b) duration of unemployment by

detailed tabulations; and secondly, the duration of unemployment is further analyzed by fitting an unemployment function. The results support the following findings: (1) given a comparable length of exposure to education, the duration of unemployment varies significantly among the different categories of professional manpower (viz, scientists, engineers, doctors, and agricultural and veterinary scientists); (2) in each category the duration of unemployment is less among those with higher academic performance than those with lower academic performance; and (3) the females face a longer duration of unemployment compared to the males.

1313. Rao, M. J. Manohar and Ramesh C. Datta. "Human Capital and Hierarchy." Economics of Education Review 4, no. 1 (1985): 67-76.

Investigates the relationships among schooling, experience, job status, and earnings in a large, private company in India. Results indicate that job status rises monotonically with experience and channels the transmission effects of schooling and experience onto earnings. Marginal productivity theory and the weak version of the screening hypothesis are supported.

1314. Ritzen, Jo M. "Manpower Targets and Educational Investments." Socioeconomic Planning Science 10, no. 1 (1976): 1-6.

Discusses the use of quadratic programming to calculate the optimal distribution of educational investments required to closely approach manpower targets when financial resources are insufficient to meet manpower targets completely. Demonstrates use of the quadratic programming approach by applying it to the training of supervisory technicians in Bangladesh.

1315. Saradomoni, K. "Education, Employment, and Landownership: Role of Caste and Economic Factors." Economic and Political Weekly 16 (September 1981): 1466-69.

An attempt is made in this paper to present intra-caste and inter-caste differences in education, employment, and landownership in a village population near Trivandrum in Kerala with the objective of examining whether these differences were predominantly influenced by caste or economic factors.

1316. Saxena, J. P. "Education Occupation Matrix in Fertilizer Industry." Manpower Journal 16 (April-June 1980): 79-90.

Studies the relationship between education and occupation
in the fertilizer industry, using industry-occupation and
education-occupation matrices. The study is based on data
collected from employees employed in large fertilizer
manufacturing units. Comments on the mismatching between
educational qualifications and occupation.

1317. Sharma, G. D. and M. D. Apte. "Graduate Unemployment in
       India." Economic and Political Weekly 11 (June 1976):
       915-25.

       This paper examines the pattern and incidence of
       unemployment among the educated, by faculty and by region.
       These two aspects of unemployment are examined in two
       parts: (1) the problem at present; and (2) the problem in
       perspective, covering the period up to 1985-86.

1318. Sharma, Harsha and V. K. Berry. "Manpower Study of the
       Fertilizer Industry." Manpower Journal 16 (April-June
       1980): 1-24.

       Suggests improvements in educational and training programs
       to match the technological advances in the fertilizer
       industry. Examines the existing employment situation, the
       matching of education with the job requirement, the future
       manpower requirements and the training needs of the industry.
       Recommends measures to improve the recruitment and investment
       pattern.

1319. Sharma, N. L. and Surendra. "Job Oriented Training and
       Specialization in Geology." Journal of Higher Education 3
       (Autumn 1977): 173-80.

       Analyzes the growing importance of geological education and
       the growth in the number of institutions imparting it.
       Discusses the question of pure versus applied geology and the
       need for prolonged training in applied geology. Mentions
       recommendations of the seminar on "Teaching and Research in
       Earth Science" held in Delhi University (1973), regarding the
       selection of courses. Suggests certain measures to improve
       the existing system.

1320. Tilak, Jandhyala B. G. "Wastage in Education in India: A
       Case Study of Andhra Pradesh." Indian Educational Review
       17 (April 1982): 58-85.

1321. Varghese, N. V. "Some Conceptual Problems in Manpower
       Planning." Manpower Journal 17 (July-September 1981): 39-
       56.

NEPAL

Book

1322. Sharma, Swash Raj. Education and Employment Policies in
       Nepal; A Perspective View. Bangkok: UNESCO, 1981.

PAKISTAN

Books

1323. Floysted, Gunnar. The Labour Market and Training Programmes
       for Diploma Holders from the Polytechnic Institutes in
       Pakistan. Pakistan Institute of Development Economics
       Research Report No. 87. Karachi: The Institute, 1968.

1324. Karwanski, Ryszard A. Education and Supply of Manpower in
       Pakistan. (National Commission on Manpower and Education
       Research Study No. 2.) Karachi: Manager of Publication,
       1970.

1325. Khan, Mohammad Mohabbat and Habib Mohammad Zafarullah. The
       Recruitment and Training Systems in the Civil Service of
       Pakistan and the United States Federal Civil Service: A
       Historical-Analytical Study. Dhaka: Center for
       Administrative Studies, University of Dhaka, 1978.

1326. Rurd, Kaare. Manpower and Educational Requirements of
       Pakistan, 1961-90. Islamabad: Planning Commission,
       Government of Pakistan, 1970.

1327. Seminar on Agricultural Education and Manpower Requirements,
       West Pakistan Agricultural University, 1965. Papers
       Presented at the Seminar on Agriculture Education and
       Manpower Requirements Organized by Faculty of Agricultural
       Economic and Rural Sociology, West Pakistan Agricultural
       University, Lyallpur. Lyallpur: The University, 1966.

1328. Zaki, Wali Muhammad. Educational Development in Pakistan: A
       Study of Educational Development in Relation to Manpower
       Requirements and Resource Availability. Islamabad: West
       Pakistan Publishing Co., 1968.

This study highlights the major problems in educational
planning in Pakistan and takes into account demographic and
resource factors of the country. The first part of the study
begins with an examination of the present schooling process;
school-age populations and projections for education and the
future. The study further examines the requirements and
supply of educated and trained manpower such as engineers and
technicians in light of development projects. Also looked at
are education budgets and available resources which are based
on the national economy. The author concludes by stressing
some of the problems that need to be addressed immediately:
illiteracy, lack of girls' schooling, dropout, examination
systems, and lack of specialist instructors.

SRI LANKA

Books

1329. Deraniyagala, C., R. Dore, and A. W. Little. Qualifications
and Employment in Sri Lanka. Sussex: University of
Sussex, 1978.

1330. Sanyal, Bikas C. and Others. University Education and
Graduate Employment in Sri Lanka. Paris: UNESCO/Colombo,
Marga Institute, 1983.

Explores the relationship between development of higher
education and employment of graduates. Findings reveal
information on what goes on inside Universities, and raise
issues that should receive urgent attention.

1331. Youth, Land, and Employment. Colombo: Marga Institute,
1974.

Article

1332. Mace, J. "Qualifications and Employment in Sri Lanka."
Comparative Education 15, no. 1 (1979): 116-27.

CHAPTER 31

THE "BRAIN DRAIN" AND RELATED ISSUES

INDIA

Book

1333. Kabra, K. N. Political Economy of Brain-Drain. New Delhi:
Arnold Heineman, 1976.

Presents the phenomenon of brain drain as a reverse
technology transfer from the developing countries to the
developed ones. Describes the situation as a process of
migration of highly qualified manpower (HQM) which is a kind
of almost unilateral transfer of the technology and personnel
for the achievement of technology. Analyzes the following
basic tenets: (1) economic growth of the West, coupled with
the emergence of the socialist system and the developmental
urge of the third world, (2) emphasis on research and
development and the resultant growth in demand for HQM, (3)
strengthening of the neo-colonial grip of capitalist
countries over developing nations, through instruments such
as technical and financial collaboration, unequal trade and
treaties, etc. Considers the impact and consequences of
brain drain and mentions certain policy objectives for
improvement.

Articles

1334. Dandekar, V. M. "Brain Drain: The Indian Situation."
Economic and Political Weekly 2 (July 29, 1967): 1337-41.

1335. Nayar, B. K. and others. "Indian Students and Trainees in
Scientific and Technical Fields who Went Abroad During
1965-1975." Journal of Higher Education 4 (Autumn 1978):
171-86.

1336. Roy, K. "Unemployment and Brain Drain." Economic and
       Political Weekly 6 (September 25, 1971): 2059-63.

PAKISTAN

Book

1337. Ahmad, Mahmud S. and S. M. Hasan. Estimation of Brain Drain.
       Karachi: Manager of Publications, 1971.

CHAPTER 32

COMPARATIVE EDUCATION

INDIA

Books

1338. Belok, M. V. and K. Gopal. Educational Systems: Occidental and Oriental. Meerut: Anu, 1981.

1339. Hommadi, A. H. University Administration in Developing Countries. Delhi: Indian Bibliography Bureau, 1984.

1340. Joshi, R. N. Education - Elsewhere and Here: A Key to Prosperity. Bombay: Bharatiya Vidya Bhavan, 1979.

Identifies the weaknesses of the Indian education system and suggests remedies in light of the experience of Britain, U.S.A., West Germany, Russia, and Japan. The comparative analysis is related to socioeconomic context. Underlines the importance of activising vocational education in India, both technical and non-technical.

1341. Read, Hadley. Partners with India: Building Agricultural Universities. Urbana, Illinois: University of Illinois College of Agriculture, 1974.

Describes a unique international experience in higher education involving two countries--India and the United States--in establishing nine agricultural universities in India. Part I establishes the historical setting for the partnership. It reviews the origin of the U.S. land-grant universities, relates this origin to the strikingly similar needs of India after her Independence, and traces the creation and early progress of the AID-university technical assistance efforts in India. Part two recounts how the six involved U.S. universities helped nine states in India build their new agricultural universities. Part three summarizes

327

the dimensions of the U.S. university efforts in India,
analyzes the progress made by the nine assisted Indian
agricultural universities, and presents the author's view on
some aspects of the Indo-American Experience.

1342.   Sodhi, T. S. Comparative Education: Philosophy, Patterns
        and Problems of National Systems. Ludhiana: Mukand, 1979.

        The first part deals with the philosophy of comparative
        education and the educational structures--pre-primary,
        primary, secondary, higher and teacher education--of the
        U.K., U.S.A., U.S.S.R. and India. The second part discusses
        the educational problems of these countries in a comparative
        perspective.

1343.   Tickoo, Champa. Indian Universities: A Historical,
        Comparative Perspective. Bombay: Orient Longmans, 1980.

        This volume considers the current problems of Indian higher
        education from both historical and comparative perspectives.
        The experience of the colonial university in India as well as
        other nations including the Soviet Union and the United
        States is discussed in the context of contemporary Indian
        higher education. Chapters deal with undergraduate
        education, postgraduate education and research, the
        governance of universities and student life. A new
        university model is called for along with a strengthened UGC.

        Articles

1344.   Arnove, Robert F. "A Comparison of the Chinese and Indian
        Education Systems." Comparative Education Review 28
        (August 1984): 378-401.

        The study of educational policies in China and India
        provides insight into the possibilities and limits of
        educational reform in countries pursuing different paths to
        development. The article reviews efforts and outcomes in the
        two countries with regard to these salient problems: 1)
        massive illiteracy, 2) lack of universal access to primary
        education and iniquities in educational opportunities and
        outcomes (based on gender, residence, class or caste), 3) a
        hierarchical, elitist, examination-oriented education system
        unrelated to economic needs and productive labor, 4) a large
        number of unemployed school leavers, and 5) dependence on
        foreign models, particularly at the higher education level.

1345. Driver, Edwin D. "Self and Society: Attitudes of Students in India, Iran, Trinidad-Tobago and the United States." Sociological Bulletin 30 (September 1981): 117-36.

1346. Shahidullah, Muhammad. "Institutionalization of Modern Science and Technology in Non-Western Societies: Lessons from Japan and India." Knowledge 6 (June 1985): 437-60.

1347. Shukla, S. "Comparative Education: An Indian Perspective." Comparative Education Review 27 (June 1983): 246-58.

Argues comparative education as practiced presently is singularly ill-equipped. Most history of education reveals the story of dissemination from and domination by the developed mainly European and western world vis-a-vis the underdeveloped world. The comparative approach tends to presume basic similarities, whereas the condition in the developing countries is of conflict and probably also basic dissimilarities. The author argues that the comparative studies of the relation of education to national and social development are as legitimate as comparative education; they are useful in forseeing the new international order and its relation to education.

CHAPTER 33

SOUTH ASIAN EDUCATION: PERSPECTIVES

Books

1348. Combining Education and Work: Experiences in Asia and
       Oceania. Bangkok: Unesco Regional Office for Education in
       Asia and Oceania, 1978. Vol. 2-Bangladesh, Vol. 6-Nepal,
       Vol. 8-Pakistan.

1349. Das, A. K. Unemployment of Educated Youth in Asia: A
       Comparative Analysis of the Situation in India, Bangladesh
       and the Philippines. Paris: Unesco; International
       Institute for Educational Planning, 1981.

       This study of unemployment among university graduates in
       West Bengal (India), Bangladesh, and the Philippines provides
       socioeconomic and educational characteristics of these areas,
       a comparative analysis of unemployment, and suggested
       measures for reducing unemployment. The International
       Institute for Educational Planning studies, focusing on
       university students, employed and unemployed graduates, and
       employers provided the data base. Differences in the
       questionnaires used in the three countries and failure to
       consider the unemployment situation of secondary school
       graduates are among the study's limitations. Socio-economic
       characteristics include statistics on population size and
       growth rate, gross national product (GNP) per capita, and GNP
       growth rate. Educational characteristics considered include
       the percentage of the population that is illiterate, public
       education expenditures, and rates of return to various levels
       of education. Comparative unemployment data examined are
       time spent waiting for employment, a profile of unemployed
       graduates (by sex and area of residence), guardian's
       education and income, reasons for unemployment (such as
       inadequate training, financial support, career information,
       and placement services), and a lack of self-employment
       opportunities. Suggested measures for reducing unemployment
       include better interaction between employers and educational
       institutions, improved career and educational counseling,

331

improved placement services, and promotion of self-employment
opportunities.

1350. Dutta, S. C. Adult Education in South Asia. New Delhi:
       Indian Adult Education Association, 1965.

1351. Huq, M. Shamsul. Education and Development Strategy in South
       and Southeast Asia. Honolulu: East-West Center Press,
       1965.

1352. Huq, M. Shamsul. Education, Manpower and Development in
       South-East Asia. New York: Praeger, 1975.

       Contends that the deepening crisis in education was a part
       of the larger crisis in development. Therefore, reform
       efforts in education cannot play a worthwhile role except
       within a broader growth model aimed at the development and
       utilization of human capital. It identifies and analyzes the
       major challenges in the field of education as well as the
       social and economic factors to which they are related.
       Examines the implications of the multi-dimensional concept of
       development along with the various approaches to study of the
       dynamics of development indicating that growth is not static.
       The need for an educational system designed to fit the
       economic and social requirements of a nation is raised and
       several approaches to the development of theoretical plan-
       models to meet this challenge is tackled. The book also
       examines the developing economic and social situation in the
       light of the provisions of the national developmental plans
       and analyzes the educational structures in the region of
       South and South-East Asia.

1353. Jayasuriya, J. E. Education in the Third World: Some
       Reflections. Bombay: Somaiya, 1981.

       Part 1, entitled 'Educational Strategies for the Third
       World Countries', analyzes possibilities and constraints and
       suggests modes for the re-organization of certain sectors of
       education for the achievement of a better future. A pattern,
       not based on a copy of Western models which are adopted in
       many Asian countries, is formulated. Part two surveys
       educational development in Sri Lanka from the Pre-Christian
       era to the present.

1354. Sanyal, Bikas C. Higher Education and the Labor Market in
       Asia. Paris: UNESCO, 1982.

       This 1971-76 study of the employment markets in Bangladesh,
       India, Indonesia, the Philippines, and Sri Lanka reveals

that, except in the Philippines, unemployment is increasing
at a very fast rate relative to the level of education per
person. In the Philippines and in India, enrollment ratios
for higher education have been substantially higher than in
the other countries. As social pressure has led to expansion
in higher education, the majority of students have enrolled
in arts-based rather than science-based subjects. Although
arts-based studies cost less, developing nations need more
science-based students to further resource development. The
role of education in each country and region is best
ascertained, according to the author, by analyzing available
physical and human resources potentials. Such analysis needs
to consider what types of skills will be in increasing
demand, and to develop strategies for matching needed skills
with the training content of higher education. Findings of
the International Institute for Educational Planning
Conference to which this paper was presented include a
general lack of coherent and comprehensive national policies
toward higher education and a significant mismatch in all the
countries studied between the expected educational career of
the student and the actual educational career.

Articles

1355. Adieshiah, Malcolm. "Future Asian Education: The Challenge
       of Numbers." Prospects 10, no. 4 (1980): 471-80.

1356. Dutt, Luithi Ela. "Education, Unemployment and Youth Unrest:
       The South Asian Syndrome." Prospects 9, no. 1 (1979): 85-
       90.

       Discusses that the quantitative expansion of education in
       South Asia did not necessarily result in expanding job
       opportunities. It was precisely because educational
       expansion was not directly linked to employment creation and
       also the low rate of growth of these economies failed to
       absorb the growing number of graduates from the educational
       system. Consequently, underemployment and unemployment
       become a widespread feature, which created youth unrest in
       the area. There is then a direct link between socioeconomic
       development and the functionalism/dysfunctionalism of formal
       education. Also, formal education provided unequally in an
       underdeveloped economy accentuated the inequalities in income
       distribution and ways of living.

1357. Fisher, Marguerite J. "Higher Education of Women and
       National Development in Asia." Asian Survey 8, no. 4
       (1968): 263-69.

       This is a report on higher educational aspects of a 1966
       seminar on Asian women and development sponsored by the
       United Nations. It includes table of statistics on female
       students and staff in the various Asian countries for years
       1955, 1958, and 1963.

1358. Kirpal, Prem. "Modernization of Education in South Asia:
       The Search for Quality." International Review of Education
       17, no. 2 (1971); 138-50.

       This paper explains how the right kind of education could
       improve the quality of life--satisfaction, harmony and
       comprehension--that may elude a more prosperous society. The
       author argues that the quality of education lies at the heart
       of educational change, for only a good education can both
       serve as an effective instrument of economic and social
       development and enrich the quality of life by integrating
       society and giving more scope and freedom to individuals. He
       then discusses some educational strategies of South Asian
       countries in general and India in particular in achieving the
       quality of education.

1359. Patel, Surendra, J. "Educational Miracle in Third World 1950
       to 1981." Economic and Political Weekly 20 (August 3,
       1985): 1312-18.

1360. Sanyal, Bikas, C. "Higher Education and the Labour Market in
       Asia." Journal of Higher Education 8 (Autumn 1982): 167-
       77.

1361. Tilak, Jandahyala. "Political Economy of Investment in
       Education in South Asia." International Journal of
       Educational Development 4, no. 2 (1984): 155-66.

1362. Wang, Bee-Lan Chan. "Positive Discrimination in Education:
       A Comparative Investigation of Its Bases, Forms, and
       Outcomes." Comparative Education Review 27 (June 1983):
       191-203.

       Explores some basic theoretical questions pertaining to
       positive discrimination in education, drawing from empirical
       experiences of several countries that have practiced it in
       one form or another--the United States, India, Malaysia and
       Sri Lanka. Encompasses policies and practices that have

variously been called reverse discrimination, preferential treatment, or affirmative action.

1363. Wickramasignhe, Shanti and David Radcliffe. "Women and Education in South Asia." Canadian and International Education 8, no. 2 (1979): 117-25.

Reviews the status of women's education in South Asia, with special reference to Sri Lanka. It considers such matters as the rise in absolute levels of illiteracy as contrasted with a relative improvement in the literacy of women, and relates the educational qualifications of women to the degree of opportunity available to them for commensurate employment, and social and political participation. Consideration is also given to the hidden contribution of women as unpaid family and agricultural workers, an economic as well as a social contribution that is not easily reflected in traditional indicators. The paper concludes with some reflection on religious and cultural traditions and their significance for the status of women in South Asian development.

CHAPTER 34

REFERENCE AND OVERVIEWS

BANGLADESH

Books

1364. Bureau of Educational Information and Statistics. Education
System of Bangladesh: An Introduction. Dhaka: Bureau of
Educational Information and Statistics, 1982.

Article

1365. Education Directorate, Government of the People's Republic of
Bangladesh, Education in Bangladesh. Dhaka: Bangladesh
Government Press, 1974.

This volume provides a short account of the system of
education in Bangladesh and also statistical data on the
different types of institutions for the year 1972-73.
Primary schools are brought under the Government control
during this period. At present, there are 36,537 primary
schools with a total enrollment of 7,793,905 students. The
number of primary school teachers, who are government
servants, are 155,742. In secondary level, there are 7,717
secondary schools with an enrollment of 1,834,095 students.
The government of Bangladesh is giving adequate attention to
the expansion of higher education. There are four
universities for general education with total enrollment of
22,552 students. The agricultural University of Mymensingh
has an enrollment of 1,936 and the University of Engineering
and Technology at Dhaka has an enrollment of 1,902 students.
The universities of general education have 256 degree
colleges including thirty-one government colleges affiliated
with them.

1366. "Education in Bangladesh." <u>Bulletin of the Unesco Regional</u>
       <u>Office for Education in Asia and Oceania</u>. no. 20, (1979).
       The article provides an overview of general educational
       conditions of Bangladesh. Apart from discussing structure
       and situation of primary, secondary, tertiary, teacher
       education and technical education, the situation of nonformal
       education and adult literacy programs are discussed. Some
       light also thrown on experiments in rural education.

INDIA

     Books

1367. Biswas, A. and D. C. Aggarwal. <u>Education in India</u>. New
       Delhi: Arya Book Depot, 1971.

1368. Biswas, A. and D. C. Aggarwal. <u>Encyclopedia Dictionary and</u>
       <u>Directory of Education</u>. New Delhi: Academic, 1971.

1369. Kirpal, Prem. <u>A Decade of Education in India</u>. Delhi:
       Indian Book Co., 1968.

1370. Naik, J. P. <u>The Search for a National System of Education:</u>
       <u>The Indian Experience</u>. New Delhi: ICSSR, 1974.

1371. Roy, N. R. <u>Some Current Educational Problems</u>. New Delhi:
       S. Chand, 1971.

1372. Sarkar, S. <u>Education in India: A Perspective</u>. Calcutta:
       World Press, 1978.

NEPAL

     Book

1373. Mohsin, Mohammad and Prem Kasaju, eds. <u>On Education in</u>
       <u>Nepal: A Topical Compilation</u>. Kathmandu: Office of the
       National Education Committee, 1974.

Reference and Overviews

Article

1374. "Education in Nepal." Bulletin of the Unesco Regional Office for Education in Asia. 6, no. 2 (March 1972): 140-46.

PAKISTAN

Books

1375. Iqbal, Muhammad. Education in Pakistan. Lahore: Aziz, 1977.

1376. Iqbal, Muhammad. Education in Pakistan: A Teacher Speaks on Education. Rawalpindi: Religious Book Society, 1967.

1377. Multi, A. G. Human Resource Development Through Education in Pakistan. Islamabad: Pakistan Manpower Institute, 1980.

Traces the development of education in Pakistan. The major areas discussed are: orientation towards Islamic ideology, primary education and literacy, orientation towards science and technology, quality improvement, and reduction of inequality in educational opportunities.

1378. Qureshi, Ishtiaq Husain. Education in Pakistan: An Inquiry into Objectives and Achievements. Karachi: Ma'aref, 1975.

Article

1379. "Education in Pakistan." Bulletin of the Unesco Regional Office for Education in Asia. 6, no. 2 (1972): 147-65.

SRI LANKA

Book

1380. Jayasuriya, J. E. Some Issues in Ceylon Education, 1964. Peradeniya: Association Education, 1964.

Article

1381. "Educational Development in Ceylon." Bulletin of the Unesco
       Regional Office for Education in Asia 6, no. 2 (March
       1972): 25-36.

CHAPTER 35

BIBLIOGRAPHICAL AND STATISTICAL REFERENCES

BANGLADESH

Books

1382. Bangladesh, Ministry of Education. _Statistical Profile of Education in Bangladesh._ Dhaka: Bangladesh Bureau of Educational Information and Statistics, 1978.

1383. Bangladesh. Ministry of Planning. _Statistical Pocketbook of Bangladesh, 1978, 1979._ Dhaka: Statistics Division and Bangladesh Bureau of Statistics, 1979, 1980.

Statistics on education are found under the chapters on "Education, Health and Social Welfare" and "Labour and Manpower."

INDIA

Books

1384. Brembeck, Cole. S. and E. W. Weidner. _Education and Development in India and Pakistan: A Select and Annotated Bibliography._ East Lansing, Mich.: College of Education and International Programs, 1962.

1385.   Deo, Pratibha and others. Educational Research in the
        University of Bombay. Bombay: University of Bombay,
        Department of Education, 1981.

        A compendium of 892 titles and authors of research work
        submitted for the M.Ed. degree from 1938 to 1980, of eighty-
        seven titles and authors of researches submitted for the
        Ph.D. degree from 1943 to 1980 and of abstracts of these
        Ph.D. thesis covering objectives, methods, tools, data
        collection and analysis, and major findings. Research topics
        have been classified into twelve areas: educational
        philosophy, sociology, psychology, economics, history;
        teacher education; organization and administration of
        schools, curriculum methods and textbooks; guidance and
        counseling; tests and measurement; comparative education, and
        adult and social education.

1386.   Fourth All-India Educational Survey: Some Statistics on
        School Education. New Delhi: National Council of
        Educational Research and Training, 1980.

1387.   Govind, Vijay and Chhotey Lal. Higher Education in India: A
        Bibliography. New Delhi: Ess and Ess, 1978.

        Helps people working in this field to find material
        appearing in 125 journals and newspapers published between
        1972-77. Includes a 2123 entries under twenty subject heads,
        such as comparative education, curriculum, sociology of
        education, and politics of education.

1388.   Jafar, S. M. Student Unrest in India: A Select Bibliogra-
        phy. New Delhi: Indian Document Service, 1977.

        This bibliography is intended to meet the research need on
        student unrest in India, which is caused by the education
        explosion. In this work, 1415 articles from periodicals and
        books have been listed systematically. Articles on nature,
        causes, remedies, etc., of student unrest have been indexed
        in it. A brief survey of the historical background has also
        been included.

1389.   Kamalavijayan, D. Problems of Higher Education in India: An
        Annotated Bibliography of Source Material. Gurgaon:
        Indian Documentation Service, 1979.

        A select annotated bibliography of source material on the
        subject. Covers the period 1947 to 1977 and lists 250
        entries covering Indian and foreign literature in English,
        including governmental and non-governmental publications.

Areas covered are obstructing services, bibliographies and catalogs, dictionaries and encyclopedias, directories, handbooks, indexing services, yearbooks and annual reviews, journals, books, conference and commission reports. Also contains a list of important higher education organizations.

1390. Kaula, P. N. Bibliography on Workers' Education. New Delhi: Ministry of Labour and Employment, Government of India, 1958.

A bibliography covering 378 items on different aspects of the subject, with respect to India and other countries. Classified according to subjects.

1391. Khandawala, Vidyut K., ed. Education of Women in India: 1850-1967: A Bibliography. Bombay: SNDT Women's University, 1968.

1392. Kothari, V. N. and P. R. Panchamukhi. "Economics of Education: A Trend Report." A Survey of Research in Economics: Vol. VI: Infrastructure. Bombay: Allied, 1980.

The survey discusses important published and unpublished works in the field of economics of education by Indian and foreign authors, on India problems. The accompanying bibliography lists 280 items appearing in the field till about 1975.

1393. Literacy Statistics at a Glance. New Delhi: Ministry of Education and Social Welfare. Directorate of Adult Education, 1979.

This compendium of literacy statistics reports on: the stage of literacy in the States and Union Territories; the district-wise literacy position of the adult groups; the literacy solution among the scheduled castes and scheduled tribes; the comparative literacy position for each district in terms of sex, rural and urban areas, and castes and tribes.

1394. National Council of Educational Research and Training. Fourth All-India Education Survey. New Delhi: NCERT, 1982.

The present report provides the findings of the educational survey which was conducted during 1978-1979 with a view to providing data on the existing educational facilities at the school level. The specific objectives of the survey were:

1) To assess the present position of the provision of educational facilities at various stages of school education in respect to coverage of school-going population; the distance to be covered by a child to have access to a school, especially children belonging to the disadvantaged section of society; 2) To assess the availability of minimum basic facilities in the schools, such as a building, furniture, library, equipment, health and sanitation, and incentives; 3) To prepare block maps with existing schooling facilities and to identify clusters of habitations where institutions need to be opened or existing schools need to be upgraded; 4) To prepare the ground for conducting quarterly monitoring of information relating to school attendance.

1395.   National Council of Educational Research and Training. Fourth All-India Educational Survey; Some Statistics on School Education. New Delhi: NCERT, 1980.

The present survey, unlike the third survey which was conducted in 1973, is limited to school education. While the findings have been compiled for preparation of the Sixth Five-Year Plan with regard to education, persons interested in the development of education of the country will find the book a useful source of information.

1396.   Parker, Franklin, ed. American Dissertations on Foreign Education: A Bibliography with Abstracts: Vol. II, India. Troy, New York: Whitston, 1972.

One hundred ninety-one bibliographic entries with abstracts of American dissertations on India are incorporated in this volume.

1397.   Patole, N. K., ed. Educational Research in Universities in Maharashtra. (Platinum Jubilee Publication). Bombay: S. T. College, 1982.

A compilation of theses and dissertations approved by six universities in Maharashtra state, for awarding the Master and Doctoral degrees. Covers the period 1939 to 1981 and enumerates a total of 157 doctoral thesis and ninety-nine theses for the M.Ed. degree in total fulfillment and 1783 dissertations for M.Ed. degree in partial fulfillment of the requirements.

1398.   Rokadia, B. C. and others (compilers). Adult Education in India: A Bibliography. New Delhi: Directorate of Adult Education, 1981.

Covers the existing literature on adult education for the period 1951-80. The information sources are: bibliographies, periodicals and newsletters, reports of conferences and seminars, and reports of committees and commissions. The references cover the following areas: policy planning and administration of institutions of adult education, their history and organization. Literature on methods, contents and materials relating to adult education, post-literacy follow-up and continuing education, personnel and their training, evaluation of statistics and research in this field, and the international situation are also included.

1399. Shanker, Laxmi and S. Hamid Husain, eds. Education and Educational Psychology. Bhopal: Council of Oriental Research, 1979.

A bibliography of researchers for which degrees and diplomas have been awarded in Indian universities since 1970. Includes research in progress and covers over 1800 items in areas such as psychology, sociology, economics and history of education; the teacher, curriculum, courses and methods, examinations, organization and administration of education.

1400. Srivastava, L. R. N. An Annotated Bibliography on Tribal Education in India. New Delhi: Tribal Education Unit, Department of Adult Education, NCERT, 1967.

An annotated bibliography on the subject that includes books, articles, and government publications.

1401. Tyagi, K. G., ed. Indian Education Index: 1947-1978. New Delhi: Archaran Prakashan, 1980.

A comprehensive subject and author index of the contents of twenty-six Indian, English language, educational journals. Gives access to more than 20,000 published items and suggests the libraries where the journals might be available.

1402. University Grants Commission. Directory of Scientific Research in Indian Universities. New Delhi: University Grants Commission, 1979.

Contains information on 9,930 research projects carried out by 66,333 scientists on physical sciences, bio-sciences, engineering, agriculture, management, transport, chemical technology, and architecture.

1403. University Grants Commission. University Development in
       India: Basic Facts and Figures 1972/73-1976-77. New
       Delhi: University Grants Commission, 1979, 1980, 1981,
       1982.

       (1) Part I Sec. A: Universities Colleges and Enrollment,
       1979; (2) Part I Sec. B: University Departments, University
       Colleges and Affiliated Colleges, 1980; (3) Part I Sec. C.:
       Post-graduate and Research Enrollment, 1981; (4) Part II Sec.
       A: Examination Results 1973 Annual + 1972 supplementary;
       1974 Annual + 1973 supplementary, 1980; (5) Part II Sec. B:
       Examination Results 1975 Annual + 1974 supplementary, 1981;
       (6) Part II Sec. C: Examination Results 1976 Annual + 1978
       supplementary, 1981; (7) Part I Sec. D: Post-graduate and
       Research Enrollment, 1982.

1404. Vijai, Govind and C. Lal. Higher Education in India: A
       Bibliography. New Delhi: Ess and Ess, 1978.

Articles

1405. Altbach, Philip G. "Bibliography on Higher Education in
       India." Pp. 419-48 in The Higher Learning in India, eds.
       Amrik Singh and Philip G. Altbach. New Delhi: Vikas,
       1974.

1406. Anderson, C. Arnold. "Organising Indian Educational
       Statistics for Action." Economic and Political Weekly 7
       (November 1972): 2250-52.

       By capable mobilization of appropriate educational data,
       building upon its historic base in nationwide statistics on
       social topics, India can lead the way to some decisive
       answers about the part that education plays or can play in
       development: economic, political, cultural, community, or
       social.

1407. "New Publications in the field of Educational Research:
       Selected Bibliography." Indian Education 30 (1984): 128-
       35.

1408. Sharma, R. C. "Educational Innovation and Change in India:
       Trends and Bibliography." University Administration 3, no.
       1 (1976): 76-86.

NEPAL

Book

1409. Tribhuvan University, Research Centre for Educational
       Innovation and Development. Bibliography on Education in
       Nepal. Kathmandu: Tribhuvan University, 1980.

PAKISTAN

Books

1410. Institute of Education and Research. Punjab University.
       Statistical Profile of Education in West Pakistan.
       Karachi: Manager of Publications, 1971.

1411. Pakistan. Bureau of Educational Planning and Management.
       Statistics on University Education, 1968-1974. Islamabad:
       The Bureau, 1976.

1412. Pakistan. Central Bureau of Education. Pakistan Education
       Statistics, 1947-48 to 1972-73. Islamabad: The Bureau,
       1975.

1413. Saad, Geti. Selected Bibliography and Abstracts of
       Educational Materials in Pakistan, Vol. 15, No. 3 July-
       September, 1981. Washington, D.C.: Educational Resources
       Information Center (ERIC), 1981.

       Government publications, newspaper articles, monographs,
       and syllabi published between July and September 1981 and
       dealing with Pakistani education are cited in this annotated
       listing. Entries are organized by the following topics:
       educational administration, organization, and financing;
       curriculum; educational development; educational goals,
       planning and reforms; elementary and secondary education;
       examinations; higher education; educational history; Islamic
       education; teaching of languages; libraries; literacy;
       medical education; educational philosophy; professional
       education; psychology; teachers; teaching methods and media;
       technical education; textbooks; women's education; and
       general. The document ends with a writers' index.

1414. South Asia: A Selected Bibliography of Theses and
       Dissertations, University of the Punjab, 1947-1979.
       Lahore: Center for South Asian Studies, The University,
       1981.

1415. West Pakistan. Bureau of Education. Bibliography on
       Education in Pakistan. Lahore: The Bureau, 1970.

       Includes references to English language books, pamphlets,
       government reports, documents, surveys, periodicals,
       articles, doctoral theses, dissertations, etc. Entries have
       been classified into just under 200 subjects covering almost
       every aspect of education in Pakistan.

1416. Zaki, Wali Muhammad and M. Sarwar Khan, comps. Pakistan
       Education Index. Islamabad: Central Bureau of Education,
       1970.

SRI LANKA

   Books

1417. Amarasinghe, N. comp. Thesis presented for higher degrees of
       the University of Ceylon, 1942-1971, deposited in the
       Library of the University of Ceylon: A Classified List
       with Author and Title Index. Peradeniya: University of
       Ceylon Library, 1971.

1418. De Silva, Chandra Richard and Daya de Silva, comps.
       Peradeniya Research: A Bibliography of Research
       Publications by the Academic Staff of the Faculties of Arts
       and Oriental Studies, University of Ceylon, Peradeniya,
       1952-1974. Peradeniya: Ceylon Studies Seminar, 1974.

1419. Jayasuriya, J. E. Ceylon Education Abstracts: Period
       Covered January 1, 1966--December 31, 1967. Washington,
       D.C.: Educational Resources Information Center (ERIC),
       1979.

       "Ceylon Education Abstracts" attempts a coverage of the
       more significant materials published in Ceylon on various
       aspects of education. This is the fourth and concluding part
       of Volume 1. The four parts of Volume I have dealt with the
       materials published during the period January 1, 1957 to
       December 31, 1967. Where the title of the entry is not in
       English, it is in Sinhalese with an English translation. A

few titles are in Tamil and in such cases the words "in Tamil" appear at the end of the abstract. A list of the newspapers and the periodicals from which material has been selected, and an author index are given at the end.

Numbers refer to entries, not pages.

ABOUT THE AUTHORS

Philip G. Altbach is Professor and Director of the Comparative Education Center and Chairman of the Department of Educational Organization, Adminstration and Policy, State University of New York at Buffalo. He is editor of the Comparative Education Review, author of Comparative Higher Education, Publishing in the Third World and other books. Dr. Altbach has served as Fulbright Research Professor at the University of Bombay. He is co-editor (with Amrik Singh) of The Higher Learning in India and (with Suma Chitnis) of The Indian Academic Profession.

Denzil Saldanha is Lecturer in the Unit for Research in the Sociology of Education at the Tata Institute of Social Sciences, Bombay and Associate Editor of the Sociological Bulletin. He has served as Lecturer at M.D. College and as invited Lecturer in the Department of Applied Psychology, University of Bombay. He was Deputy Director of the Center for Studies in Decentralized Industries.

Jeanne Weiler is a doctoral student in comparative education at the State University of New York at Buffalo. She has taught at the University of Kuwait and has been on the staff of the Institute of International Education, New York.